STUDIES IN ENGLISH LITERATURE

Volume LXVI

T.

DISSENTING REPUBLICAN

*Wordsworth's Early Life and Thought
in their Political Context*

by

LESLIE F. CHARD, II

University of Cincinnati

1972

MOUTON

THE HAGUE · PARIS

LIBRARY OF CONGRESS CATALOG CARD NUMBER: 78-159463

Printed in The Netherlands by Mouton & Co., Printers, The Hague.

For ANNE

PREFACE

I wish to acknowledge some of my many sources of support for this study. J. B. McNulty of Trinity College, Connecticut, first led me to the social and political elements in *Lyrical Ballads*. Benjamin Boyce, Lewis Patton, Lionel Stevenson, and the late Merle Bevington gave generously of their time at the dissertation stage of this project. My subsequent revisions have been greatly assisted by the work of recent Wordsworth scholars; to single out two among many, I am especially indebted to Mark Reed's *Wordsworth: The Chronology of the Early Years* and to Chester Shaver's revised edition of the early *Letters*. Funds to carry out my research have come from the Graduate School of Duke University, the Faculty Research Committee of Emory University, and the University of Cincinnati. The staffs at the university libraries of Cincinnati, Cornell, Duke, and Emory and at the British Museum, Dr. Williams's Library, the Wordsworth Library at Grasmere, and the New York Public Library have been gracious in their assistance. Mrs. Mary Anne Meeker assisted me in compiling the Index, and Mrs. Arden Rosenthal helped with proofreading. Special acknowledgment should be made to the Duke University Library for permission to make use of William Godwin's Diary, and to the Taft Committee of the University of Cincinnati for supporting the publication of this book. Finally, I thank my wife for her unfailing support and encouragement.

L. F. C.

TABLE OF CONTENTS

INTRODUCTION

This study examines three dimensions of Wordsworth's career in the 1790's: the poet's biography, his intellectual development, and his creative growth. The first dimension entails particularly an investigation of Wordsworth's life at Cambridge, in France, and during his several visits to London. The second is concerned with his debt to seventeenth-century English Republicanism, eighteenth-century French political thought, and (most central to this study) the tradition of English Dissent. Developing from the other two, the third dimension arrives at certain assertions about the evolution of *Lyrical Ballads* and about the reliability and the structure of *The Prelude*. These three dimensions are united by one essential point: that Wordsworth's revolt against Locke and his eighteenth-century heritage in evolving his concept of the creative imagination and the active universe (to mention but two of the concerns most occupying scholarly attention today) was not a total one. It was not total if we are to trust *The Prelude*, trust it in ways that some critics have been all too reluctant to do, despite their agreement about the poem's "imaginative" accuracy. It is my contention that *The Prelude* contains a degree of reliability seldom acknowledged and that to understand this Wordsworth's London career and his connections with English Dissent must be examined in detail.

By thus studying the Dissenting world, we may come to see that, while Wordsworth revolted against the eighteenth-century establishment in literature, religion, politics, and society, he did not therefore revolt from self, from nation, or from all aspects of his intellectual heritage. Just as a long-standing tradition of literary "dissent" existed in such a form as the novel from Defoe through Sterne (and after), so in religion and politics the Protestant Dissenters represent a tradition of revolt that, like its Establishment opposition, was dependent on Locke and Newton. While clearly respectful of Locke's empiricism, English Dissent by the late eighteenth century was manifesting signs of impatience with a mechanical universe. In a similar way, Dissenters tended to the left in politics, but as moderate liberals, not as subversives. Consequently Wordsworth could find in them exactly the compromises he was to make in the late 1790's as he began to compose the poetry in *Lyrical Ballads*: Lockean empiricism colored by a sense of the transcendental, liberalism moderated by a respect for place and for tradition. It would seem, then, that the primary source for the world-view inherent in *Lyrical Ballads* was neither Godwin's materialism (which for Wordsworth was but a temporary aberration) nor his Coleridgean rebellion from Godwin, but rather the liberal humanitarian tradition of English Dissent.

Wordsworth's career prior to *Lyrical Ballads* has long needed a detailed, full-length study, not simply to re-evaluate the hypotheses of previous students, but more particularly to probe into areas that have never before received adequate attention. The neglect of Wordsworth's debt to such French writers as Montesquieu and others more clearly contemporary with the poet (notably Condorcet) is amazing, especially since he spent a year in France at a time alive with the ideas of these political thinkers and since he openly admits in *The Prelude* that under Beaupuy's influence he turned to the work of previous theorists. But even more outstanding is the fact that no one has ever thought to take a close look at Wordsworth's first publisher – not even a short note has ever been written about the relationship between Wordsworth and the Dissenting circle that surrounded Joseph Johnson. For that matter, nothing has ever been written in any detail about his various early trips to London.

In many ways, Garrod's forty-years-old study of Wordsworth is closer to the mark than some newer works. If he does oversimplify, Garrod at least stresses the essential "rightness" of *The*

Prelude and he properly resists the temptation to psychoanalyze every inch of Wordsworth's career. Besides Mrs. Moorman, too few recent scholars have approached the poet as a reasonably sane, balanced young man, subject to the same feelings and the same stages of psychological growth that most young men undergo. Wordsworth was indeed sensitive and intelligent, but psychological abnormality is not a requisite for poetic creation. Nor is there any evidence that he was unbalanced: *The Prelude* is not the record of a guilt-ridden mind, nor do the letters or the poems of his youth indicate guilt or excessive rebellion. It is doing no more than justice to Wordsworth to acknowledge that his actions were the consequence of intelligent deliberation; that his various states of mind were as much the product of his intellect as they were the result of physical and emotional forces. Further, presupposing an intelligent approach to his time on the part of the poet, it is logical to assume that he was aware of most of the intellectual conditions of the 1790's; there is enough evidence in the works to prove this. Yet few literary scholars have studied the age in any detail and correlated it with Wordsworth's thought. Whether or not specific references to them appear in Wordsworth's writings, the political events, the controversies, and the published works of the period must all be evaluated in terms of the poet's development.

As will have been gathered by now, Wordsworth's early works and *The Prelude* are the basis for this study. Certainly his "Letter to the Bishop of Llandaff", the early letters, and the various poems of the period are indisputably valid sources. Likewise, there is no reason whatsoever to doubt that Wordsworth intended to tell the truth, insofar as his memory permitted, in *The Prelude*. He wrote the poem primarily for Coleridge, and in the knowledge that only his immediate family and friends would read it in his lifetime; he had no motive for dissembling. Moreover, *The Prelude* cannot be regarded as merely a simple autobiographical account of the poet's early years, though neuroses-hunters often accuse Wordsworth of dishonesty for leaving out episodes of his life. Coleridge and the poet's family did not need to be told of details they already knew – and which in all probability had little permanent effect on his mental development. (The Annette Vallon affair is most pertinent here.) Instead, Wordsworth's great poem must be regarded as no more or no less than what he wanted it to be and what its subtitle says it is: an account of the growth of the poet's mind. And, for a study of his intellectual development, it is unassailable evidence.

Unless otherwise noted, all allusions to *The Prelude* refer to the first version (MS. A), which was composed between 1798 and 1805. Although poetically inferior to the published version of 1850, MS. A is consistently more explicit than the revised text. Moreover, as the poet's revisions indicate, his first draft retains much of his youthful political enthusiasm; in the subsequent manuscripts he repeatedly deleted his political criticisms and colored his thought with his later religious orthodoxy. Further, Professor de Selincourt has shown that, since it was addressed to Coleridge, MS. A is more personal, having "the tone of intimate conversation", while the later versions often suppress the more private glimpses.[1] This is particularly true of the aspects of his early life that are most pertinent to this study: the details of his first long sojourn in London, the motives for his trip to France in 1792, and incidental revelations of character.

It is also worth noting that MS. A was composed within a few years after Wordsworth underwent the experiences which he describes, so that it is unlikely his memory failed him with regard to many particulars. Nevertheless, it must be admitted that Wordsworth frequently did view the past from a changed perspective when he wrote the poem. This granted, it will still be seen in the following pages that he consistently distinguishes (through both structure and changes of tense and tone) between description of former states of mind and "editorial" expressions of his point of view while writing the poem.

In order to focus directly on Wordsworth's mental growth, the organization is chronological from chapter to chapter, and within

---

[1]   *The Prelude, or Growth of a Poet's Mind*, Ernest de Selincourt, ed.; 2nd ed., revised by Helen Darbishire (Oxford: Clarendon Press, 1959), pp. lxii-lxiii; see also pp. lxiii-lxxiv for de Selincourt's comments on Wordsworth's "changes of idea".

the chapters as far as is possible; otherwise the various influences on Wordsworth form the basis of organization: his associates, his reading, the political conditions around him. As a consequence, the reader's indulgence must be asked for the opening chapter, where the argument is essentially a negative one, demonstrating that Wordsworth's childhood did not make him a rebel against everything conventional and traditional and that his Cambridge days were not the direct occasion of his liberal ideology. But the final proof of these contentions must come later; Chapter III studies his political awakening during his trip to France in 1792, while Chapter IV deals with his revolt against English society – one that was intellectual in origin and decidedly moderate and ethical in nature – and with his concurrent involvement in London Dissenting circles.

My aim in this work is not to present a final or exhaustive study of these aspects of the early Wordsworth. Rather I hope to begin – or less presumptuously to continue – the exploration of his political sources, his personal life in the 1790's, and the origin of *Lyrical Ballads* and *The Prelude*. The absence of a detailed biographical study of Wordsworth's early career, emphasizing his London visits, his Dissenting connections, and his reading of political literature, is alone sufficient justification for this undertaking. Yet much more than this results as well. His early poems and the "Letter to the Bishop of Llandaff" can now be put in a new perspective – one that relates them more directly to his mental development; and some clues as to their times of composition consequently come to light. Likewise, his early intellectual stages are delineated more accurately, and the development of *Lyrical Ballads* out of his youthful liberalism has been traced in more detail, than has hitherto been the case. But, above all, this study is a reassertion of the mature Wordsworth's strength of mind. It shows that his later philosophy was reached, not by the blind gropings of a sick and tormented mind, but by deliberate intellectual endeavor.

I.

CHILDHOOD AND CAMBRIDGE: THE CONSERVATIVE BACKGROUND

Early Wordsworth scholars tended to romanticize the poet's childhood. Concerned as they were with his philosophy of nature, they emphasized his boyhood haunts, tracing to them his love of nature, more particularly of the Lake Country.[1] Certain recent scholars have gone to the other extreme, resorting to a psychoanalytical interpretation in their efforts to plant the seeds of Wordsworth's radicalism in his childhood experiences. As a consequence, they have rejected *The Prelude*, when they have found it necessary, in the belief that the poem was meant to be a simple autobiographical narrative and that its conclusions were motivated by feelings of guilt. In effect, such scholars focus on what, in their estimation, *should* have gone into the poem, rather than on what *is* in it.

Although Wordsworth never mentions the subject, Meyer believes that the death of the poet's father and the hardships incident upon Lord Lonsdale's refusal to settle his debts were little short of traumatic for the boy.[2] Todd goes to even greater extremes to show that the poet was a radical from the first; Wordsworth's hatred for tyranny, Todd maintains, was occasioned by his early relationship with Christopher Crackanthorpe, his uncle and guardian, while the example of Lord Lonsdale was instilling in the boy anti-aristocratic sentiments.[3]

---

[1] Émile Legouis, *The Early Life of Wordsworth* (London: J. M. Dent, 1932), pp. 22-24; George McLean Harper, *William Wordsworth, His Life, Works, and Influence*, 2 vols. (New York: Scribner's, 1916), I, 18-53.

[2] George Wilbur Meyer, *Wordsworth's Formative Years* (Ann Arbor: University of Michigan Press, 1943), pp. 7, 8-12.

[3] F. M. Todd, *Politics and the Poet, A Study of Wordsworth* (London: Methuen, 1957), pp. 17-18.

A less extreme view is taken by Hayden, who says that Wordsworth's

early economic experiences may not have *made* him a revolutionary, but they most certainly were of a sort to help him to prepare to accept the idea of the Revolution .... We have already seen that Wordsworth considered his love of personal freedom associated with political equality. [In *The Prelude*, especially with regard to the walking trip with Jones through France and Switzerland.] Here again, his experiences in economics are paralleled by the French Revolution, which partly mirrored his own rebellious spirit: here was to rise the common man (Wordsworth) against the tyrannous lords of landed aristocracy (Lonsdale). [4]

F. W. Bateson's view is explicitly psychoanalytical: "So far from surrendering to the neurotic elements in his personality, as so many Romantic poets have done, Wordsworth's early life was one long desperate struggle against them." [5]

Two more recent studies also reveal, if not psychoanalytical excesses, at least a reluctance to give *The Prelude* its due. David Ferry states that there is a "collision between the poet's powerful and honest sense of fact and his thematic preconceptions", so that one feels *The Prelude* is not "a piece of scrupulous biographical reporting". [6] And in discussing "The Vale of Esthwaite", Geoffrey Hartman makes the following assertion: "That Wordsworth's first original poem reverts so often to a gothic and visionary gloom reveals the strength of the conflict in him between the homeless and the naturalized imagination, a conflict never to be quieted." [7]

[4] Donald Hayden, *After Conflict, Quiet: A Study of Wordsworth's Poetry in Relation to His Life and Letters* (New York: Exposition, 1951), pp. 11-12.
[5] F. W. Bateson, *Wordsworth, A Re-interpretation* (London: Longmans, Green, 1954), p. 199. Mrs. Mary Moorman, Wordsworth's latest biographer, gives a balanced, straightforward account of Wordsworth's childhood, without attempting to make the details extravagantly significant. *William Wordsworth, A Biography* (Oxford: Clarendon Press, 1957), pp. 1-85.
[6] David Ferry, *Limits of Mortality: An Essay on Wordsworth's Major Poems* (Middletown, Conn.: Wesleyan University Press, 1959), pp. 125-131. See also Herbert Read, *Wordsworth* (London: Faber and Faber, 1949), p. 41: "in a wider sense altogether I tend to distrust the evidence of the *Prelude*".
[7] Geoffrey Hartman, *Wordsworth's Poetry, 1787-1814* (New Haven: Yale University Press, 1964), pp. 88-89. I do not necessarily object to Hartman's distinction between "the homeless and the naturalized imagination". Rather,

Even if the over-simplification of most of these interpretations is discounted, they each still contain serious distortions of Wordsworth's childhood. And in every case, these exaggerations appear because *The Prelude* is renounced as a reliable source of evidence. In the course of the poem Wordsworth included all the elements he felt were important in shaping his views of man and the universe; to be sure, he is occasionally euphemistic, but no evidence indicates that he did not give a truthful account of his experiences, as much as anyone can be truthful about himself. Nowhere does he mention these supposedly severe childhood crises that some scholars have hypothesized; and no tangible external corroboration of them exists either.

Instead, the first two books of his poem repeatedly stress the unfailing delight which the young boy felt in the presence of nature and in the company of his playmates. His childhood joys, he notes, were a theme he could pursue

> through every change
> Of exercise and play, to which the year
> Did summon us in its delightful round.
> *(The Prelude*, I, 502-504).

Even when he had lost his parents and felt alone in the world, his environment gave him solace; he was still able to exult over the beauty of life:

> Wonder not
> If such my transports were; for in all things
> I saw one life, and felt that it was joy.
> (II, 428-430).

Wordsworth's extant juvenilia support his statements in *The Prelude*. Although some of his early poems occasionally contain

---

I fail to see any evidence in the juvenilia of such a conflict, and I feel he is in effect making a connection between the early and the later verse that simply does not exist.

Although Hartman elsewhere alludes to the reliability of *The Prelude* (p. 365), the net effect of his book is to undermine the poem's authority; his analysis of "An Evening Walk", for instance, posits a mood, a world-view even, wholly at odds with that which *The Prelude* presents for the same years. See pp. 90-101.

a gothic pose, this is clearly a conventional form of landscape description and not an indication of intellectual or emotional malaise, as is true of the gothicism in *Guilt and Sorrow* and *The Borderers*. Both in "Lines Written as a School Exercise at Hawkshead" and in "The Vale of Esthwaite", the two most extended expressions of his boyhood mind, the prevailing mood is one of confidence and joy. In the latter poem he particularly indicates his delight in gothic feelings.[8]

The poet's early environment was evidently a moderately conservative one. His father was an agent for Sir James Lowther, the richest landowner in Cumberland, and from all accounts John Wordsworth was a dedicated employee.[9] Something of the political atmosphere surrounding the young poet is implied in *The Prelude* when he refers to Pitt:

> One, of whose name from Childhood we had heard
> Familiarly, a household term.
> (VII, 525-526).

This is confirmed by the political sympathies of the other children. Richard, who became a lawyer in London, ignored the reform agitation that fascinated his younger brother and later admonished him to be more discreet in his radicalism.[10] Likewise, Christopher went to Cambridge when the University was alive with political ferment; he occasionally met Coleridge, yet he never sympathized with the young liberals.[11] After ingratiating himself with the university authorities by his scholarship, he took orders and he later became Master of Trinity College, thus tacitly indicating his acceptance of the political and religious establishments of the late

---

[8] *The Poetical Works of William Wordsworth*, Ernest de Selincourt and Helen Darbishire, eds., 5 vols. (Oxford: Clarendon Press, 1940-1949), I, 259-261, 270-283. See especially lines 240-241, 268-273, of "The Vale of Esthwaite".

[9] Mrs. Moorman, pp. 5-9.

[10] *The Letters of William and Dorothy Wordsworth. The Early Years 1787-1805*, Ernest de Selincourt, ed., 2nd ed., revised by Chester L. Shaver (Oxford: Clarendon Press, 1967), p. 121 and n. Hereafter cited as *Early Letters*.

[11] Christopher Wordsworth, *Social Life at the English Universities in the Eighteenth Century* (Cambridge: Deighton, Bell, 1874), pp. 587-599: "Extracts from the Diary of Christopher Wordsworth".

eighteenth century. And Dorothy, despite her affection for her poetic brother, was an enthusiastic admirer of the royal family; of the king she wrote:

I own I am too much of an aristocrate ... not to reverence him because he is a Monarch more than I should were he a private Gentleman, ... I say it is impossible to see them *at Windsor* without loving them, because at Windsor they are seen unattended by Pomp or State. [12]

All this suggests that Wordsworth's early upbringing was politically conservative. In fact, his entire intellectual climate as a child was conventional. As will be shown in detail later, his philosophical training was centered in the tradition of Bacon, Newton, and Locke. His religious orthodoxy is indicated both by his later, temporary interest in becoming a clergyman and by certain passages in his juvenilia, particularly "Sonnet Written by Mr. ——— Immediately after the Death of His Wife" (ll. 11-14) and "A Ballad" (ll. 29-32).[13] From *The Prelude*, it is known that at Hawkshead Wordsworth was taught science and enough mathematics to ignore the subject during his first year at Cambridge. In addition, Mrs. Moorman shows that while a schoolboy he read not only the older poets of the eighteenth century – notably Thomson, Gray, Collins, and Goldsmith – but also some of those more contemporary with him who are lesser known today, such as Helen Maria Williams, Elizabeth Carter, and the poets of the gothic and sentimental school generally. *The Annual Register* for 1783, Mrs. Moorman believes, was the source of Wordsworth's first knowledge of Crabbe.[14] Wordsworth's debt in his early poems to the eighteenth century, especially Pope, is shown by Miss Potts.[15]

---

[12] *Early Letters*, p. 83. I know of no direct evidence suggesting the political views of the third brother, John. Although he admired Wilberforce, like his sister, he expressed directly contradictory feelings about Pitt. *The Letters of John Wordsworth*, Carl H. Ketcham, ed. (Ithaca: Cornell University Press, 1969), pp. 85, 141.

[13] *Poetical Works*, I, 265, 265-266.

[14] Mrs. Moorman, pp. 51-55.

[15] Abbie Findlay Potts, *Wordsworth's Prelude: A Study of Its Literary Form* (Ithaca: Cornell University Press, 1953), pp. 33-38.

As described, Wordsworth's formal education and his personal reading were conventional, and the extent to which his early verse derives from the traditional eighteenth-century poets and from the currently popular gothic and sentimental poets would indicate his total acceptance of established literary values. While he later attacked certain educational theories, he nowhere repudiates his education at Hawkshead. Rather, he was thankful for his schooling, both formal and natural:

> I was rear'd
> Safe from an evil which these days have laid
> Upon the Children of the Land, a pest
> That might have dried me up, body and soul.
> This Verse is dedicate to Nature's self,
> And things that teach as Nature teaches, then
> Oh where had been the Man, the Poet where?
>   (*The Prelude*, V, 226-232).

Wordsworth later rebelled against this literary tradition, just as he rebelled against the political and intellectual establishments of the eighteenth century; but we must be careful to distinguish between revolt against externals and revolt against self, or one's past. His repudiation of the literary tradition was prompted by the same condition that occasioned his political revolt – the absence of intellectual and human values in both areas. There is no reason to suppose that he was thus repudiating himself, that is, something he once was, or that *this* revolt involved anything more or less than an objective intellectual process (for example, some sort of mental crisis or neurosis).

Since his brothers and his sister were subjected, as young children, to the same environment without ever rebelling from it, Wordsworth's later liberalism (both in politics and in other spheres) must be regarded, not as a revolt from his childhood, but as a consequence of particular experiences which he did not share with them: his early sensitivity to nature, his second trip to France, and his liberal associates in London.

Scholars have been too prone to interpret Wordsworth through the eyes of Dorothy, who spent virtually her whole childhood under the heavy domination of her guardians. Her bitterness at

their severe discipline and their parsimoniousness is understandable, and she was later even more embittered by their indifference
to her brother.[16] But Dorothy, being a young woman, was at the
mercy of her guardians to a much greater extent than her brothers;
financially, she was totally dependent on them, and she seldom
escaped their immediate supervision. Nothing suggests that as a
young boy Wordsworth felt so strongly about his guardians, or
that his childhood was warped by poverty, neglect, and traumatic
experiences. It must be remembered that his Hawkshead days
began at Whitsuntide, 1779, little more than a year after his
beloved mother died and while his father was still alive, so that,
in comparison with Dorothy, he was seldom subjected to the
direct surveillance of his guardians.

At Hawkshead, likewise, he led a relatively cheerful life, at a
school that had admirable standards for his day,[17] under a school-
master he admired and loved all his life, and among schoolmates
who were his social equals.

> It was my fortune scarcely to have seen
> Through the whole tenor of my School-day time
> The face of one, who, whether Boy or Man,
> Was vested with attention or respect
> Through claims of wealth or blood.
>
> (*The Prelude*, IX, 221-225).

In sum, Wordsworth became a liberal both because young men
naturally tend in that direction and because of the particular
social and political *milieu* of his time; he did not need to be
subjected to tyrannical relatives in order to hate tyranny. This is
substantiated by *The Prelude* (Books I and II), where he pictures
his childhood, not as idyllic to be sure, but at least as unrestrained
and, more important, as a period of imaginative growth.

While Wordsworth's childhood did not make him an embittered
republican, certain distinctive habits of mind characterized his
early thinking. These were partly responsible for the period of

---

[16] *Early Letters*, pp. 3-4, 8, and 9-10.
[17] Mrs. Moorman, pp. 26-28; and especially Ben Ross Schneider, Jr.,
Wordsworth's Cambridge Education (Cambridge: Cambridge University
Press, 1957), pp. 4-7.

depression that overcame him from 1794 until 1796, but they were ultimately integral components of the noble and comprehensive view of life which supplanted his despair. What needs to be stressed at this point is that such a continuity exists in Wordsworth's thought and that from the first it contains radical political implications. Taken together, these habits of mind were sources of permanence to which Wordsworth would recur time and again, as succor or as inspiration. And in the very process of recurring to them, he was to construct yet another source of permanence, not inherent in his childhood but a result of adverting to it. This source was a sense of temporal continuity, "tradition" when elaborated beyond the self. Thus the poet's sense of tradition came, not from direct acceptance of his conservative childhood environment, but by analogy with his mental development; the one would have led him to a conservative view of life, while the other brought him to liberalism. Further, that he did so often find memory a source of comfort, that he looked upon his early years as an exemplum of a healthy past-present relationship, tells us as much about his childhood as it does about his maturity.

The most elementary characteristic of Wordsworth's thought, almost from the very first, was a heavy emphasis on external reality, an unidealistic preoccupation with physical qualities, molded alike by the sensuous awareness that he early possessed and then by the grounding he received as a schoolboy in empirical thought. Locke and Newton, as well as Bacon, must have been in his mind when he composed his "Lines Written as a School Exercise at Hawkshead":

> And has the Sun his flaming chariot driven
> Two hundred times around the ring of heaven,
> Since Science first, with all her sacred train,
> Beneath yon roof began her heavenly reign? . . .
> [Not] that vile wretch who bade the tender age
> Spurn Reason's law and humour Passion's rage;
> But she who trains the generous British youth
> In the bright paths of fair majestic Truth.

And at Hawkshead particularly, the poet notes,

> immortal Science reigns; ...
> To teach, on rapid wings, the curious soul
> To roam from heaven to heaven, from pole to pole,
> From thence to search the mystic cause of things,
> And follow Nature to her secret springs. [18]

An important passage in *The Prelude* (I, 571-640) describes the poet's early relationship to nature in similar terms. Having presented specific details about his childhood landscape, Wordsworth proceeds to generalize and to distinguish between "extrinsic passion" (or "vulgar joy"), of which he was early conscious, and "joys/Of subtler origin",

> Those hallow'd and pure motions of the sense
> Which seem, in their simplicity, to own
> An intellectual charm, that calm delight
> Which, if I err not, surely must belong
> To those first-born affinities that fit
> Our new existence to existing things,
> And, in our dawn of being, constitute
> The bond of union betwixt life and joy.
>   (I, 578-585).

His early poetry makes abundantly clear, and in doing so reinforces such passages as the above, that while the young boy gloried in the rational faculties of the mind, he also found delight in the world of his "fancy":

> Through what sweet scenes did fancy rove
> While thus her fairy dreams she wove.
> Compared with fancy what is truth?
> And Reason, what art thou to Youth? [19]

[18] *Poetical Works*, I, 259-261. Hoxie Neale Fairchild has also noted the "Baconian, Newtonian" point of view here. *Religious Trends in English Poetry*, 4 vols. (New York: Columbia University Press, 1949), III, 140-141. See also: *The Early Wordsworthian Milieu: A Notebook of Christopher Wordsworth with a Few Entries by William Wordsworth*, Zera S. Fink, ed. (Oxford: Clarendon Press, 1958), p. 97; Arthur Beatty, ed., *Wordsworth: Representative Poems* (New York: Odyssey Press, 1937), pp. xxvi-xxvii; Kenneth MacLean, *John Locke and English Literature of the Eighteenth Century* (New Haven: Yale University Press, 1936), pp. 1-4.
[19] *Poetical Works*, I, 276-277 (lines 294-297). See also the above-quoted lines from "Lines Written as a School Exercise", *Poetical Works*, I, 259-261.

Thus, over Wordsworth's childhood preoccupation with external reality was suffused a sense of mystery in nature and a feeling of profound kinship with her, in part foreshadowing the animism of his later thought. More important, he discovered, despite the fears that *The Prelude* amply documents, the power of nature, her eternal forms, that permitted him to achieve the "calm delight" which is both peace and growth. The license which enabled the young boy to respond so fully to nature helped him to develop a unique freedom of the imagination. Having experienced imaginative scope and growth as a boy, and so becoming convinced of the inherent power of the mind, he was later able to assimilate not only the rational schemes of the necessitarians but also the Platonic and Unitarian concepts that inform his mature poetry. Worth particular note here is his early insistence on Truth as a transcendent ideal combined with his awareness of nature's "secret springs" lying beyond external appearances.

Parallel to his incipient love of nature was Wordsworth's youthful faith in the inherent nobility of man; in *The Prelude* he tells of witnessing the simple and upright shepherds tenaciously working for their livelihood:

> Thus was Man
> Ennobled outwardly before mine eyes,
> And thus my heart at first was introduc'd
> To an unconscious love and reverence
> Of human Nature; hence the human form
> To me was like an index of delight,
> Of grace and honour, power and worthiness.
> (VIII, 410-416).

Years later he realized, thankfully, the benefits his mind derived from these men; knowledge (at least the absolute truths Wordsworth sought) to him came from seeing the ideal first (*The Prelude*, VIII, 428-471). This faith in man was valuable in several ways, for it helped to make him habitually aware that elementary components were more important in evaluating an object than superficial appearances; it gave him the basic ingredients of his later concept of the hero; it enabled him to attain a greater education in human nature, for man perverted was thus the more understandable, if at first painful to behold; and, consequent to this last, it anticipated his belief in perfectibility.

Finally, Wordsworth's concept of unity must be regarded as a legacy of his childhood. John Jones is certainly right in saying that "The large and lazy assumption that the Romantic poets were all striving to express unity has obscured the structure of distinct but related things which is the world of Wordsworth."[20] Nevertheless, that Wordsworth's idea of unity originated in his increasing awareness of the value to him of the interaction of the mind and external objects – "distinct but related things" – is implicit in the first books of *The Prelude*. Further, unity was manifested in his childhood in at least three ways: in terms of the senses, it was revealed in what he calls "pure organic pleasure" (*The Prelude*, I, 591); in human terms, it appeared in the form of sympathy; and in intellectual terms, it was apparent in his early ability to synthesize. Thus unity as a philosophical concept may be vague and may be invoked lazily; but as a quality perceived in nature and in the mind, it is essentially and vitally Wordsworthian.

Nature taught him, he tells us in *The Prelude* (XII, 1-55), the reconciliation of opposites; its agency was a power which he learned to reverence because it lifts "The Being into magnanimity". This consciousness of natural unity acquired through intellectual power and resulting in a state of harmony is alive with political implications. The whole of Books I and II emphasizes joy and happiness, the personal equivalents of political peace; all result from natural harmony. As a child, too, the poet was free to be himself – a prime source of his personal harmony. The poet's later commitment to peace and freedom may be seen as a natural development from this early sense of personal harmony and joy. And that he was able later to discover a peace and freedom that transcended the political may be explained in the same way.

On the other hand, no evidence indicates that the social, economic, and political conditions in the North of England left any impression on the young Wordsworth, except insofar as the life

[20]   *The Egotistical Sublime* (London: Chatto and Windus, 1954), pp. 32-33.

of the Lake Country shepherds later, in retrospect, came to be an ideal in light of his experiences elsewhere. As he states in *The Prelude* (VIII, 413-414), these shepherds introduced him to "an *unconscious* love and reverence/ Of human Nature" (italics mine). At the time, he did not respond one way or the other to them – or to the other aspects of his environment; he accepted it and unknowingly found joy in it. The impression given by the whole of *The Prelude* is that as a boy Wordsworth saw man solely as a noble being in a healthful if humble state; nothing in the early verse confutes this. Economic and social historians seem to be in agreement that the North of England was relatively un- touched by the agrarian distresses which ravaged other parts of the country about this time.[21] Further, Wordsworth was far re- moved as a child from the debates over the rights of Dissenters and from the threat of rebellion in the army and navy. Even by the 1790's, in comparison with the burning issues of the time, the problems of agrarian reform and poor relief were given rela- tively little attention in the newspapers and magazines. Nor were the various reform groups, usually alert to injustices of any kind, especially interested in them. Ashton, who has made a careful economic analysis of the whole eighteenth century, may well be right in dismissing accounts of agrarian depression from 1781 to 1795.[22]

It would probably be safe, then, to say that Wordsworth first became aware of the social issues of his day only after he arrived at Cambridge. But even here it would be dangerous to place much emphasis on these issues, for Wordsworth was habitually aloof, often virtually indifferent; and, by his own account in *The Prelude*, he hints that he generally remained apart from the various factions and conflicts of the university world (III, 626- 643). The great issues of society in Wordsworth's first years at Cambridge, until the advent of the French Revolution, were by and large concerned with specific reforms, in none of which he

[21] See G. D. H. Cole and Raymond Postgate, *The British People, 1746- 1946* (New York: Knopf, 1947), pp. 107-110, for some reasons why the south of England was more severely depressed than was the north.
[22] T. S. Ashton, *An Economic History of England: the Eighteenth Century* (London: Methuen, 1955), p. 40.

ever expresses more than passing interest. If parliamentary debates, newspapers, and magazines are accurate indices, the two most debated subjects while Wordsworth was an undergraduate were the Regency crisis and the repeal of the Corporation and Test Acts.[23] A relatively small number of subordinate political and social issues completes the list: the state of taxation and revenue; the election of 1788 – especially in the borough of Westminster, where Fox and Horne Tooke waged a bitter campaign; the trial of Warren Hastings; the abolition of the slave trade; and occasional motions in Commons for Parliamentary reform, all of them Foxite appeals to 1688, not to particular abstract rights of man.[24] Another significant trend was the Yorkshire reform movement which had begun about 1780 primarily through the impetus of Christopher Wyvill; while this program was supported by the Dissenters at Cambridge, it was also backed by the entrenched reactionaries.[25] The extent of Wordsworth's concern with these issues, all of which surely were argued among the undergraduates, is uncertain;[26] but judging from the account in *The Prelude*, where Wordsworth indicates that his first real concern with politics did not begin until his second trip to France, it is probable that they were of little interest to him. Further, the issues on the whole were not the kind to attract Wordsworth. But a more detailed examination of the poet's university career will better substantiate this contention.

---

[23] *The Parliamentary History of England, from the Earliest Period to the Year 1803* (London: Hansard, 1816-1817), XXVIII-XXIX, May 8, 1789-December 13, 1792; hereafter cited as *Parliamentary Debates*. See also *The Monthly Review*, I-XXIX (1790-1799), and *The Morning Chronicle* and *The Times* for these years.

[24] Simon Maccoby agrees that the repeal of the Corporation and Test Acts monopolized the pamphlet world during the winter of 1789-1790. *English Radicalism, 1786-1832; from Paine to Cobbett* (London: George Allen and Unwin, 1955), pp. 33-34.

[25] John Steven Watson, *The Reign of George the Third, 1760-1815*, The Oxford History of England, XII (Oxford: Clarendon Press, 1960), pp. 228-234.

[26] Even Schneider, who tends to over-emphasize Wordsworth's political interests at Cambridge, is cautious about the poet's first years at the university. See *Wordsworth's Cambridge Education*, p. 13, especially.

Every conceivable interpretation of Wordsworth's academic life has been rendered by scholars. Harper, at one extreme, believes that the poet on the whole enjoyed his life at the university.[27] Schneider, making the most of Wordsworth's account in *The Prelude* of his withdrawal from the active life of the university, claims that the poet in his first year made an instinctive revolt against the predominant environment there of "cynical self-interested unrighteousness", a revolt that "foreshadows, parallels, and helps to explain his revolt in 1798 against eighteenth-century culture".[28] This withdrawal on Wordsworth's part is the primary thesis of Schneider's book; yet much the greater part of his work is spent in speculating about the extent of Wordsworth's connection with political and religious dissentients at the university and showing what he considers to be their pervasive influence there.

Certain more recent scholars side with Schneider against Harper on this point.[29] Yet Wordsworth's accounts of his Cambridge years give no indication of any extreme reaction, whether conscious or unconscious, psychological or intellectual. In *The Prelude* he consistently implies that his withdrawal from the formal academic course of study was as much due to indolence as it was to his over-preparedness. Indeed, he states specifically that he was by nature sociable and "lov'd idleness and joy", so that he and his colleagues, "unburthen'd, unalarm'd" by serious matters

> saunter'd, play'd, we rioted, we talk'd
> Unprofitable talk at morning hours,
> Drifted about along the streets and walks,
> Read lazily in lazy books.
>
> *(The Prelude*, III, 202-258).

Although Wordsworth did wish that the curriculum "had an ampler range,/ And freer pace" (III, 509-510) – a wish logically

---

[27] Harper, I, 59-63, 66-67.

[28] Schneider, pp. 17-18.

[29] Hayden, p. 7; Meyer, pp. 14-19; Todd, p. 21. See also H. W. Garrod, *Wordsworth*, 2nd ed. (Oxford: Clarendon Press, 1927), p. 37. At the same time, another extreme is exemplified by Herbert Read, who argues that since Wordsworth's crisis occurred from 1793 until 1798, his Cambridge years are thus rendered insignificant. *Wordsworth*, pp. 51-55.

stemming from his indolence and over-preparedness – he expresses no fundamental opposition to the curriculum; his exception here is but a passing note that he does not emphasize. Similarly, the "not for that hour,/ Nor for that place" passage has often been quoted as proof of Wordsworth's alienation from Cambridge. But the full passage does not suggest anything so severe as hostility to the university at large:

> Not seldom I had melancholy thoughts,
> From personal and family regards,
> Wishing to hope without a hope; some fears
> About my future worldly maintenance,
> And, more than all, a strangeness in my mind,
> A feeling that I was not for that hour,
> Nor for that place.
>
> (III, 75-81).

The "thoughts" and "fears" to which Wordsworth alludes are perfectly normal for an undergraduate – he does not suggest otherwise. In effect, Wordsworth is saying that while his college years were on the whole pleasant, he did have periods of doubt, like any other student. That he did have fears about his future is not to be denied, and these undoubtedly were complicated by his guardians. But, in its overall proportions, Book III of *The Prelude* gives far greater weight to the poet's pleasures at the university than it does to his discontent. Above all, the concluding lines of this passage – particularly the words "strangeness" and "feeling" – point not to conscious rebellion but to an intuitive, dimly felt sense of being out of place. This sense of displacement could have been the result of any number of factors. Most plausibly, *The Prelude* may be taken at face value: the source of his withdrawal was the undergraduate climate, which Wordsworth would have felt most immediately and constantly and which would very likely have made him feel inferior and "countrified", unlike his formal studies that could only have made him aware of his academic accomplishments. It should also be stressed that this disaffection was only an initial reaction, that it later disappeared as he became more involved in the undergraduate world. His continued aversion to his studies may be taken not as a sign of rebellion but simply as an indication of his nature and his taste: aside from the subjects he was already well versed in, the formal curriculum was of little interest to him. (See especially III, 94-104, 139-144, 206.)

Later in *The Prelude* Wordsworth describes how he read widely but with little discipline at the university, which

> Gave treacherous sanction to that overlove
> Of freedom planted in me from the very first
> And indolence, by force of which I turn'd
> From regulations even of my own,
> As from restraints and bonds.
>   (VI, 44-48).

This reaction against regulations, then, was not prompted by external circumstances but by his inner nature and his earlier conditioning – a conclusion both consistent with the above account of Wordsworth's childhood and supported by circumstantial evidence as well. It was a "rebellion" brought on neither by intellectual premises nor by psychological duress.

The same conclusion may be inferred from the absence of radical elements in the portions of *An Evening Walk* which date from the poet's Cambridge days; as far as is known, every political overtone in the poem was added after he went to France.[30] Moreover, there are absolutely no criticisms – either of the university or of the government – in his letters to William Mathews, an undergraduate friend, to whom Wordsworth wrote frequently in 1791; in fact, after his return from France at the end of 1792 he had to declare formally his political ideals to Mathews – a good indication that they were the result of his year away from England.[31]

Even if Cambridge was affected by political ferment, it is entirely possible that Wordsworth escaped its influence. Such was the case with Henry Gunning, who preceded the poet to the university and who was in fact a radical before entering, and with Christopher Wordsworth, who followed his brother there. Although they were more scholarly than Wordsworth, they both

---

[30] *Poetical Works*, I, 4-39.
[31] *Early Letters*, pp. 48-50, 55-57, 57-59, 61-63, 75-78, 118-120.

had many undergraduate acquaintances and yet neither one alludes to any atmosphere of rebellion at Cambridge.[32]

When the poet and his friend Jones traveled on the continent in the summer of 1790, three years after Wordsworth entered Cambridge, he was excited at the sight of France in revolution, but he felt no intellectual affinity with the cause of the insurgents:

> A Stripling, scarcely of the household then
> Of social life, I look'd upon these things
> As from a distance, heard, and saw, and felt,
> Was touch'd, but with no intimate concern.
>
> (*The Prelude*, VI, 681-705).

This is confirmed by a long letter he wrote to Dorothy in September, 1790, which describes his reactions to France and Switzerland; his attention was centered wholly on the beauty of the countryside and on the characteristics of the people, to the virtual exclusion of the political events.[33]

In short, everything that is known about the poet's early years points to the conclusion that he had been brought up in an atmosphere of political conservatism and religious orthodoxy, and that he did not renounce either until he went to France at the end of 1791; as will be seen, until he turned to republicanism, he even intended to become an Anglican clergyman.

Instead of criticizing the political conservatism at Cambridge, Wordsworth objected to the social snobbery and intellectual aridity of the undergraduates, to laxness in enforcing rules in the statute book, and above all, to any factor whatsoever that might be inimical to nurturing a love of learning among the students (*The Prelude*, III, 614-643). "Let Folly and False-seeming", he says,

> parade, among the Schools, at will;
> But spare the House of God. Was ever known
> The witless Shepherd who would drive his Flock
> With serious repetition to a pool

---

[32] Henry Gunning, *Reminiscences of Cambridge, A Selection Chosen by D. A. Winstanley* (Cambridge: Cambridge University Press, 1932), pp. 5-63; Christopher Wordsworth, *Social Life at the English Universities*, pp. 587-599.

[33] *Early Letters*, pp. 32-38.

Of which 'tis plain to sight the never taste?
A weight must surely hang on days begun
And ended with worst mockery: be wise,
Ye Presidents and Deans, and to your Bells
Give seasonable rest; for 'tis a sound
Hollow as ever vex'd the tranquil air;
And your officious doings bring disgrace
On the plain Steeples of our English Church,
Whose worship 'mid remotest village trees
Suffers for this. Even Science, too, at hand
In daily sight of such irreverence,
Is smitten thence with an unnatural taint,
Loses her just authority, falls beneath
Collateral suspicion, else unknown.
This obvious truth did not escape me then,
Unthinking as I was.

                            (*The Prelude*, III, 410-433).

In this attack on compulsory chapel it must be noticed that Wordsworth is making no comment whatsoever on religious worship; his criticism is just the reverse, that the irreligious spirit of the undergraduates makes a mockery of genuine religion, and science as well.

Much the same criticism of undergraduate attitudes and habits is implicit throughout the whole of Book III of *The Prelude*. It appears again by contrast when Wordsworth describes his idealized conception of the early Cambridge:

                            Princes then
At matins froze, and couch'd at curfew-time,
Train'd up, through piety and zeal, to prize
Spare diet, patient labour, and plain weeds.
                            (*The Prelude*, III, 467-470).

A similar passage appears later in Book III (626-643) in which he regards Cambridge as a microcosm of the world at large, specifically commenting on political and social abuses; but he does not indicate that this was his undergraduate opinion, and there is no reason to believe that it was. Near the end of Book III Wordsworth explicitly states

            Of these and other kindred notices
            I cannot say what portion is in truth

> The naked recollection of that time,
> And what may rather have been call'd to life
> By after-meditation.
>
> (III, 644-648).

This important insertion shows how scrupulous Wordsworth is trying to be to differentiate between his original feelings and his present thoughts. To the extent that Book III does criticize the "system" at Cambridge, the comments appear to reflect the opinions of an older alumnus, not the initial reactions of the original student.

In sum, the "rebellion" Wordsworth does describe in *The Prelude* was against the atmosphere of insincerity, social conventions, and indifference to learning.[34] He reacted, then, against undergraduate attitudes and customs, not against the traditions and the curriculum of the university, and what they represented; as will be seen, he then revered the Milton-Newton-Locke heritage at Cambridge, and his favorite subjects were mathematics and the classics, the very heart of the school's curriculum.

The argument that Wordsworth's political opinions were first formulated at Cambridge inevitably centers on the several well-known Dissenters associated with the university. As Schneider notes, "the dissentient movement at Cambridge grew out of the Newtonian-Lockean revolution at the beginning of the century".[35] Most of the leaders in the movement were Unitarians, although they were not able to publicize their views because of the university statutes. Yet they did occasionally agitate for the removal of subscription and for the reform of the university at large. In politics, they were invariably liberals, supporters both of the American and of the French Revolution.

Schneider makes the most detailed analyses of these men, spending the greater part of his book on discussing the careers of Paley, Jebb, Bishop Watson, Horne Tooke, William Frend,

---

[34] In this one respect, at least, the poet's nephew, Christopher Wordsworth, appears to be correct in stating that Wordsworth was primarily disgusted with undergraduate life at Cambridge, especially with the prevailing indifference to rules. *Memoirs of William Wordsworth*, 2 vols. (London: Moxon, 1851), I, 46-47.

[35] Schneider, pp. 117-118.

Robert Robinson, and George Dyer, and hypothesizing their influence on the young undergraduate radicals who were known to be friends of Wordsworth by 1795, if not earlier: James Losh, William Mathews, Basil Montagu, and Francis Wrangham.[36] But Schneider still can adduce no evidence proving that a direct connection existed between Wordsworth and the dissentients during the poet's undergraduate years.[37] As a result, Wordsworth's supposed conversion to liberalism at Cambridge must be doubted both because no tangible evidence suggests that he did convert then, and because much evidence indicates that he did so later.

Wordsworth's grandnephew Christopher presents a view of the political situation at Cambridge far removed from that presented by Schneider:

For the remainder of the century [after the 1760's] both Universities became assimilated to the new tory party, . . . So that even at Cambridge by 1793, the friends of the first french Revolution were in such discredit that even a whig was scarcely to be found. [38]

Yet Coleridge, at exactly the same time, was immersed in political controversy at Cambridge; by 1793 the university was embroiled in the controversy over William Frend's publication of *Peace and Union*, and the country at large was debating the French Revolution and Pitt's policies. The point is not that Christopher Wordsworth is "right" or "wrong", but that at least some people could be surrounded by such debate and yet remain indifferent to it, even unaware of it. If such was the case with the first Christopher Wordsworth in 1793, it could even more understandably have been the case with his brother between 1787 and 1791.

Nevertheless, Wordsworth's Cambridge days were not devoid of intellectual development beyond that of his formal studies. He

---

[36] *Ibid.*, pp. 113-149.
[37] *Ibid.*, particularly pp. 145-146. An instance parallel to this is "the revival of Platonic studies" at Cambridge during these same years, which a number of people have observed. Here, too, although this revival occurred while Wordsworth was at the university, he was patently unaffected by it. See John H. Muirhead, *Coleridge as Philosopher* (New York: Macmillan, 1930), p. 38.
[38] *Social Life at the English Universities*, pp. 80-81.

revered the traditions and the memory of the great men who had preceded him:

> I could not print
> Ground where the grass had yielded to the steps
> Of generations of illustrious Men,
> Unmov'd.
>
> (*The Prelude*, III, 261-264).

Singled out for special, and significant, adulation are Newton and Milton, significant primarily because Wordsworth was proud to be their countryman, something scholars forget when they exaggerate Wordsworth's affinities with France in 1793; they are judging him from the example of more extreme revolutionaries. Newton is the first to be honored by Wordsworth:

> And, from my Bedroom, I in moonlight nights
> Could see, right opposite, a few yards off,
> The Antechapel, where the Statue stood
> Of Newton, with his Prism and silent Face.

And years later, about 1832, the aging poet added to this two of his finest lines:

> The marble index of a mind for ever
> Voyaging through strange seas of Thought, alone.
>
> (*The Prelude*, III, 56-59).

This is more than a lover of mathematics speaking. He is obviously proud of Newton, his imagination captured by the scientist's ability to build what Wordsworth later called

> an independent world
> Created out of pure Intelligence.
>
> (*The Prelude*, VI, 186-187).

The tradition of Locke and Newton pervaded Cambridge in the late eighteenth century, as is evidenced by the account of Henry Gunning, who was an undergraduate from 1784 to 1788, and by Christopher Wordsworth's diary; it is worth noting that the latter's other references to his reading are almost wholly to science and mathematics.[39] When such external evidence is com-

---

[39] Gunning, pp. 5-63; *Social Life at the English Universities*, pp. 587-599.

bined with the allusions to Newton and Locke in Wordworth's
early works, it is clear that the mechanical philosophy of the early
eighteenth century surrounded the poet at Cambridge, as well as
at Hawkshead, and that he came to believe in it. This explains
his readiness to accept the schemes of the political reformers
whom he met after graduating, for they all, by using Newton and
Locke as their models, presupposed that the mind of man could
both lead to his improvement and synthesize all realms of human
experience. From mathematics, he tells us,

> I drew
> A pleasure calm and deeper, a still sense
> Of permanent and universal sway
> And paramount endowment in the mind,
> An image not unworthy of the one
> Surpassing Life, which out of space and time,
> Nor touch'd by welterings of passion, is
> And hath the name of God. Transcendent peace
> And silence did await upon these thoughts
> That were a frequent comfort to my youth.
> (*The Prelude*, VI, 150-159).

Such feelings would have confirmed for him his boyhood faith
in the mind's capacity, and by a simple transformation would
have helped to lead him to his later philosophy centered on intuitive awareness.

Wordworth's praise of Milton also offers an insight into his
mental development. His admiration for Milton was so great that
he became intoxicated the first time he attended a gathering in
the rooms his idol had occupied. While his description stresses
Milton's political ideals, Wordsworth does not suggest that his
undergraduate love for the poet was prompted by the latter's
republicanism; here again, we must distinguish carefully between
description of the past and later authorial commentary:

> our blind Poet, who, in his later day,
> Stood almost single, uttering odious truth,

Schneider rightly states that everything Wordsworth "read at Cambridge
came to him with a materialist-mechanist colouring". *Wordsworth's Cambridge Education*, p. 111.

Darkness before, and danger's voice behind.

(The Prelude, III, 284-286).

As will be seen, the emphasis here on Milton's sense of alienation from his time was probably occasioned by the fact that Wordsworth later shared the same feeling. Nevertheless, his undergraduate adoration of the man was an important foreshadowing of his subsequent interest in the seventeenth-century Republicans. This adulation made him more receptive to their political thought when he met it in France. Such is implied by another passage in *The Prelude*:

> nor was it least
> Of many debts which *afterwards* I owed
> To Cambridge, and an academic life
> That something there was holden up to view
> Of a Republic, where all stood thus far
> Upon equal ground, that they were brothers all
> In honour, as in one community,
> Scholars and Gentlemen, where, furthermore,
> Distinction lay open to all that came,
> And wealth and titles were in less esteem
> Than talents and successful industry.
>
> (IX, 225-235; italics mine).

The "afterwards" here is significant. When his political thought matured, largely through the influence of the English Republicans, Cambridge in retrospect served as an example for him of the ideal commonwealth. Once again, then, we have confirmation of two points: that he was not alienated from Cambridge at large, and that his political development came after his graduation.

Wordsworth's youthful aesthetic and literary principles also indicate his acceptance of the conventional point of view of the eighteenth century. His undergraduate taste was thoroughly traditional:

My Spirits have been kept in a perpetual hurry of delight by the almost uninterrupted succession of sublime and beautiful objects which have passed before my eyes during the course of the last month, . . . Among the more awful scenes of the Alps, . . . my whole soul was turned to him who produced the terrible majesty before me.[40]

[40]   *Early Letters*, pp. 32-34.

Similarly, his early poems, particularly *An Evening Walk*, were modeled on the poets who had preceded him immediately: their verse form is the heroic couplet; their language is the artificial diction of the age, complete with the double epithets; their structure is that of the descriptive landscape poem.[41] The extent of Wordsworth's intellectual indebtedness to the century must be kept in mind, for it reveals that his later reaction was not an impulsive, emotional one originating in any psychological torment within him; it was instead a conscious, thoughtful repudiation of the entire intellectual *milieu* in which he grew up.

By the same token, the character of the undergraduate poet did prepare him for his later rebellion. Through his sensitivity to nature and his early observations of the Lake Country farmers, he had attained an idealistic humanitarianism which readied him for the prevailing political theory of perfectibility. At Cambridge, and then in London, he discovered men in various stages of dissipation; his faith in nature and man was so great, however, that he ascribed their corruption to their surroundings, not to any inherent flaws in them. (By thus refusing, or failing, to perceive evil Wordsworth was of course adopting if not orthodox Anglicanism, then at least what was the conventional view on the part of many eighteenth-century Anglicans.) With this background, it was inevitable that Wordsworth, subsequently reading the many political theorists from Locke on who related national characteristics to such influences as government, climate, or topography, should decide that external conditions are determinants of the quality of men. And thus he was prepared to seek the political and social

---

[41] De Selincourt, *Poetical Works*, I, 317-329, and Legouis, pp. 120-160, record the many borrowings from the poets of the eighteenth century which Wordsworth's early poems contain. I concur with the fine studies of this poem made by Geoffrey Hartman and Frederick A. Pottle, although I must qualify the latter's assertion that the poem represents a "struggle of a new sensibility with an old literary diction". This "new sensibility", at this stage of Wordsworth's career, must be viewed primarily as a product of his personal nature and of his non-political youthful experience; it is not a conscious intellectual development. See *Wordsworth's Poetry, 1787-1814*, pp. 90-101, and *The Idiom of Poetry*, rev. ed. (Ithaca: Cornell University Press, 1946), pp. 109-134.

improvement of humanity, while still believing in the essential, or potential, nobility of man.

But a careful distinction must be made at this point. Havens epitomizes the common interpretation of Wordsworth's undergraduate concept of man in stating that his Cambridge years were detrimental to his lofty view of human nature.[42] This is not sufficiently precise. Vice and folly are indeed emphasized in his account of Cambridge in *The Prelude* (especially VIII, 641-677); but the effect they had on Wordsworth was not negative. He was sobered by the experience, coming to realize that man was weak unless he conscientiously attempted to make moral decisions, that life could be loved only "by acting well/ And understanding" (*The Prelude*, VIII, 675-676). Wordsworth clearly indicates that a new awareness resulted from his insights into Cambridge society. He at first adopted the gaudy, elaborate undergraduate style of dress (and, presumably, an equivalent behavior),[43] until, spending his first summer vacation at Hawkshead, he came to realize that he had been seduced away from the ideals of simplicity and naturalness:

A freshness also found I at this time
In human Life, the life I mean of those
Whose occupations really I lov'd.
(*The Prelude*, IV, 181-183).

This is a meaningful passage, showing clearly that Wordsworth had now coupled a reverence for simple, sincere endeavor with a belief in the genuineness of word and action. The hint of utilitarianism is worth noticing, too, for it indicates his readiness to accept one of the primary tenets of the Dissenting reformers.

All this is simply to say that, by the time he left Cambridge, Wordsworth was not a radical, evidently being unaware of and even uninterested in the world of English politics. But he had acquired, by combining his Hawkshead and his Cambridge experiences, a fairly realistic ideal of man, an awareness of the

[42] Raymond Dexter Havens, *The Mind of a Poet* (Baltimore: The Johns Hopkins Press, 1941), p. 469.
[43] See also *The Collected Writings of Thomas De Quincey*, David Masson, ed., 14 vols. (London: Black, 1896-1897), II, 266.

depravity men were subject to, and the enthusiasm to raise humanity out of its depravity to that ideal. His next years were spent in search of the means to effect this transition.

II.

LONDON, EARLY 1791: TOWARDS POLITICAL
COMMITMENT

> With deep devotion, Nature, did I feel
> In that great City what I owed to thee,
> High thoughts of God and Man, and love of Man,
> Triumphant over all those loathsome sights
> Of wretchedness and vice.
>
> *(The Prelude*, VIII, 62-66).

Wordsworth's political development really began in January, 1791, when he left Cambridge and went to London, thus for the first time coming in touch actively with the political controversies of the day. If color and excitement were his objects, he could not have picked a more opportune moment in history.

The primary object of everyone's interest was, of course, France. By the end of 1790 Mirabeau and Robespierre were leading their respective factions to a direct encounter; Danton, Desmoulins, and Marat had begun to influence the mob, using it as an instrument of vengeance; together, the mob and the Jacobins were casting an ominous light on the future of revolutionary ideals.[1] In England, reformers and radicals alike had quickly identified themselves with the moderate Girondins, and from 1789 onwards there was frequent intercourse between the various revolutionary societies of England and the Girondist groups.[2]

Beginning in January, 1791, exactly at the time when Wordsworth came to London, Robespierre started to achieve a clear ascendancy, to the despair of English followers of the Revolution.

[1] François Victor Alphonse Aulard, *The French Revolution, A Political History, 1789-1804*, Bernard Miall, trans., 4 vols. (New York: Scribner, 1910), I, 46-47.
[2] Watson, pp. 358-359.

The final tragedy struck the moderate camp on April 2, 1791, when Mirabeau suddenly died, leaving Robespierre to push through the Assembly a series of devastatingly extreme measures in the ensuing weeks. In the face of this crisis, the king began to negotiate openly with the powers of Europe to come to his aid, and the émigrés started to prepare for war on the borders of France. Then, on the night of June 20, 1791, came the unsuccessful attempt by Louis to escape from his kingdom.[3] All in all it was a suspenseful period in the history of the Revolution, as the ideals which had precipitated it seemed about to disappear amid confusion and vengeance.

A rival, and more immediate, field of interest was the English Parliament, then holding its first session since the publication of Burke's inflammatory *Reflections* in November, 1790. Fox and many of his followers had unhesitatingly spoken out in behalf of the Revolution, so that all eyes expectantly waited for the almost inevitable clash between the two leaders of the Opposition in Commons. They were not disappointed, though the split did come under rather unexpected circumstances.

The session, which started on February 4, 1791, was in many ways simply a long series of debates over reform, beginning with Wilberforce's renewed efforts to abolish the slave trade and concluding with the debate over Fox's libel bill. But on none of these was there any serious rift in Fox's ranks. The break came, rather, during debate over the seemingly harmless Quebec Government Bill, when Burke, on May 6, 1791, made his sensational, if irrelevant, denunciation of the French Revolution and then publicly announced that he and Fox were friends no more. The fireworks were all that a young enthusiast could ask for: Burke's highminded tirade; Fox's emotional outburst, torn as he was between his friend and his principles; and Pitt's adept maneuvering to keep the two going until their breach was irreparable.[4]

Overshadowed though they were by these histrionics, the many reform measures cannot be ignored, for behind each of them was a large group of agitators. After Wilberforce's bill was reintro-

3   Aulard, I, 47-49.
4   *Parliamentary Debates*, XXIX, 351-430.

duced, Horne Tooke's petition protesting the "undue" West-minster Election of 1789 was brought before a committee.[5] The election had been a lively and bitter contest, primarily through the rivalry of Fox and Horne Tooke. Tooke never stood a chance of having his petition acknowledged, but he did have a goodly number of sympathizers among liberal thinkers, closely associated as he was with many of them.[6]

Two other reform measures were introduced in February, 1791, alone – during Wordsworth's first month in London. On the ninth came a motion to inquire into the merits of Botany Bay as a penal colony. And on the twenty-first Mitford and Windham introduced a bill for the "relief" of Roman Catholics, a measure that was supported by many of the London Protestant Dissenters. Burke in the meantime had brought up again the subject of Warren Hastings' impeachment, thus rekindling one of the most heated controversies of the time.[7]

Another series of reform bills appeared in April and May, while Wordsworth was still in the city. Grey's motion to inquire into Pitt's plans for war with Russia was not exactly a reform measure, but in the debate over it were introduced many of the idealistic anti-war arguments that later were used against the war with France.[8] Later in April the slave trade Abolition Bill was badly defeated, undoubtedly a hard blow to all proponents of reform. Finally, in May came motions to repeal the Test Act in Scotland and to study the efficacy of imprisonment for debt; the latter passed, but the former was defeated easily.[9]

Outside Parliament in 1791 several groups of reformers had begun to organize. The London Society for Constitutional Information, which had been suspended since 1784, was revived in this year primarily through the efforts of Horne Tooke. It is

---

[5] *Ibid.*, XXVIII, 1210-1221.
[6] Godwin's Diary is one index of the extent to which Tooke mingled with the prominent men of philosophy and science. See also Minnie Clare Yarborough, *John Horne Tooke* (New York: Columbia University Press, 1926), p. 155.
[7] *Parliamentary Debates*, XXVIII, 1221-1269.
[8] *Ibid.*, XXIX, 164-218.
[9] *Ibid.*, 250-359; 488-514.

doubtful, however, if Wordsworth ever associated with this or any of the later, similar societies, for they were interested mainly in constitutional reform, particularly of suffrage, and were decidedly political, not literary or intellectual, in nature. But one group differed radically from these – the Society for Commemorating the Revolution of 1688, a moderate organization composed mostly of liberal Dissenters. This Society was largely interested in creating the image of a traditional English reform movement, and with this object they republished earlier political tracts, such as those of Locke, Sidney, Trenchard, and Lord Somers. The Republicans of the seventeenth century were their especial ideals, and in this and in their reform program they varied little from the view that Wordsworth came to hold in 1793.

In 1791 a resident of London could not have ignored this Society, for it had been responsible for starting the most fiercely waged debate of the time. On November 14, 1789, Dr. Richard Price had delivered a sermon before the 1688 Society, in which he not only called for continued reform efforts in the name of the tradition of the Glorious Revolution, but also highly extolled the French Revolutionaries for approximating the ideals of their English predecessors. It was in reply to Price that Burke wrote his *Reflections*, the most controversial book of the period. Many an author gained temporary fame wholly on the basis of his attack on Burke and defense of the Revolution. Most notable, and notorious, was Paine, whose first part of the *Rights of Man* was published on February 20, 1791,[10] in the very middle of this first London stay of Wordsworth. Paine just then was alternating between Paris and London; in the latter city about the spring of 1791 "he became the centre of an active company of reformers, which included Horne Tooke, Rickman, Priestley, Mary Wollstonecraft, and Romney".[11]

The vast majority of the other replies to Burke came out either shortly before or during Wordsworth's visit to London in 1791;

---

[10]   Godwin's Diary, 1791. Typescript in the possession of Professor Lewis Patton, Duke University.

[11]   F. J. C. Hearnshaw, ed., *The Social and Political Ideas of Some Representative Thinkers of the Revolutionary Era* (New York: Barnes and Noble, 1950), pp. 104-105.

he cannot have avoided some notice of them. A brief list will help to keep some of the more significant names in mind: Capel Lofft, *Remarks on the Letter of the Right Hon. Edmund Burke* (December, 1790); Mary Wollstonecraft, *A Vindication of the Rights of Men* (December, 1790); Joseph Priestley, *Letters to the Right Hon. Edmund Burke* (January, 1791); Thomas Christie, *Letters on the Revolution in France* (early 1791); James Edward Hamilton, *Reflections on the Revolution in France, . . . considered* (early 1791); James Mackintosh, *Vindiciae Gallicae* (early 1791).

With the primary exception of Mackintosh, the most important of these replies to Burke came from the publishing house of Joseph Johnson between late 1790 and June, 1791. It is crucially significant that, the next time Wordsworth was in London, his first published poems appeared over Johnson's imprint within a month and a half after the poet's arrival.

More should be known about this discerning publisher of Cowper, Blake, Wordsworth, Coleridge, and many other of the best writers of the time. In 1791 Johnson was primarily famous for his publication of works in three areas, areas in which he must have been especially interested, to judge from his emphasis on them: political philosophy, especially that defending the French Revolution or supporting a reform of representation at home; the cause of the Dissenters; and science, notably the experiments of Priestley. Whenever Wordsworth became a liberal, at Cambridge, in London, or in France, his decision to enlist in Johnson's camp clearly places him with the moderate political, religious, and social reformers.

Scholars have generally ignored Wordsworth's activities during his London stay in 1791. Mrs. Moorman's extensive biography spends just eight pages on this period – and all of her material comes from *The Prelude*; Todd can manage only three quick pages in his analysis of the poet's political development.[12] Yet

---

[12]   Mrs. Moorman, pp. 153-160; Todd, 35-37. Mrs. Moorman's interpretation of Wordsworth's thought at this time is that his "opinions were quite unfixed"; Todd concludes "that his convictions were already strong". This is dangerous ground to tread. David Perkins, *Wordsworth and the Poetry*

many obvious inferences, not only about Wordsworth's activities but also about his mental state, may be made about this time. Aside from two letters to Mathews written after he had left the city, *The Prelude* (Books VII and VIII) is our only direct source of information about Wordsworth's London visit of 1791. Nevertheless, his account of his state of mind then is plausible in light of the external circumstances just described and from what we can infer about a new university graduate's reaction to the great city, especially when he is on his own and undecided about a career. Also, his description is consistent with his account of his mental state at Cambridge and later in France, the former uninvolved, the latter committed, and the London period representing the transition between the two. While Books VII and VIII of *The Prelude* are a kind of synthesis of Wordsworth's reactions to London over a number of years, there can be no doubt that the account of his state of mind and of his activities applies almost entirely to 1791, emphasizing as it does the impressions of a newcomer to the city.

The Prelude indicates that for the most part Wordsworth lived humbly and alone while in London, just as he initially remained aloof at Cambridge:

> now it pleas'd me my abode to fix
> Single in the wide waste, to have a house
> It was enough (what matter for a home?)
> That own'd me.
>
> (*The Prelude*, VII, 75-78).

As to pastimes, he seems to have enjoyed most of all watching the crowds and getting caught up in the excitement of the city (*The Prelude*, VII, 121-135). At the theater, he saw Mrs. Siddons perform in several tragedies – some of them Shakespeare's, judging from the echoes at this point in *The Prelude*. But above all (and this is the longest description of his 1791 activities in the poem) he viewed

---

of Sincerity (Cambridge: Belknap Press, 1964), pp. 119-123, discusses Wordsworth's reactions to London, but without distinguishing one visit from another.

> that great Stage
> Where Senators, tongue-favor'd Men, perform,
> Admir'd and envied. Oh! the beating heart!
> When one among the prime of these rose up,
> One, of whose name from Childhood we had heard
> Familiarly, a household term.
>   (*The Prelude*, VII, 516-542).

Noteworthy here is his metaphor of the theater, implying that he attended Parliament only to witness the spectacle, not out of any intense political convictions. When he first visited Parliament, he was prepared to admire Pitt, the subject of these lines, since that statesman had been "a household term" in the Wordsworth family. Instead he found a hollow and pompous man, although the poet's description must have been colored in part by his distaste for Pitt's apostasy from the reform cause, with which Wordsworth may well have come to sympathize during his stay in the city. This would explain his satirical treatment of Pitt:

> like a Hero in Romance
> He winds away his never-ending horn,
> Words follow words, sense seems to follow sense;
> What memory and what logic! till the Strain
> Transcendent, superhuman as it is,
> Grows tedious even in a young Man's ear.
>   (*The Prelude*, VII, 537-542).

After line 542 of the original manuscript of Book VII Wordsworth later added impressions of Burke and Fox, strongly suggesting that he had been on hand for some of the fiery debates these two engaged in during the 1791 session. Unfortunately, his opinion of them by the 1820's was no longer a valid index of the feelings he originally felt:

> Genius of Burke! forgive the pen seduced
> By specious wonders, and too slow to tell
> Of what the ingenuous and the sensitive,
> All wise men wishing to grow wiser caught
> Rapt auditors! from thy most eloquent tongue . . .
> I see thee stand, stricken with many years . . .
>   Who sits
> Listening beside thee–no–no longer near

Yet still in heart thy friend. Illustrious Fox
Thy grateful Pupil. In the power of words
Thundering and light(e)ning [sic] when *his* turn
    shall come
A British Pericles. The times were big
With change that nightly failed not to provoke
Keen struggles, and black clouds of passion raised.
Yet Wisdom like the Goddess from Jove's brain
Broke forth in armour of resplendent words.
                    (*The Prelude*, VII, after 542: i-xix).

Whether or not Wordsworth actually witnessed the Burke-Fox
rupture, that event was certainly uppermost in his mind here. This
is obviously a first-hand description, but it would be foolish to
attempt any conjectures as to the approximate date of Wordsworth's attendance at Parliament.[13] Several suggestive clues, however, may be garnered from the above passage. For one, the lines
show clearly how much Wordsworth was aware of the momentous time he was living in, an awareness inevitably dependent
upon an active interest in current events. Moreover, the satire is
absent from Wordsworth's portraits of Burke and Fox; his admiration for the former came much later, as the lines attest, but
that for Fox may well have originated in 1791, when Fox stood
virtually alone in behalf of high political principles and the rights
of man.

Ten years later Wordsworth sent a copy of *Lyrical Ballads* to
Fox, which he accompanied with a letter that revealed both his
intimate knowledge of the recent course of events in Parliament
and his sympathy with Fox's principles. After referring to the
latter's efforts in behalf of poor-law reform, Wordsworth con-

---

[13] A notation in the diary of B. R. Haydon, May 23, 1815, contributes
another bit of information: that Wordsworth must have attended Parliament
several times, as the wording implies: "I Breakfasted with Wordsworth &
spent delightful two hours. Speaking of Burke, Fox, & Pitt, he said, 'You
always went from Burke with your mind filled, from Fox with your feelings
excited, from Pitt with wonder at his making you uneasy, at his having
had the power to make the worse appear the better reason. Pitt preferred
power to principle,' he said." But this could easily be a composite view
developed over a period of years. *The Diary of Benjamin Robert Haydon*,
Willard Bissell Pope, ed., 2 vols. (Cambridge: Harvard University Press,
1960), I, 446.

cludes with the wish "that the time may come when the country may perceive what it has lost by neglecting your advice".[14]

In the 1790's, Fox and those few around him were the only politicians toward whom the reformers could look for satisfaction. In 1795, Wordsworth despaired of politics entirely, thanks to the apostasy of many M.P.'s from their reform principles and to the private lives of others, notably Fox. Therefore, the idealized picture drawn in *The Prelude* is almost certainly a reproduction of the poet's feelings of 1791 and 1793, when he might well have regarded Fox as a "British Pericles". The analogy is suggestive, for it shows how the recent university graduate judged Fox, not only as a reformer and law-giver (even if his efforts were futile), but also as a classicist and a lover of the arts. The result is indicated by Wordsworth's deep insight into, and sympathy for, Fox's personal feelings: "still in heart thy friend. Illustrious Fox/ Thy grateful Pupil."

It is important to realize, however, that for the most part the indolence of Wordsworth's Cambridge career was still with him, as *The Prelude* and especially the letters indicate. He was as "Yet undetermin'd to what plan of life/ I should adhere" (VII, 63-64). Indignation at social and political conditions was yet to stir him into action. He seems to have been at loose ends, increasingly aware of the world of action and gradually more involved in it, but still unsure what direction his involvement should take. A note of confusion and perhaps frustration about his destiny is revealed in a letter he wrote to his friend Mathews on June 17, 1791:

I quitted London about three weeks ago, where my time passed in a strange manner; sometimes whirled about by the vortex of its *strenua inertia*, and sometimes thrown by the eddy into a corner of the stream, where I lay in almost motionless indolence. Think not however that I had not many very pleasant hours; a man must be unfortunate indeed who resides four months in Town without some of his time being disposed of in such a manner, as he would forget with reluctance. [15]

---

[14] *Early Letters*, p. 315.
[15] *Early Letters*, p. 49; see also *Ibid.*, pp. 55-56, and *The Prelude*, IX, 20-23.

This last sentence is worth notice, for it shows that at one time, at least, the city was not totally repugnant to Wordsworth. By reading between the lines and by remembering Wordsworth's fondness for social intercourse, it would probably be correct to assume that these "pleasant hours" were owing to his London acquaintances.

On June 26, 1791, Dorothy Wordsworth wrote to Jane Pollard about her family's suit with Lord Lonsdale:

We have got a very clever man on our side but as he is young he will not have much authority, his name is Christian, he is a friend of my Uncle, knows my brother William very well and I am very well acquainted with him and a charming man he is; ... You may perhaps have seen his name in the reviews; a pamphlet which he published lately upon the question whether Hastings' trial was to go on was highly spoken of. He is professor of common law in the university of Cambridge. [16]

Dorothy is referring to Edward Christian, a brother of Fletcher Christian of H. M. S. *Bounty* fame. In late 1790 Stockdale published the pamphlet which Dorothy mentions, *An Examination of Precedents and Principles; by which It Appears that an Impeachment is Determined by a Dissolution of Parliament*; a second edition appeared in January 1791, published by Deighton.[17]

Christian had many connections with Wordsworth; in fact, he and the poet were distantly related.[18] He, too, had come from the Cockermouth area. His college was also St. John's, where he was a fellow until 1789 and where he received his B.A. and M.A. in 1779 and 1782 respectively. From 1788 until 1800 he was professor of the Laws of England at Cambridge, so that he was in some way associated with the university during Wordsworth's entire career there. For a short while he was master of Hawkshead school, most likely in 1781, but certainly during Wordsworth's years at the school.[19] And in 1796, when Christian was endeavoring to exonerate his brother from the charges of Captain

---

[16] *Ibid.*, pp. 52-53.
[17] The *Critical Review* noticed both editions, but gave only grudging praise to the second. I, 114, 234.
[18] C. S. Wilkinson, *The Wake of the Bounty* (London: Cassell, 1953), p. 14.
[19] *Gentleman's Magazine*, CXXXIV (1823), 569-570; *DNB*, X, 276-277.

Bligh, Wordsworth took an intimate part in the cause by writing to the *Weekly Examiner* of Sherborne and protesting the publication of some forged letters purportedly written by Fletcher Christian.[20]

Since Dorothy was writing on June 26, 1791, Christian had probably been engaged by the Wordsworths while William was still in London. The manager of such family matters was their older brother, Richard, then a lawyer in London. This fact, coupled with Christian's current publishing concerns and Dorothy's statement that he "knows my brother William very well", would make it probable that Christian and Wordsworth associated in London.

Although probably no radical, Christian may well have been a supporter of the Whigs and of the cause of reform in general, to judge from his pamphlet on the Hastings controversy. At the very least he was something of an anti-aristocrat, as his part in the Wordsworth-Lonsdale case shows. Moreover, his ancestors had been Commonwealthmen, and the Republican tradition of the seventeenth century was said to be very much alive in his family.[21] On all of these counts he would have attracted Wordsworth, and possibly helped to direct him towards republicanism.

Another point of interest, which also accounts for Wordsworth's interest in the Christian family, is supplied by Edward Christian's first cousin, John, who changed his last name in 1790 to Curwen. This latter became a politician of some note, beginning his career by unsuccessfully striving to lessen Lord Lonsdale's political power in Cumberland – a goal which would have endeared Curwen to Wordsworth.[22] Curwen's daughter later married the poet's oldest son, John.

As to Wordsworth's other possible friends in London in 1791, *The Prelude* supplies a small clue:

---

[20] Mrs. Moorman, pp. 299-300; see also J. R. MacGillivray, "An Early Poem and Letter by Wordsworth", *Review of English Studies*, N.S. V (1954), 62-66.

[21] *Times Literary Supplement*, July 15, 1965, p. 594. Noted in a review of Edward Hughes, *North Country Life in the Eighteenth Century: Cumberland and Westmoreland, 1700-1830.*

[22] Wilkinson, pp. 9-11.

> Obscurely did I live,
> Not courting the society of Men
> By literature, or elegance, or rank
> Distinguish'd.
>
> *(The Prelude*, IX, 20-23).

The emphasis here is significant, for it shows that Wordsworth withheld himself consciously from men of that false distinction he had seen at Cambridge, that he took a certain pride in living humbly. But the implication in the reference to men of "literature" is a strange bias. It is supported by a letter Wordsworth wrote a few months later to William Mathews, summarizing his recent reading:

> my incursions into the fields of modern literature, excepting in our own language three volumes of *Tristram Shandy*, and two or three papers of the *Spectator*, half subdued – are absolutely nothing. . . . The truth of the matter is that when in Town I did *little*, and since I came here I have done nothing. [23]

But another letter by Dorothy of the same period mentions that her brother has been reading poetry and history;[24] this would suggest that Wordsworth was referring to the novelists of his day, and that the excesses of their work were unattractive to him.

One group of men particularly thought "elegance" and "rank" were distasteful, and gloried in their virtually enforced "obscurity" – the reformers. More precisely, one group of literary men also found the contemporary cults of the gothic and sentimental to be no more than symptoms of the trivial and false values of an aristocratic society. They were the Dissenting reformers. The foremost Dissenting publisher, Johnson, perfectly reflected these attitudes in his choice of authors and works; he rarely published novels, especially those of the sentimental or gothic schools. And the occasional volumes of poetry that he accepted were almost consistently political, theological, or of a generally didactic nature.

Johnson's publication of Wordsworth's *Descriptive Sketches* and *An Evening Walk* immediately after the poet's return from France does not necessarily suggest that the two knew each other

[23]   *Early Letters*, p. 56.
[24]   *Ibid.*, p. 52.

in 1791. But it does imply that Wordsworth either knew some of Johnson's associates prior to 1793 or else was well acquainted with the ideals of that group. Both in the 1793 version of *An Evening Walk* and in *Descriptive Sketches* we see a general tendency on Wordsworth's part to make his poetry more relevant, to become more involved through poetry in the "real" world. As part of this attempt, he uses noticeably fewer gothic and sentimental devices and descriptions than appear in his earlier poems; and when he does resort to the gothic or the sentimental, he frequently attempts to evoke horror or pity in sociological terms.[25] Also to be noticed here is the way in which Wordsworth belittles drama (at least that contemporary to him) as a literary form (*The Prelude*, VII, 507-517). Johnson, too, very evidently thought little of contemporary drama, for he rarely published plays.

The next spring the poet wrote to Mathews from France to give his friend some advice about publishers:

Would it not be possible for you to form an acquaintance with some of the publishing booksellers of London, from whom you might get some hints of what sort of works would be the most likely to answer? [26]

Since he advised Mathews to do so, it is likely that Wordsworth in 1791 had at least acquainted himself with the principles of the various publishers; the striking similarities between Wordsworth's first publications and the other works issued by Johnson strongly suggest that the poet had discovered the latter in 1791 and had admired his ideals.

Moreover, Wordsworth's description of his friends, sketchy as it is, does recall the humble self-effacement of many Dissenting personalities. Typical of the Dissenters were such men as Richard Price, Joseph Priestley, and Robert Robinson, all of whom were middle-class intellectuals, liberals in politics, and outspoken ene-

---

[25] *Poetical Works*, I, 4-90. A notebook dating from the poet's Cambridge days contains a number of earlier drafts of portions of *An Evening Walk*; these are almost consistently more sentimental and gothic, and less explicit in their descriptions, than the parts of the poem that first appeared in 1793. See de Selincourt's Notes, *Ibid.*, I, 319.

[26] *Early Letters*, p. 76.

mies of the idea of an Established church. In politics, they were descended from the Whigs of the Glorious Revolution and from the Republican theorists of the Commonwealth. Dissenting congregations by and large called themselves Baptists, Independents, or Presbyterians, although during the later eighteenth century a decided tendency towards Unitarianism appeared among them, especially on the part of Dissenting intellectuals. Despite these doctrinal differences, the Dissenters were united by certain basic ideals, notably their insistence upon freedom of conscience in religion.[27]

As will be seen, Godwin's Diary proves that Wordsworth was closely connected with a number of Dissenters during the 1795 stay in London; circumstantial evidence, particularly Johnson's publication of *Descriptive Sketches* and *An Evening Walk,* strongly suggests that he knew some of them in 1793. As Wordsworth was so rarely in London, it is highly possible that these associations were originally formed in 1791.

More specifically, Wordsworth states in the Fenwick note to *The Excursion* that as a young man he was friendly

with Mr. Nicholson of Cateaton Street, Strand, who at a time, when I had not many acquaintances in London, used often to invite me to dine with him on Sundays; . . . (Mr. N. being a Dissenter). [28]

Scholars have generally agreed that Wordsworth is here referring to his 1793 visit to London, although the 1791 stay is better described as "a time, when I had not many acquaintances in London". After all, in 1793 Wordsworth was staying with his brother (and possibly thus meeting Richard's London friends, though they were undoubtedly of an alien political philosophy), and he was familiar with his relatives the Rawsons and with Johnson. Moreover, if he did first associate with Nicholson in 1791, the

[27]   A good summary of the origins and of the general principles of the Dissenters may be found in Anthony Lincoln, *Some Political and Social Ideas of English Dissent, 1763-1800* (Cambridge: University Press, 1938), pp. 4-65. Generally speaking, the Dissenters had little in common with the Methodist movement, which was largely centered in the lower classes and which had none of the liberal intellectual characteristics that the Dissenters manifested.

[28]   *Poetical Works,* V, 374-375.

publication of his poems by Johnson immediately after he returned from France becomes more understandable – as does the fact that the poems he submitted were in every way conformable to Johnson's demands, though they had been written months before.

It should also be noted that Wordsworth's activities in London, on all of his visits during the 1790's, seem to have been centered in Holborn. Nicholson lived in Cateaton Street, while Johnson's shop was near-by in St. Paul's Churchyard, then the center of the booksellers. The presence of the Old Jewry meetinghouse on the edge of Holborn undoubtedly made the area something of a Dissenting community as well. If Wordsworth associated with his brother in 1791, as is likely since it was his first protracted visit to the city, he was then first brought in contact with the area, since his brother's quarters were in Gray's Inn at that time. It is entirely possible, then, that his familiarity with the Dissenting community began in 1791 as a consequence of his visits to Holborn.

At this point another criterion is pertinent. In *The Prelude* Wordsworth makes no reference to his career between his leaving London and his moving to France about six months later. This would indicate that no sudden crisis prompted his French trip, that the essential motives for going were with him while he was in London, and that the intervening months were of little importance to his mental development. Indeed, *The Prelude* implies exactly this (IX, 18-39). Without analyzing these motives as yet, it may still be surmised that Wordsworth's interest in France, and more particularly in the Revolution, had to be aroused before he would undertake such a trip at that time. A decided stigma was attached to all Englishmen who ventured across the Channel at this time. From this it may be gathered that Wordsworth's London associates, whether Dissenters or former Cambridge friends, were probably sympathizers with the Revolution, men who won Wordsworth's admiration for their indifference to public opinion. Just such indifference was evidenced at this very time by one of Wordsworth's current heroes, C. J. Fox, who virtually destroyed his party by aligning it with an unpopular cause. Significantly,

Fox was the spokesman in Parliament for the Dissenters.[29]

Much may be said about Wordsworth's social and political thought at this time – thanks primarily to Books VII and VIII of *The Prelude*. Almost all scholars have contradicted Wordsworth here and stated that he went to France already filled with revolutionary fervor.[30] This does not seem defensible to me. Although Wordsworth surely was interested in the Revolution by then and was more aware of politics than he had been at Cambridge, he does not seem to have gone to France filled with revolutionary zeal. His wanderings of the summer intervening between his London visit and his departure from England suggest indecisiveness, not hardened dedication or passionate interest. Certainly Wordsworth had acquired no systematic political philosophy before going to France.

Nevertheless, from the available evidence, it is apparent that Wordsworth in early 1791 was inclined to be a republican, having encountered – at least in name – the prominent figures in reform circles, as well as their central ideas; but he was not stirred to action until a year later, when he began to shape his ideas into finished form. Even if *The Prelude* did not substantiate this interpretation, peripheral circumstances strongly suggest that Wordsworth must have sympathized with the radical cause in 1791 while he was in London.

Unlike his Cambridge *milieu*, London surrounded him with political controversy of every type; and in this atmosphere Wordsworth clearly did not remain aloof, even if he did live alone. The whole of this section of *The Prelude* emphasizes how he was caught up by the excitement and the moving currents of life and thought in the city. With such involvement he could not have ignored the primary subjects of the day: the French Revolution and political reform. During this time he first witnessed Parliament in action; it is almost unnecessary to say that, since he later apologized to Burke for his youthful hostility, if he then sided

---

[29]   Maccoby, pp. 31-34.

[30]   H. W. Garrod, *Wordsworth*, pp. 58-61, makes Wordsworth a disciple of Rousseau in 1791, though *The Prelude* states explicitly that the poet read no formal political thought until he came under the influence of Beaupuy (X, 658-689).

with any group it was the Foxites and the "French" party. He was sufficiently involved in the cause of replying to Burke's attack at this time so that two years later he penned his own "Apology for the French Revolution" (as Grosart entitled it) in reply to another "apostate". In fact, Wordsworth's "Apology" (properly "Letter to the Bishop of Llandaff") is strongly reminiscent of Milton's *Ready and Easy Way to Establish a Free Commonwealth*, which was republished by Johnson while the poet was in London in 1791; one of the many similarities between Wordsworth and the Dissenters was that they both looked to the political tradition of Milton. Wordsworth must have had enough familiarity with Johnson's circle to know their ideals, or else he would not have submitted to him his *Descriptive Sketches* and *An Evening Walk* – poems which few London publishers would have accepted, and not just for their political implications.[31]

Wordsworth's readiness to sympathize with the English liberals when he first became aware of them was the result of two quite understandable motives. As was shown, he suffered no significant privations as a child; and at Cambridge he was able from his own account to dress *à la mode* and to join in student activities, if he so deigned. An economic crisis, and indeed a psychological one, was almost inevitable when once he left the university and went to London. He was an orphan, left to the guidance of his uncle guardians, and withheld from his rightful inheritance by an aristocrat. Now, too, he was undergoing something of a crisis concerning his choice of a career. It was at this point, and not during his Cambridge days, that Wordsworth would have been made miserable by and rebelled against the hostility of his conservative, narrow-minded uncles and the flouting of English law by the apparently power-mad Lord Lonsdale. As a matter of fact, although Lonsdale had been avoiding the law ever since the Wordsworths' claim had been presented to him in 1786, it was in the spring of 1791 that he openly revealed his intention – to

[31] Johnson only rarely published authors whose views were not his own, and the remainder he cultivated carefully in his circle. Wordsworth must have known this too, prominent as the members of the group were, so that submitting his poems to Johnson *may* have been an effort to enter this select company.

oppose any settlement with the Wordsworths with all his force, which was almost unlimited.[32] The poet's obsession with misused power must be regarded as largely a result of the example of Lord Lonsdale.

In the second place are the actual conditions in which Wordsworth must have existed. Since his guardians were increasingly indifferent, his only means of continued financial support was his older brother, himself just beginning his career. *The Prelude* nowhere mentions Wordsworth's economic situation while in London, such details being ignored throughout the whole poem. But the implication is there, nonetheless: "Obscurely did I live" suggests financial distress as much as an undistinguished social life. And at times in Books VII and VIII of the poem, he reveals a note of malaise about life and a certain anxiety about his future that are not apparent in the earlier books, though they by no means approach the profound depression recorded in Book X of the 1805 version. For the first time living apart from others, among economic conditions new and distasteful to him, and with Lord Lonsdale manifesting the inequity of the established order, Wordsworth may well have gradually turned to republicanism.

Hostility to the Establishment is implicit through the whole of the London part of *The Prelude*. In fact, here alone does satire appear, a significant reversion in 1805 to the methods of political ridicule he learned in the early 1790's. The corruption of the established church (but not religion per se) is attacked through the famous satire of the hollow and pompous cleric (VII, 543-565); and he effectively mocks the political system also, and more especially Pitt, by imitating the grandiose yet meaningless phrases of the statesman:

> Silence! hush!
> This is no trifler, no short-flighted Wit,
> No stammerer of a minute, painfully
> Deliver'd. No! the Orator hath yoked
> The Hours, like young Aurora, to his Car;
> O Presence of delight, can patience e'er

---

[32] *Early Letters*, p. 52; see also De Quincey, II, 252, and Mrs. Moorman, pp. 167-169.

> Grow weary of attending on a track
> That kindles with such glory? Marvellous!
> The enchantment spreads and rises; . . .
> These are grave follies.
>
> (VII, 528-543).

Significant also in the London description is the sudden emergence of Miltonic echoes, which recur throughout the sections dealing with the city.[33] Since the young Wordsworth, as has already been mentioned, regarded Milton primarily as a republican, he strongly hints by these overtones that he associated London with the birth of his political ideals.

But determining when Wordsworth became a liberal is not enough; the particular nature of his political beliefs must be determined, for there were, after all, many schools of reform with which Wordsworth might have associated. No evidence indicates his thoughts about the reform of Parliament, although the satire of this body in *The Prelude* suggests a mind sympathetic to the cause of improved representation. Certainly Wordsworth shared the attitude of virtually all the radicals in supporting the many humanitarian reform plans then current, chief among them being Wilberforce's abolition bill.

Fortunately, *The Prelude* permits a greater degree of certainty about Wordsworth's more general views, especially when it is examined in terms of the various contemporary schools of thought. From this it is apparent that he regarded his London days primarily as an education in man, in his physical and spiritual nature. His first reaction to the city was a feeling of insignificance in the face of its size and "power", until he came to realize that this was but a reflection of man's own mental potentiality (*The Prelude*, VIII, 678-751). He thus was able to retain the faith in humanity essential to all social and political radicalism, despite the appalling sights that undoubtedly confronted him. But he was not an extremist, a radical such as Paine and Holcroft were, who would transform all nations into Utopian republics; he still loved England, its traditions and accomplishments:

---

[33] *The Prelude*, VII, 81-88, 228, 306, 538; VIII, 678; and IX, 12-18, to mention some of the more obvious or pertinent parallels.

that vast Metropolis,
The Fountain of my Country's destiny
And of the destiny of Earth itself,
That great Emporium, Chronicle at once
And Burial-place of passions and their home
Imperial and chief living residence.

(The Prelude, VIII, 746-751).

The reappearance of Miltonic phrases here and throughout this section of Book VIII again indicates clearly that Wordsworth later associated Milton with his own outlook at this time. He shared especially Milton's faith in moderate republicanism and in the traditions and potential greatness of the English nation.

Furthermore, Wordsworth was not in 1791 a rationalist, a member of the school later associated with Godwin, who would make man's mind an end in itself, capable of its own accord of bringing humanity to absolute perfectibility. The power that he found in the city, and therefore in man, had origins beyond the mind; it was a transcendental immanence, "a Spirit/ Living in time and space, and far diffus'd" *(The Prelude,* VIII, 763-764).

In all this – moderation, love for England, traditionalism, admiration for the Republicans of the seventeenth century, and belief in a higher power moving man – Wordsworth closely parallels many Dissenting thinkers. This is not to say that he must therefore have been influenced by them, for he obviously could have come to these ideas on his own or in other ways; but the affinity did prepare him for a later association with them and an even closer identification of ideals.

Probably the most important intellectual accomplishment of this London visit, however, was the fact that nature here first made him aware of "the unity of man", paradoxically leading him to a love of man in spite of man's urban depravity and to a sense of unity despite the city's disorder. Having shown in Book VII of *The Prelude* how the city initially revolted him, he proceeds in Book VIII to describe how "Nature ... In that great City" gave him "High thoughts of God and Man, and love of Man." At this point two questions are relevant. First, was the influence of nature in the city something that occurred at second hand, a result of his childhood experiences acting on his memory, or was it a direct influence, nature being immanent in the city? My conclusion is that the latter is correct. While his childhood is reviewed in the first part of Book VIII, Wordsworth does not suggest a causal relationship between childhood and London, but rather brings out a number of parallels between the way nature affects one in the city and in the country. If simplicity is not found immediately in the city, it does appear there as a consequence of the workings of the imagination; "power" is apparent there from the first.[34]

The second question must be dealt with fully in a later chapter, but it should be raised here. While Wordsworth's love of man can be found also in Dissenting thought (and in the thinking of all radicals of the time), is there any equivalent sense of *unity* in the Dissenting view of life? In short, were all Dissenters the apostles of the Newtonian, mechanistic philosophy that most scholars have made them, or were certain of them also arriving at an organic sense of the unity of man? Again, I think that the latter was the case, and that here as in several other instances we have significant differences between Dissenting thought and that of most other liberals.

Wordsworth foreshadows his discussion of the "unity of man" theme by noting in Book VII that "the face of every one/ That passes by me is a mystery" (596-597). From his description of the inhabitants of London, it is obvious that he objected mainly to the way they had lost their identity and were the victims of their environment:

> Oh, blank confusion! and a type not false
> Of what the mighty City is itself
> To all except a Straggler here and there,
> To the whole Swarm of its inhabitants;
> An undistinguishable world to men,
> The slaves unrespited of low pursuits,
> Living amid the same perpetual flow

[34] Perkins, *Wordsworth and the Poetry of Sincerity*, pp. 119-123, contains an excellent discussion of Wordsworth's progression to a full love of man in London, or what Perkins calls the "idea of Man". Perkins' interpretation of Books VII and VIII of *The Prelude* is roughly parallel to mine.

> Of trivial objects, melted and reduced
> To one identity, by differences
> That have no law, no meaning, and no end.
>   (VII, 695-704).

This passage cannot be passed off by saying that Wordsworth just did not like cities. He found much of worth in London, and its adverse effects on men are not insuperable obstacles. Rather he here criticizes those men who have failed to live up to their potentialities in two ways: by laboring after unworthy ends, and by failing to attain the scope of mind to distinguish attributes by themselves. And this failing can be directly related to faulty educational methods, those especially which obscure the whole by over-emphasizing the parts (*The Prelude*, VII, 707-720).

Admittedly, the two books on London (especially VII, 121-243) heavily emphasize the multiplicity of sounds, colors, faces, and action in the streets of London, the general confusion that initially prevented his senses from fully apprehending any one phenomenon and weighing its value. As in childhood, he was here unusually responsive to sense impressions, but now the sensory confusion temporarily disoriented him. Nevertheless, his mind was stimulated by the experience, and by coming face to face with the superficial differences separating man from man, he was made aware of fundamental resemblances:

> among the multitudes
> Of that great City, oftentimes was seen
> Affectingly set forth, *more than elsewhere*
> *Is possible*, the unity of man,
> One spirit over ignorance and vice
> Predominant, in good and evil hearts
> One sense for moral judgements, as one eye
> For the sun's light.
>   (VIII, 824-831; italics mine)

It was this unity of man that made educational and political reform theoretically possible to Wordsworth, just as the circumstances of the city helped to show why reform was necessary.

It must be stressed, however, that Wordsworth had no systematic political philosophy in 1791. Rather, these were more or less isolated attitudes and opinions, which prepared him for a later, more coherent philosophy. This, too, is made clear in *The Prelude*, when Wordsworth mentions the first time he heard a woman utter profanity; instinctively he was upset at "the over-throw/Of her soul's beauty", but

> farther at that time
> Than this I was but seldom led, untaught
> At these appearances habitually
> To feel that such division has no place
> And cannot have; that in society . . .
> There are no gaps, that vice whatever shape
> It may put on a breathing object is
> No statue, and doth momently send forth
> Her respirations to be blown about
> At random by the universal air.
>
> (*The Prelude*, VII, 432-434, alternate version of Ms. X).

In this obscure passage, which Wordsworth inserted in 1804 but subsequently rejected, he seems to be implying that even in 1791 he had a dim awareness of the inner goodness of all men and of the responsibility of all men to one another; and that, conversely, all men are equally subject to evil. This last point again connects him with the Dissenters but not the more radical theorists. This sense of moral relativity likewise enabled him to believe in the efficacy of reform – and in the duty of all men to seek it. But the full realization awaited the appearance of Beaupuy.

Similarly, Wordsworth came to see in London that the senses were necessary intermediaries for an awareness of spiritual forces. He was led directly to a concern with physical reality, and more especially to a sensory philosophy. By this means he was able to accept the systems of such men as Beaupuy and the Dissenters, who built ethical and political philosophies on this same foundation of eighteenth-century materialism.

III.

FRANCE, 1792: POLITICAL THEORY

Wordsworth's activities during the months in 1791 between his leaving London [1] and his departure for France are properly ignored by the poet in *The Prelude*, for his mental course for the next year or so had been charted in London during the spring. Nevertheless, emotionally these summer months must have been an important period for the young man. He had only recently become sympathetic to liberal thought and been introduced to the world of politics; the populace of London had sobered him, making him aware for the first time that extensive reforms were urgently needed, just as the follies he witnessed in Parliament convinced him that English representation was inadequate and ineffectual. Now returned to rural solitude, he was able to contemplate the state of man and society in a clearer perspective, to formulate theories from the actualities he had just seen. The material consequence was his year's stay in France – an undertaking that must be viewed in the context of the 1790's, when it would have been an extremely momentous expedition for a young man.

Nor can it be presumed that because Wordsworth went to France, or even because he had been sobered by London, he was now suffering from depression. The letters of the summer and fall of 1791 explicitly show that he was in exceptionally good spirits, almost to the point of carefreeness. Dorothy helps to explain why:

---

[1] The letters prove that Wordsworth left London in late May, and that he was in Wales shortly thereafter. *Early Letters*, pp. 48-49. See also Mrs. Moorman, p. 161.

I often hear from my brother William who is now in Wales where I think he seems so happy that it is probable he will remain there all the summer, or a great part of it: Who would not be happy enjoying the company of three young ladies in the Vale of Clewyd and without a rival? . . . then there are mountains, rivers, woods and rocks, whose charms without any other inducement would be sufficient to tempt William to continue amongst them as long as possible. [2]

If the human condition was at all the subject of his thoughts, as it must have been, he was a decided optimist about the prospects of humanity. Foremost among the reasons for this was his summer-long residence in Wales – which, as Dorothy rightly forecast in June, was the perfect place for him to commune with nature. Then, too, Wordsworth temporarily was no longer suffering from indigence. During the whole of the summer his friend Robert Jones was his host at Plas-yn-llan in Denbighshire, while from September on he was again at Cambridge, supposedly studying foreign languages, thanks to his temporary return to the good graces of his uncle and guardian, William Cookson.

Mrs. Moorman believes that the Mount Snowdon episode, recounted in Book XIII of *The Prelude* (Book XIV in the 1850 version), occurred this summer. The moon-lit scene, with the sounds of the sea issuing from the chasm before him, was later to become an "emblem of a mind/ That feeds upon infinity" (XIV, 70-71, 1850 version). But, as Mrs. Moorman suggests, he seems to have been "untouched" by the landscape, for aside from a few echoes nothing of this trip appears in the poetry of the following months.[3] This passage from *The Prelude* centers on the mind of man, not on nature, and it seems likely that man was in 1791 – as in France and in the subsequent two years – his preoccupation.

Had Wordsworth been so inclined now, he might have settled the problem of his future by becoming curate of Harwich, a position offered to him by his influential second cousin, John Robin-

---

[2] *Early Letters*, p. 51; see also pp. 49-50, 56, 62. This last is a reference to Wordsworth's final letter from England before sailing to France, and is direct proof that he was in high spirits at the time. One of the few scholars to agree that Wordsworth at this period was not in a state of abject depression is Mrs. Moorman, p. 161.

[3] Mrs. Moorman, pp. 161-163.

son. Wordsworth declined, ostensibly because he was under age, though his references to the matter in his letters indicate clearly that at the time his temperament was little inclined to the system of religious preferment then prevalent in England.[4] Yet this does not necessarily suggest, as some scholars have inferred, that Wordsworth was then hostile to religion; as the subsequent discussion will reveal, just the opposite was the case. Further, the mere task of having to decide about a career must have sobered him, causing him to think specifically about the various professions open to him and to wonder which would best enable him to serve humanity. This would explain the tone of the letters he wrote to Mathews in mid-1791, for they repeatedly reveal that the poet was searching for the proper career while castigating himself for his indolence.[5]

But if his personal affairs for the moment were promising, the prospects of an immediate settlement from Lord Lonsdale disappeared in the course of the summer. Dorothy mentions that "Lord Lonsdale has retained all the best counsel, who except one, are engaged to serve him upon all occasions",[6] a fact that must have embittered the Wordsworths, so obviously just was their claim. Likewise, Dorothy wrote to Jane Pollard on December 7, 1791, that "Poor Richard is quite harassed with our vexatious Business with that tyrannical Lord Lonsdale; he has all the Plague of it."[7] Her attitude undoubtedly reflects that of her whole family. They did indeed win the case at the Carlisle Assizes in August, 1791; yet the unscrupulous Earl had final settlement referred to an arbitrator, thus prolonging the issue until the Wordsworths despaired of all success and gave up proceedings. Lonsdale was now obviously refusing to do justice; he was, moreover, flagrantly circumventing English law. Wordsworth's subsequent open avowal of republicanism must be viewed as a reflection on the case, and more especially on the events of this summer.

[4] *Early Letters*, pp. 57-58; Wordsworth did go to the trouble of traveling to London to discuss the matter with Robinson – confessedly out of mere deference to an important man.
[5] *Ibid.*, pp. 49, 56, 58, 60-61.
[6] *Ibid.*, p. 52; see also Mrs. Moorman, pp. 168-169.
[7] *Ibid.*, p. 66.

His trip to France could plausibly have been prompted by his disgust with England's corrupt establishments and ineffective laws.

It was at Cambridge, presumably in October, 1791, that Wordsworth decided to go to France. Scholars have generally assigned two motives for the journey, one dependent upon "sources" and the other using a psychological interpretation. The former school, notably Garrod and Hayden, assumes that a reading of Rousseau prompted Wordsworth to go to France, though no evidence whatsoever indicates either a reading of Rousseau or Rousseau-istic motives for the trip. Hayden, though less extreme than Garrod, illustrates the flimsiness of such a contention: "he may have found in Rousseau the expression and the confirmation of the rightness of his own desire not to face formal preparation but to remain free and independent, unhampered in his pursuit of knowledge and life." [8] Apart from the fact that Rousseau's ideas were commonplace by 1791, a distaste for a heavy academic course of study is fairly typical of young men, as Wordsworth himself had already indicated as an undergraduate,[9] without adverting to Rousseau as a precedent.

Hayden tries to eat his cake too, for he believes that Wordsworth at the same time had an intense guilt complex occasioned by his failure to fulfill his relatives' hopes, and that the poet generally resorted to travel as an escape mechanism.[10] Hayden is seconded by most recent scholars. Meyer dogmatically asserts that "the motive of escape" was "foremost in his mind",[11] while Mrs. Moorman cautiously assents to the same view: "Poverty he did not mind, but independence was an essential part of human dignity." [12] Todd merely notes that Wordsworth contradicts himself on the subject, and concludes that, "if France did 'lure him forth', it was a France in revolution".[13]

[8] Hayden, p. 16; Garrod, pp. 58-61.
[9] Wordsworth to Miss Taylor, 9 April 1801: "I did not, as I in some respects greatly regret, devote myself to the studies of the University". *Early Letters*, p. 327.
[10] Hayden, pp. 14-15.
[11] Meyer, pp. 23-24.
[12] Mrs. Moorman, pp. 169-170.
[13] Todd, pp. 37-38.

In the first version of Book IX of *The Prelude* Wordsworth states that he quitted London

> and betook myself to France,
> Led thither chiefly by a personal wish
> To speak the language more familiarly,
> With which intent I chose for my abode
> A City on the Borders of the Loire.
>
> (IX, 35-39).

There is no reason why this cannot be accepted as the actual motive behind the poet's journey. Dorothy wrote to her friend Jane Pollard on December 7, 1791, to say that her brother should have arrived at Orleans, "where he means to pass the Winter for the Purpose of learning the French Language which will qualify him for the office of travelling Companion to some young Gentleman if he can get recommended".[14] In other words, he intended to become a "travelling Tutor", as Dorothy puts it in the same letter, a scheme which would have necessitated fluency in French.

It is possible that his desire to study French and his interest in the Revolution may have been closely connected. In writing to Mathews just before he left England, he confessed that he had attained no "discipline amongst the Western languages".[15] If he had been introduced to liberal thought while he was in London during the previous spring, he would have been at least dimly aware of the extensive influence of the French political thinkers on the English reform movement.

Of the many important French revolutionary works, relatively few had been translated into English by 1791. Helvétius' *Treatise on Man* and Montesquieu's *Spirit of Laws* had both been translated many years earlier; Voltaire had been popularized through the efforts of Smollett and Goldsmith, but several of the works of Rousseau had not been published in English (the notable exceptions being *The Social Contract, Émile,* and *La Nouvelle Heloïse*). Consequently, Wordsworth's announced intention to learn the French language may have been motivated by his desire to gain a first-hand knowledge of the French thinkers he

[14] *Early Letters*, p. 66.
[15] *Ibid.*, p. 62.

had heard about in London. His statement does not imply that he was by now a radical, but it does suggest that he was fascinated by the Revolution and that he was intellectually prepared to undertake an extensive study of political thinkers. De Quincey helps to substantiate this opinion:

Wordsworth, it is well known to all who know anything of his history, felt himself so fascinated by the gorgeous festival era of the Revolution – ... that he went over to Paris, and spent about one entire year between that city, Orleans, and Blois. [16]

The wording here suggests that De Quincey's sources were close to the poet, thus allowing him to correct misapprehensions about Wordsworth's trip.

At the same time, it must be emphasized that even if he was a liberal sympathizer, he was not an agitator in behalf of the reform cause. That his life as yet had no such clear objective is indicated by his last letter to Mathews before he left England, in which he again laments his indecision about a career and confesses that he had no "resolution".[17] Fierce dedication to a cause was as yet nonexistent in him.

The influence of his earlier London visit is reflected in all this. The mental confusion he first felt there was still with him now, but so were his sympathy with the cause of reform, his interest in politics, and his admiration for literary figures of genuine merit.

In November, 1791, Wordsworth left Cambridge to go to France. His new interest in politics and his sympathy with the republican cause are apparent from the outset. While waiting at Brighton for a favorable wind, he went out of his way to meet Mrs. Charlotte Smith, a well-known radical authoress, and to have her write letters of introduction to several of her associates in France.[18] These letters must have been addressed primarily to her liberal acquaintances, for her career in France was spent mainly with such people,[19] all of which bespeaks Wordsworth's

[16]   De Quincey, II, 274.
[17]   *Early Letters*, pp. 61-63.
[18]   *Ibid.*, p. 69.
[19]   *DNB*, VIII, 28-29; Florence May Anna Hilbish, *Charlotte Smith, Poet*

interest in meeting mainly those whose political sentiments were the same as his.

The identity of only one of these addressees is known, Helen Maria Williams, but her career amply supports the contention that Wordsworth was consciously seeking to associate with known liberals. She had been in France at least a year before Wordsworth and was an enthusiastic supporter of the Girondins; in England she became notorious for her sympathies from the very first: "From the time she went to France, not only were her works denounced as fabricated, but her reputation as a woman was attacked." [20]

Wordsworth had admired Miss Williams when he was an undergraduate, writing a sentimental and non-political sonnet about her,[21] so that his interest in meeting her may not have been entirely prompted by political zeal. Nevertheless, notorious as Miss Williams was, Wordsworth's interest reveals something of his liberal sympathies and of his unconcern with traditional social conventions. Moreover, Miss Williams, despite her sexual freedom, was closely connected with liberal Protestant groups in France – a connection which Wordsworth may have learned about if he associated with Dissenters earlier in 1791, and which may have added to his interest in her.[22] Above all, it cannot have been mere coincidence that Wordsworth decided to reside in the very city in which Miss Williams was known to live: while still in England he deliberately chose Orléans in order to meet her. When he arrived there and discovered she had only recently left the city,

---

and Novelist (1749-1806) (Philadelphia: University of Pennsylvania, 1941), pp. 112-117.

[20] M. Ray Adams, "Helen Maria Williams and the French Revolution", *Wordsworth and Coleridge, Studies in Honor of George McLean Harper*, Earl Leslie Griggs, ed. (Princeton: Princeton University Press, 1939), pp. 114-115. *The Anti-Jacobin, or Weekly Examiner*, 4th ed., 2 vols. (London: Wright, 1799), I, index, contains the following under "Wollstonecraft": "See Helen Maria Williams, Godwin, Prostitution". See also John G. Alger, *Englishmen in the French Revolution* (London: Sampson Low, 1889), p. 69.

[21] "Sonnet on seeing Miss Helen Maria Williams weep at a tale of distress", *Poetical Works*, I, 269. As de Selincourt notes, Wordsworth "does not seem to have met her, ... till 1820, when he was in Paris". *Ibid.*, p. 367.

[22] *DNB*, LXI, 404-405.

he was downcast: "a considerable disappointment", he wrote to his brother Richard,[23] to whom he was usually uncommunicative about such matters.

At any rate, Wordsworth crossed the Channel for the second time in his life on Saturday, November 27, 1791, and arrived in Paris on Wednesday, November 30.[24] Here again he manifested his new interest in politics, for though he spent just five days in the French capital he took the time to attend the National Assembly, and possibly even the Jacobin Club.[25] From Paris he went directly to Orléans, where he arrived on December 6, 1791, and rented "a very handsome appartment on the first floor"[26] of the home of a hosier named M. Gellet-Duvivier. Residing in the same house with him were three cavalry officers, all of them typically opposed to the Revolution. Subsequently came his attachment to Annette Vallon, whom he followed to her home at Blois in the early spring of 1792.[27] In Blois he made the acquaintance of Michel Beaupuy, the lone republican among four companies of the Bassigny Regiment stationed there.[28] For about four months Wordsworth associated with Beaupuy, until the latter left for the front on July 27, 1792.[29] In middle or late September Wordsworth either accompanied or followed Annette back to Orléans, where he resided "until nearly the end of October", when he went once more to Paris. After a stay of about six weeks there, he returned to England.[30]

---

[23] *Early Letters*, p. 69.
[24] Mrs. Moorman's account of Wordsworth's trip to France is by far the most complete and the most intelligent (pp. 170-210). But in the light of the evidence about Wordsworth's career at this time, it is impossible to agree completely with her interpretation of the poet's state of mind as he arrived in France: "Wordsworth in 1791 was very little more politically-minded, or less ignorant of the causes and history of the great Revolution, than he had been when he had passed through France in the previous year on the flood-tide of the Feast of Federation." Mrs. Moorman, p. 171.
[25] *The Prelude*, IX, 46-49.
[26] *Early Letters*, pp. 68-69.
[27] *Ibid.*, pp. 75-78.
[28] Mrs. Moorman, pp. 173-188.
[29] Georges Bussière and Émile Legouis, *Le Général Michel Beaupuy* (Paris: Félix Alcan, 1891), p. 43.
[30] Mrs. Moorman, pp. 187, 200-201, 208-209.

Although except for his visits to Paris Wordsworth saw little significant political activity, this was a memorable period in the course of the Revolution for anyone residing in France, and his letters testify that little of it was lost on him.[31] Before he arrived in France the old Constituent Assembly dissolved itself, being replaced on October 1, 1791, by the Legislative Assembly, which numbered among its members several of the literary spokesmen of the Revolution, notably Brissot and Condorcet. The ensuing months brought an increasing tension between revolutionaries and *émigrés*, until in early December, just at the time Wordsworth was in Paris, Narbonne became Minister of War and the Assembly voted to increase the size of the army and of military expenditures; war was quickly becoming inevitable.

On April 20, 1792, under a Girondin ministry, the Assembly declared war on Austria. But the consequent invasion of Belgium was a complete failure, culminating in the uprising of Dillon's troops, who kidnapped their general and subsequently murdered him.[32] The ensuing summer months brought continual reversals, to the point that the fall of Paris seemed imminent; and with them came an increased degree of unrest among the masses, prompted also by the hesitation of the Girondist Assembly to dethrone the king. By September mob panic and irresolute leadership combined to precipitate the September massacres. Such was the atmosphere in which Wordsworth conversed with Beaupuy and then read the works of political theorists of the previous two hundred years; it was a period of frustration for the idealists, frustration both with the Girondin leaders for their hesitance and with the mob for its failure to rise above its passions.

As France began to be more successful in the war, there arose another period of hopeful expectancy, resulting on September 21, 1792, in the formation of the Convention, a body assigned the task of giving the nation a Constitution. Again, on the extreme side was the Mountain, dedicated to national defense above all,

---

[31] *Early Letters*, pp. 70-71, 77-78.

[32] This episode was singled out by Wordsworth in a letter to Mathews, in which he lamented this turn of events foreshadowing the downfall of the moderates and, more importantly, indicating that the masses were oblivious to the higher ideals of the Revolution. *Early Letters*, pp. 77-78.

in opposition to the idealistic Girondins, who now took the opportunity of proposing every conceivable scheme of republican government, many of them, inevitably, based upon specific theoretical proposals of the past. They sought to restrain the mob in favor of constitutional reforms, and to stop short of regicide. Wordsworth's final visit to Paris on this trip thus occurred as the Revolution neared its climax, when the two sides were becoming more clearly defined and the whole nation waited anxiously for the outcome of the conflict. Fortunately for Wordsworth, he left France a few months before the declaration of war with England and the succeeding Terror.[33]

The French Revolution was probably the most important single influence on Wordsworth's political development. He himself stresses its importance both by devoting three books of *The Prelude* to his French visit (which lasted but a small fraction of the time covered by the poem) and by placing Book VIII, "Retrospect", just before these books, a way of suggesting that France represented a significant turning point in his career. It should be emphasized, also, that these three books are not just about the trip per se, but about its consequences as well. More than anything, the Revolution together with Wordsworth's readings and associations at this time combined to give him that prime requisite of all great poets – "high seriousness", a quality that was to torment him severely in the next few years. His studies of this period, not just of politics, but also of educational theory, psychology, and several forms of philosophy, reveal Wordsworth's growing interest in man. The only major step still to confront him was the correlation of this humanitarian thought with his earlier, half-conscious view of nature. Although this process took a number of years, it ultimately bore fruit in the philosophy implicit in *Lyrical Ballads*.

Wordsworth's brief stay in Paris in 1791 and his liaison with Annette at Orléans are of little account in his political development; each in its own way shows that by nature he was still carefree and impatient with authority. Todd is undoubtedly right in pointing out that Wordsworth's visit to the National Assembly

[33]   Aulard, I, 338-367; II, 31-158.

in late 1791 "indicates that his interest in the political events of
the Capital had developed since his previous visit".[34] But in the
few days Wordsworth spent in the city he would have had little
time to familiarize himself fully with the political situation. More
important, despite Todd's implications, he was not a fervid follower of the Revolution; when visiting the ruins of the Bastille, he

> pocketed [a] relick in the guise
> Of an Enthusiast, yet, in honest truth . . .
> I look'd for something that I could not find,
> Affecting more emotion than I felt.
>   (*The Prelude*, IX, 63-79).

He had become interested in the various specific reform causes
in England, but he had yet to attain the enlarged vision of the
humanitarian; it seems clear that, while he was now genuinely
interested in politics, he was still unacquainted with the political
traditions and writers that lay behind current events.

The affair with Annette has been grossly overemphasized as
an indication of Wordsworth's intellectual rebellion; little can
excuse the excesses of Todd, who makes much of Wordsworth's
"consciousness of guilt",[35] or of Bateson, who reveals more than
anyone else the dangers of connecting the affair with Wordsworth's radicalism: "Wordsworth would probably not have become an active political revolutionary, if the barriers of his
passivity had not been previously overthrown by sexual passion."[36] Yet how had Wordsworth manifested this "passivity"?
Certainly not by the manner in which he ignored his guardians,
nor, above all, by his sudden trip to France. If any one person
was most responsible for the poet's political development at this
time it was Beaupuy, who, initially as a friend and then as a
thinker, led Wordsworth to the enlightened theories of man and
society prevalent in Revolutionary thought.

A perfect prototype of the enlightened humanitarian, Beaupuy
has been described as "a follower of Rousseau in everything that

---

[34] Todd, p. 39.
[35] *Ibid.*, p. 41.
[36] *Wordsworth, A Re-Interpretation*, p. 88.

set his master apart from Helvétius and Holbach." [37] This is mis-
leading, for it suggests that Beaupuy's influence on Wordsworth
was wholly Rousseauistic – a theory that is both a distortion of
the picture given in *The Prelude* and unlikely in view of
Rousseau's pervasiveness at the time. Likewise, it is an over-
simplification to say that Beaupuy was responsible for arousing
Wordsworth's "political ardour". [38] As a man, Beaupuy made
Wordsworth eager to follow his example, to dedicate his life to the
welfare of man and to the removal of self-interest from his pursuit of reform. In short, it was Beaupuy's personal example that
made of Wordsworth an humanitarian: "Man he lov'd/ As Man"
(*The Prelude*, IX, 312-313) aptly describes both Beaupuy and
Wordsworth.

Having been impressed with Beaupuy's character, Wordsworth
was now receptive to the specific ideals which the General espoused. When Wordsworth was in Paris a few months earlier, he
probably did not bother to take sides with the major factions in
the government, even if he had been able to distinguish between
them; now, under Beaupuy's influence, he was to align himself
with a specific radical philosophy – that represented by the
Girondins.

> oft in solitude
> With him did I discourse about the end
> Of civil government, and its wisest forms,
> Of ancient prejudice, and chartered rights,
> Allegiance, faith, and law by time matured,
> Custom and habit, novelty and change,
> Of self-respect, and virtue in the Few
> For patrimonial honour set apart,
> And ignorance in the labouring Multitude.
>
> (*The Prelude*, IX, 327-335).

This is not the language of a rash extremist, or of a Rousseauistic
idealist. Rather the philosophy Beaupuy enunciated to Words-

---

[37] Fairchild, III, 148. The only biography of Beaupuy is the above-quoted
Le Général Michel Beaupuy by Bussière and Legouis.
[38] Todd, p. 42; almost all other scholars have similarly been content to
regard Beaupuy as Wordsworth's introduction to Rousseau or to political
reform.

worth was a composite of eighteenth-century French and seventeenth-century English political thought; and the latter was probably as influential as the former, for an unidealistic view of the masses, a belief in "chartered rights", in "virtue in the Few", and in "law by time matured" are commonplace in the writings of the English Republicans. Beaupuy thus appealed to the strong sense of history and tradition that Wordsworth still possessed: the poet had

> a sounder judgment
> Than afterwards, carried about me yet
> With less alloy to its integrity
> The experience of past ages.
>
> (*The Prelude*, IX, 339-342).

That experience undoubtedly included Greece and Rome as well as the English Commonwealth, for Girondist thinkers habitually depended upon the ancient republicans.[39]

All in all, it is evident from what Wordsworth says that he and Beaupuy spent much of their time evaluating various abstract schemes of government, ranging from the ancients to the most recent proposals of Girondist thinkers. It is no less evident that they concluded in favor of a state governed by a select group of the virtuous and intelligent, whose interests were identical with those of the citizens in general; in its general outlines, this concept is much more that of Harrington and Montesquieu than it is Rousseau's.

The remainder of their time was spent in speculating about man, a necessary process to give their political idealism validity:

> We added dearest themes,
> Man and his noble nature, as it is
> The gift of God and lies in his own power,

[39] Probably the most extensive study of the influence of classical thought on the French revolutionaries is that by Harold Talbot Parker, *The Cult of Antiquity and the French Revolution* (Chicago: University of Chicago Press, 1937). See also Rousseau's *Confessions* for a particular instance where a reading of Plutarch "produced that republican spirit and love of liberty, ... which rendered me impatient of restraint and servitude". *Confessions of Jean-Jacques Rousseau*, W. Conyngham Mallory, trans. (New York: Boni, n.d.), p. 10.

> His blind desires and steady faculties
> Capable of clear truth, the one to break
> Bondage, the other to build Liberty
> On firm foundations, making social life,
> Through knowledge spreading and imperishable,
> As just in regulation, and as pure
> As individual in the wise and good.
>
> (*The Prelude*, IX, 361-370).

Here their discourse was more contemporary, in the exaltation of reason and in the implied belief in perfectibility; such thinkers as Helvétius and Condorcet, in their expansions of the philosophies of Rousseau and Montesquieu, have the closest affinity with this view of man formulated by Wordsworth and Beaupuy.

Then, Wordsworth recalls, the two looked into the past once more to determine the periods when "truth" was triumphant (*The Prelude*, IX, 371-374). Doubtless they looked primarily to ancient Athens, the Roman republic, and the early days of the English Commonwealth. Significantly, Wordsworth goes on to compare Beaupuy and himself to Plato and Dion, thinking no doubt of the influence of political climates on the interchange of thought; once again, Wordsworth's associations are meaningful insights into the origins of his ideas (*The Prelude*, IX, 414-423). As Havens points out, the Girondist adulation of the heroes of Greek liberty was shared by Wordsworth; [40] but it was probably Beaupuy who actually led him to view the Greeks in such a light.

Appropriately, Wordsworth concludes the description of his connection with Beaupuy with his famous passage about the "hunger-bitten Girl", who evoked Beaupuy's exclamation: " 'Tis against *that*/ Which we are fighting" (*The Prelude*, IX, 510-519). Abstract schemes have their value, but the prime object at hand is the state of man, at once a problem of education and of economics. Wordsworth is thus ending on a note of realism; by the direction of his whole discussion of Beaupuy he is manifesting the close relationship between his poetic theory of 1798 and his political thought: to be of genuine merit, worthwhile abstractions must be made real and communicated so that mankind at large

---

[40]   Havens, *Mind of a Poet*, p. 504.

can understand them or feel their influence. And so he ends the
passage with a thought that is seldom to be found in abstract
political theorists of the previous two centuries; it is a point of
view common primarily to the heightened humanitarianism consequent upon the early days of the Revolution: Wordsworth and
Beaupuy joined in believing that poverty would be abolished, and
then

> All institutes for ever blotted out
> That legalized exclusion, empty pomp
> Abolish'd, sensual state and cruel power
> Whether by edict of the one or few,
> And finally, as sum and crown of all,
> Should see the People having a strong hand
> In making their own Laws, whence better days
> To all mankind.
>
> *(The Prelude*, IX, 519-533).

All too soon, no doubt, Beaupuy was forced to depart with his
regiment, leaving Wordsworth a new convert to republican idealism. For the next three months, secluded as he was in the provincial towns of Blois and Orléans, he did little but write poetry
and read.

Two of Wordsworth's poems may be assigned with reasonable
probability to the summer of 1792 – *Descriptive Sketches* in its
entirety and parts of *An Evening Walk*. The first is full of radical
indignation at the state of society, supported by numerous allusions to other poets and political thinkers. Although Wordsworth
states in the Fenwick note to *An Evening Walk* that the poem
"was composed at school, and during my two first College vaca-
tions",[41] I think it likely that the poem was much revised and
extended between his graduation and its publication in 1793.
While the extant portion of the Cambridge manuscript departs
little from the themes of landscape description and of melancholic
reflection in the published version, the latter does contain a significantly larger number of Miltonic references, most notably to
his political prose works.[42] External evidence supports this view,

[41] *Poetical Works*, I, 318.
[42] *Ibid.*, I, 319-323.

for Wordsworth continued to revise the poem extensively after
its publication, revisions that continue to reflect his current reading. Yet another index of Wordsworth's readings in France is his
"Letter to the Bishop of Llandaff", which he penned hastily
shortly after his return to England. These three works indicate
beyond all doubt that in France Wordsworth's interests had been
turned to the welfare of man and to political theory.

Scholarly attention has usually centered on Wordsworth's dependence upon the French writers of the mid-century, notably
Rousseau. That these writers were read by Wordsworth and influenced him heavily cannot be denied. But any would-be reformer was steeped in Rousseau; indeed, as has been noted, the
entire era was pervaded with his thought, so that all too often the
influence of other writers is overlooked.[43] Two groups of writers
especially have been underestimated, or even ignored: the English political theorists of the seventeenth century, and the psychological philosophers – both French and English – contemporary with Wordsworth.

Zera Fink has convincingly stated the case for the influence of
the seventeenth-century English Republicans on Wordsworth. Although he makes little use of Wordsworth's early poetry, Fink is
still able to support his argument with an impressive array of
data, including *prima facie* evidence, the line of reasoning in the
"Letter to the Bishop of Llandaff", and the account in *The
Prelude* of the poet's conversations with Beaupuy.[44] Although

---

[43] Harper, I, 127-134, and Legouis, pp. 55-60, are primarily responsible
for this over-emphasis; but it is still a common failing in analyses of Wordsworth's early thought.
[44] Zera S. Fink, "Wordsworth and the English Republican Tradition",
JEGP, XLVII (1948), 107-126. Another study postulating an early political
influence on Wordsworth is that of Jane Worthington, *Wordsworth's Reading of Roman Prose* (New Haven: Yale University Press, 1946).
Two insurmountable difficulties prevent any convincing comparison of
Wordsworth's thought with that of classical writings: the unspecific nature
of the vast majority of the latter, couched as they were in vague abstractions, and the fact that almost all political writings subsequent to them
manifest a heavy use of classical republicans. Such writers as Sallust, Cicero,
and Livy were a common denominator in political liberalism throughout
the seventeenth and eighteenth centuries.

much of the following discussion is dependent upon Fink's article, in a number of cases it goes beyond Fink.

As a Girondin, Beaupuy would have been well versed in the idealistic schemes of Harrington and Milton and in the much publicized careers of Sidney and Ludlow; he cannot have avoided mentioning these writers. Further, aware as Wordsworth came to be of the political trends in France while he was in the country, he would have known that the Girondins were frequently attempting to apply English Republican theory to the Revolution. This was especially true after the Convention formed in September, 1792, for then a series of specific constitutional schemes, modeled on those of Harrington and his contemporaries, were proposed.

Another area of evidence more specifically supports the theory that Wordsworth early developed a significant, and abiding, interest in the Republican writers of his own nation: his later letters indicate that, more than any other group, these English Republicans were Wordsworth's political ideals throughout his career; any thorough defense of the poet's contention that his political principles never changed would have to begin with this continued faith in the writers of the Commonwealth. That he admired them highly, regarding them virtually as prophetic law-givers, is evident. He frequently manifests a wide knowledge of these writers and their works, suggesting that his acquaintance with them was long-standing:

surely you will allow that martial qualities are the natural efflorescence of a healthy state of society. All great politicians seem to have been of this opinion; in modern times Machiavel, Lord Brooke, Sir Philip Sydney, Lord Bacon, Harrington, and lastly Milton. [45]

Further, it is worth noting that the poet's "Letter to the Bishop of Llandaff" of the next year was subtitled "By a Republican", and that his later poems often refer to the political writers and warriors of the seventeenth century. His famous sonnet on liberty, "Great men have been among us", singles out for praise "The

[45] *Letters of William and Dorothy Wordsworth, The Middle Years*, Ernest de Selincourt, ed., 2 vols. (Oxford: Clarendon Press, 1937), II, 748. Hereafter cited as *Middle Years*.

later Sidney, Marvel, Harrington,/ Young Vane, and others who called Milton friend", while his "Lines on the Expected Invasion", written in 1803, alludes to those who,

> like the Pyms and Miltons of that day,
> Think that a State would live in sounder health
> If Kingship bowed its head to Commonwealth. [46]

And in *The Excursion* he accounts for the exalted wisdom of the Wanderer by stating that he lived "among the hills" and "gazed upon that mighty orb of song,/ The divine Milton." [47]

Yet many of these writers were not represented in Wordsworth's library until late in his life. Dorothy wrote to De Quincey in 1808 to say that her brother's "library is in fact little more than a chance collection of old books (setting aside the poets, and a few other Books that are to be found everywhere)", and to ask De Quincey to "look out for" old books for Wordsworth: "Clarendon – Burnet – any of the elder Histories – translations from the Classics chiefly historical – . . . Lord Bacon's Works – Milton's Prose Works – in short, any of the good elder writers." [48] Shortly thereafter Wordsworth himself wrote: "I also wish much to see Lord Brooke's Life of Sir Philip Sidney. It is not an uncommon Book, and perhaps a bookseller could procure it." [49] The inference to be gained from both these quotations is that Wordsworth was already familiar with these writers, perhaps through books belonging to his associates, since in the case of the former he had already made allusions to them in his works, and since the latter indicates clearly that he had already seen the book; the associates most likely to possess such works were Beaupuy in 1792 and his London acquaintances of 1793 – both periods when Wordsworth's economic status would have necessitated borrowing, rather than buying, books.

By the time of his death, Wordsworth's library contained an

---

[46] *Poetical Works*, III, 116, 121.

[47] *Ibid.*, V, 16.

[48] *Middle Years*, I, 233-234.

[49] *Ibid.*, I, 258. It is worth noting that Lord Brooke (Fulke Greville) paints Sidney as an ideal patriot, and incidentally details his own political development in the course of the work.

impressive collection of political and educational works, almost
all of them dating from the seventeenth century; it included
Newton's and Bentley's Milton, a complete edition of Milton's
prose, Bacon's *Advancement of Learning*, Hobbes, Locke, Har-
rington's *Oceana*, "along with many Royalist and Puritan accounts
of the Civil War, including the King's speech on the scaffold,
Burnet, Clarendon, Fuller, Hooker, Baxter, Stillingfleet, Jeremy
Taylor, Prynne, various seventeenth-century works on Charles I,
Bates's *Rise and Progress of the Late Troubles*, and *Mercurius
Rusticus*." [50]

But the most revealing sources of Wordsworth's knowledge
of seventeenth-century republicanism – indeed, of his familiarity
with all political writers – are his writings of 1792 and 1793.
Here, too, his dependence upon the political thinkers of his own
country has been ignored, or at best underestimated.[51]

In general, the English Republicans display several concepts
which they share with Wordsworth, but frequently not with the
French thinkers of the eighteenth century. Foremost among these
is the fact that the Republicans consistently manifest an awareness of religious qualities in the universe; an integral part of their
political schemes is the acceptance, not merely of a deity, but
also of inherent spiritual qualities in man. To them, an ideal
government takes these into account: it accepts without question
the essential nobility of humanity. In effect, then, government
itself is sacred.[52] Wordsworth likewise, though at times his ortho-

[50] Henry Crabb Robinson, *Correspondence*, Edith J. Morley, ed., 2 vols.
(Oxford: Clarendon Press, 1927), Appendix, "Wordsworth's Library", II,
867-874.
[51] The works mentioned in the subsequent analysis were all readily available to Wordsworth through eighteenth-century editions; in each case, the
work emphasized was selected because it was well known in Wordsworth's
time and because it typifies its author's thought. I make no pretense of an
exhaustive analysis of each writer's influence on Wordsworth.
[52] James Harrington, *The Political Writings of James Harrington, Representative Selections*, Charles Blitzer, ed. (New York: The Liberal Arts Press,
1955), p. 21; John Milton, *The Works of John Milton*, Frank Allen Patterson, ed., 18 vols. (New York: Columbia University Press, 1931-1938),
"Ready and Easy Way to Establish a Free Commonwealth", VI, 120;
Algernon Sidney, *Discourses Concerning Government*, 2 vols. (Philadelphia:
C. P. Wayne, 1805), I, 93.

doxy might have been questioned, came to believe in a fundamental element of divinity in man, and in the religious qualities of government. *An Evening Walk* and *Descriptive Sketches* may be compared meaningfully in this regard. The former, in common with all of Wordsworth's extant poems written before 1792, manifests no concern with spiritual values, whether in man or in nature, whereas the whole of *Descriptive Sketches* emphasizes heavily the religious qualities surrounding and within man. The contrast with *An Evening Walk* is apparent from the first:

> Were there, below, a spot of holy ground,
> By Pain and her sad family unfound,
> Sure, Nature's GOD that spot to man had giv'n. [53]

It was this new point of view that occasioned Wordsworth's savage denunciation of social wrongs in the poem: they are now not just pitiable, as was the case in the earlier poem; they are to be condemned for being unnatural and immoral.

Though not central to this study, an important insight into the chronology of these two poems is established by this analysis, if the above premises are correct. *Descriptive Sketches* consistently reflects a greater knowledge of political theorists than *An Evening Walk*, and so was almost certainly written during the latter part of Wordsworth's stay in France. The earlier poem was written in part while the poet was at Cambridge; but certain portions, with their increased debt to Milton (above all, *Areopagitica*), were likely added in France when he first began to study politics. Further, the later sections of the poem, notably the lines telling of the poor woman's dead husband (241-254), manifest a strong, and new, anti-war sentiment, a point of view probably prompted both by the similar sentiment in most English Republicans and by the fear that the *emigrés* in league with Austria would destroy all that the Revolution had accomplished – a fear Wordsworth himself felt.[54]

Nor must it be forgotten that Milton, Harrington, and their associates were countrymen of Wordsworth, writing in behalf of

[53] *Poetical Works*, I, 42. Unless otherwise noted, all references to *Descriptive Sketches* allude to the 1793 edition.
[54] *Early Letters*, pp. 77-78.

their most revered political institution, Parliament.[55] Their ideal of government was a supreme House of Commons, one composed of the most gifted men of the kingdom, not of those with hereditary or financial distinction. Moreover, the members were to have the welfare of the entire nation in mind, to be above all temptations of private interest. In *Descriptive Sketches* Wordsworth makes no specific comment on governmental machinery; but he does clearly connect loss of freedom, and all its attendant miseries, with monarchy and aristocracy:

> As despot courts their blaze of gems display,
> Ev'n by the secret cottage far away
> The lily of domestic joy decay. [56]

The implications here are verified in the "Letter to the Bishop of Llandaff", for Wordsworth there makes it obvious that he is writing, in large part, as a Parliamentary republican and as an Englishman; after generalizing about political theory, using France as his primary illustration, he concludes – for obvious dramatic emphasis – with the particular situation in England, decrying corruption and sympathizing with the lot of the persecuted and misunderstood advocates of Parliamentary reform.[57] But earlier in the essay Wordsworth has been careful to suggest his ideal government, one that is totally centered on Parliament. The members of that body will be selected only for their "virtues, talents, and acquirements"[58] – decidedly Republican language. The main guarantee of continued effectiveness from the legislators is the separation of private interest from public interest; in this regard, Wordsworth holds that, on more important matters, the legislators should only propose and deliberate, lending their wisdom but leaving final enactment to the people.[59]

[55] Ludlow reveals this as well as any of the Republicans in his bitterness at Cromwell's usurpation of power that Ludlow felt belonged rightly with Parliament. *Memoirs of Edmund Ludlow* (London: T. Beckett, 1771), pp. 189-208.

[56] *Poetical Works*, I, 84.

[57] *The Prose Works of William Wordsworth*, Alexander B. Grosart, ed.; 3 vols. (London: Moxon, 1876), I, 19-23. Hereafter cited as *Prose Works*.

[58] *Ibid.*, I, 11.

[59] *Ibid.*, I, 9-10.

In all of this Wordsworth is one with the English Republicans, both in asserting the supremacy of Parliament and in specific details as to its members and its sphere of activity. Harrington's language is particularly close to Wordsworth's:

a commonwealth where the wisdom of the nation proposes, and the interest of the people resolves, can never fail in whatever shall be further necessary for the right constituting of itself. [60]

In contrast to their French successors, the English Republicans consistently looked upon power, not in terms of rights, or justice, or economic necessity, but in terms of the natural. Parliamentary rule being divinely sanctioned, any infringement upon its operation would be contrary to the nature of things. Harrington especially dwells on this point: "Unnatural force is an external or adventitious opposition to the vigor of principles and their necessary working which, from a violation of nature, is called violence." [61] Hence, implicit in the thought of these Republicans is a detestation of war, except when its object was the foundation of a republic. Needless to say, a good Republican violently opposed Cromwell's excesses, as was the case with Ludlow, whose objections to Cromwell are in perfect harmony with Republican theory: "This that they called a government had no other means to preserve itself, but such as were violent; which, not being natural, could not be lasting." [62]

All this, again, is essentially Wordsworth's point of view. Throughout both *Descriptive Sketches* and the "Letter to the Bishop of Llandaff" he connects lack of freedom with the misuse of power; he continually attacks war as a means of attaining unjustified power; and, above all, he refers to freedom and republican government in terms of nature. As has been seen, Wordsworth discovered in his youth the power of nature; but, before that insight could be applied to the individual man, he first had

[60] Harrington, *Political Writings*, p. 150; see also Sidney, *Discourses*, II, 375-384.
[61] *Political Writings*, pp. 3-4; see also Sidney, *Discourses*, I, 100, 163.
[62] Ludlow, *Memoirs*, p. 208. Algernon Sidney reveals the same emphasis: "The common notions of liberty are not from school-divines, but from nature." Again, "man is naturally free", and "he cannot justly be deprived of that liberty without cause". *Discourses*, I, 4-5.

to relate natural power to man's social realm at large. A comparison of *An Evening Walk* and *Descriptive Sketches* illustrates this process, for the former ascribes to nature no more than an aesthetic influence; in it, nature is not seen to harmonize sympathetically with the moods or states of man. At the opposite extreme, in the "Letter to the Bishop of Llandaff" monarchy is specifically seen as an unnatural abuse of executive power, inevitably producing tyranny.

The English Republican most concerned about the interrelationship of education and politics was Milton. Like Harrington, he believed in a supreme senate composed only of the wisest and best qualified men of the nation:

the ground and basis of every just and free government... is a general council of ablest men, chosen by the people to consult of public affairs from time to time for the common good. In this Grand Council must the sovereignty, not transferred, but delegated only, and as it were deposited, reside. [63]

But Milton also was explicit in his demand for a national system of education, enlightenment to him being the surest safeguard of liberty:

To make the people fittest to choose and the chosen fittest to govern, will be to mend our corrupt and faulty education, to teach the people faith not without virtue, temperance, modesty, sobriety, parsimony, justice; not to admire wealth or honour; to hate turbulence and ambition; to place every one his private welfare and happiness in the public peace, liberty, and safety. [64]

This, certainly, is far removed from the more abstract, idealized educational theory of Rousseau. To the extent that Wordsworth believed in the ability of education to ennoble man, he shared the indebtedness of his time to Rousseau; but he was a disciple of Milton in his grounding of education on decidedly Christian ethics and in his relating education to freedom.

---

[63] Milton, *Works*, VI, 125-126.
[64] *Ibid.*, pp. 131-132; Harrington similarly sought a governmental system of education for the continuance of an "able ministry" by having the universities "prudently reformed" – perhaps by now an ideal Wordsworth sought. *Political Writings*, p. 160.

In its very style and language, *Descriptive Sketches* manifests
Wordsworth's new concern with Milton; his debt is obvious not
only in the specific borrowings from Milton but also in the epic
style apparent in the passages on liberty and slavery:

> Ev'n here Content has fix'd her smiling reign
> With Independance child of high Disdain.
> Exulting mid the winter of the skies,
> Shy as the jealous chamois, Freedom flies,
> And often grasps her sword, and often eyes. [65]

That these Miltonic influences were occasioned by Wordsworth's
admiration for Milton as a Republican is evident. Throughout the
poem, liberty is related to education, while slavery is regarded
both as the consequence of ignorance and as the cause of further
mental degradation:

> While Slavery, forcing the sunk mind to dwell
> On joys that might disgrace the captive's cell,
> Her shameless timbrel shakes along thy marge,
> And winds between thine isles the vocal barge. [66]

The moralistic overtones in this are likewise typical of the entire
poem, again indicating a point of view shared by the two poets.

The emphasis on the moral and political benefits of education
is continued in Wordsworth's "Letter to the Bishop of Llandaff",
where he laments the "debauched" state of the English mob, a
state wholly a result of the perverting influence of monarchy.[67]
Of a nation with total representation, Wordsworth says:

> their administration would require much less of what is usually
> called talents and experience, that is, of disciplined treachery and
> hoary Machiavelism; and at the same time, as it would no longer be
> their interest to keep the mass of the nation in ignorance, a moderate
> portion of useful knowledge would be universally disseminated. [68]

---

[65]   *Poetical Works*, I, 60-62; in his note to the poem, de Selincourt points
out the more obvious borrowings from Milton. I, 326-329.
[66]   *Ibid.*, I, 52.
[67]   *Prose Works*, I, 10.
[68]   *Ibid.*, I, 11-12; elsewhere in the "Letter" Wordsworth gets more specific
about education's political functions: "It is the province of education to
rectify the erroneous notions which a habit of oppression, and even of
resistance, may have created, and to soften this ferocity of character, pro-

Here another important area of inquiry is introduced: the inevitable weaknesses of monarchy. In this regard the French
writers generally were again concerned with human rights, as well
as with the inability of any one man to govern an entire Kingdom
justly. Their English forerunners, however, took at once a more
moralistic and more pragmatic position. Wordsworth clearly
helped himself to the arguments of both schools in his attack on
monarchy.

On this subject, Milton is again most similar to Wordsworth.
The central idea of *The Tenure of Kings and Magistrates*, as expressed in the sub-title, is "That it is lawful, . . . for any, who have
the Power, to call to account a Tyrant, or wicked KING, and
after due conviction, to depose, and put him to death."[69] This is
exactly the primary object of Wordsworth's "Letter to the Bishop
of Llandaff", and he cannot have helped recalling the most famous
English defense of regicide in writing one of his own.

In singling out for censure the moral evils of courts, Milton also
attacks their wastefulness:

a king must be ador'd like a Demigod, with a dissolute and haughty
court about him, of vast expense and luxury, masks and revels, to
the debauching of our prime gentry both male and female. [70]

Once more, this viewpoint is suggested in *Descriptive Sketches*
(especially ll. 792-803) and then developed more fully in the
"Letter to the Bishop of Llandaff"; whether referring to the court
of France or to that of England, Wordsworth consistently objects
to the immoral influence and to the economic extravagance of
courts.

Even beyond the realm of kingly courts, the Republicans held
that virtue flourished better in a democracy; whether on the part
of the people or their representatives, a republic "produces virtue,

---

ceeding from a necessary suspension of the mild and social virtues; it belongs
to her to create a race of men who, truly free, will look upon their fathers
as only enfranchised." *Prose Works*, I, 6.

[69] Milton, "Tenure of Kings", *Works*, V, facing p. 1.
[70] Milton, "Free Commonwealth", *Works*, VI, 120; see also Sidney, *Discourses*, I, 256-266.

order, and stability".[71] Sidney's words suggest the very way in which general morality is obtained – through a balancing of all forces in the nation, thus producing peace and subverting self-interest. This explains the Republican juxtaposition of material and moral elements, for stability is consequent only upon an equal distribution of property: "where there is equality of estates, there must be equality of power, and where there is equality of power, there can be no monarchy."[72]

The same rationale subsists throughout Wordsworth's "Letter to the Bishop of Llandaff", the key Republican words – virtue, nature, property, and power – appearing everywhere in meaningful juxtaposition. Monarchy only results in immorality, the unnatural, disproportion of wealth, and tyranny; a republic is conducive to morality, naturalness, equality of property, and freedom.

Yet again, the Republicans attack kingship on the ground that it is a trial beyond the realm of human nature to endure; as Sidney puts it, "absolute power . . . is a burden which no man can bear; and . . . no wise or good man ever desired it".[73] Wordsworth uses approximately the same argument, and in language that is markedly Republican, in writing of Louis XVI:

the prejudice and weakness of mankind have made it necessary to force an individual into an unnatural situation, which requires more than human talents and human virtues, and at the same time precludes him from attaining even a moderate knowledge of common life, and from feeling a particular share in the interests of mankind.[74]

One of the more famous disputes among the Republicans was that between Harrington and Milton. They both believed in a "commonwealth", but the former, unlike Milton, refused to sanction perpetual legislators, advocating instead annual elections and prescribed durations of tenure. Interestingly, Wordsworth goes out of his way to state explicitly the same ideals, and for exactly the same reasons: to subvert private interest and to anticipate

---

[71]   Sidney, *Discourses*, I, 182.
[72]   Harrington, *Political Writings*, p. 102.
[73]   Sidney, *Discourses*, I, 121.
[74]   Wordsworth, *Prose Works*, I, 5.

"the natural tendency of power to corrupt the heart of man".[75] It is here that Wordsworth and Harrington are closest – in their mutual distrust of power, which they regard as at best a necessary evil essentially antagonistic to humanity.

The foregoing evidence, while by no means absolutely conclusive, does indicate at least that Wordsworth read the English Republicans during or after his association with Beaupuy, and that he adopted many specific Republican ideals. In fact, *Descriptive Sketches* is a virtual index of Wordsworth's gradual awakening to these political ideals, for at the opening is only a hint of radical fervor, while by the end Wordsworth is enunciating a full and fairly specific political credo. That the "Letter to the Bishop of Llandaff" is an expansion of the poem may be explained primarily by the very nature of the work and partly by the simple fact that it was written several months later; but another significant reinforcement must be remembered: Joseph Johnson and his fellow Dissenters, who also adulated the Republicans and who likewise reveal a peculiar combination of the moral and the pragmatic. The extent of Wordsworth's reading in these Republican writers, however, and his detailed knowledge of their arguments prove beyond all doubt that he did not hurriedly read them on his return to England at the prompting of his Dissenting associates. The "Letter to the Bishop of Llandaff" reveals a mind that has become thoroughly familiar with these earlier thinkers, and that has developed and refined their ideas.

Yet all this is not to say that the English Republicans were the sole objects of Wordsworth's attention while he was in France. Beaupuy undoubtedly influenced Wordsworth's reading in every direction that would assist the poet's political development, and the thinkers of his own nation would not have been neglected, least of all Rousseau. But it would be foolhardy to attempt to say where Wordsworth was influenced by Rousseau as a consequence of his reading, and where he was merely sharing Rousseau with his age as a whole; none of his parallels with Rousseau is so detailed as to indicate that Wordsworth was ever more of a dis-

[75] *Ibid.*, p. 10; see Milton, "Free Commonwealth", *Works*, VI, 126-131; and Harrington, *Political Writings*, pp. 17-18.

ciple of Rousseau than the average English radical. In fact, what can be said with safety is that Wordsworth departs from Rousseau at least as often as he follows him. And, again, when Wordsworth does disagree with Rousseau, he usually concurs with the English Republicans.

For one, like the English Republicans Wordsworth seldom emphasized the social contract theory that came into prominence late in the seventeenth century and that was to become so central to Rousseau's thought. The French philosopher's differentiation between the legislature and the government, or active principle of law, is also ignored by Wordsworth – as are most of Rousseau's more idiosyncratic theories.

Nor does Wordsworth share Rousseau's attitude toward war. True, both regard it as inevitable in crises, but to Rousseau "War . . . is a relation, not between man and man, but between State and State",[76] whereas Wordsworth regards war as necessary only when the people are in conflict with their governors; it is an expediency to be used in overcoming tyranny: "Liberty . . . is too often obliged to borrow the very arms of Despotism to overthrow him, and, in order to reign in peace, must establish herself by violence".[77] Wars between states, to Wordsworth, would merely negate one of the primary advantages of liberty.

But above all, Wordsworth, unlike Rousseau, refuses to limit liberty to certain types of nations; the "Letter to the Bishop of Llandaff" simply refers to man as a whole and to his natural right to be free. Whether or not Rousseau meant his words to be taken literally, he still joined Montesquieu in stating that monarchy was best suited for large and wealthy states and republics for small and poor nations.[78] Both to Wordsworth and to the Republicans this would have been illogical, for one of their primary objections to monarchy was that one man was incapable of thoroughly governing a nation – and certainly his inability would only be magnified the larger the nation he ruled.

---

[76] Jean Jacques Rousseau, *The Social Contract*, G. D. H. Cole, trans. (London: Dent, 1938), pp. 10-11.
[77] *Prose Works*, I, 6.
[78] *Social Contract*, pp. 68-73.

In line with this, Rousseau's heavy emphasis on the rule of law, itself without parallel in Wordsworth's thought, led him to several concepts that were anathema to Wordsworth and to the English Republicans. Most pertinent here is Rousseau's belief that privilege may rightfully exist in a state – an idea Wordsworth repudiates indirectly in *Descriptive Sketches* and explicitly in the "Letter to the Bishop of Llandaff".[79]

Aside from trivial similarities, only three important tenets particular to Rousseau may be found in Wordsworth's early thought; and in each case Wordsworth significantly modified Rousseau's ideas. The most important of these tenets is that of the general will, almost a commonplace in political thought by Wordsworth's time. To Rousseau, the general will was a manifestation of a sort of collective self-interest, a point of view reflecting the prevailing mid-century French concept of man's primary motive, his selfishness.[80] But though Wordsworth adopts the idea of a general will, the term is always used by him in juxtaposition with "reason" and "utility", or at least in such a context as to indicate that he regarded these two criteria as necessary guides for the general will.[81]

Likewise, Rousseau's concept of man in the state of nature appears without modification in *Descriptive Sketches*. Here Wordsworth manifests all the idealistic enthusiasm of a new convert to political radicalism:

> Once Man entirely free, alone and wild,
> Was bless'd as free – for he was Nature's child.
> He, all superior but his God disdain'd,
> Walk'd none restraining, and by none restrain'd. [82]

Pure, natural, and free – here are the primary conditions of the Rousseauistic view of man as he was. But by the time Wordsworth wrote his "Letter to the Bishop of Llandaff" he was more deeply versed in political philosophy, and in the social and political situation of his day. The "Letter" is not the product of a

---

[79] *Ibid.*, p. 33; Wordsworth, *Prose Works*, I, 15-16.
[80] *Social Contract*, pp. 22, 26-27.
[81] *Prose Works*, I, 7-8, 12, 13-14.
[82] *Poetical Works*, I, 72.

youthful and over optimistic enthusiast, and it totally ignores Rousseau's noble savage. Instead, Wordsworth now sees natural urges in man which society at large must repress.

The third significant Rousseauistic concept which Wordsworth may have adopted was that of the law-giver, whom Rousseau saw as necessarily a kind of superhuman being. But again, where Rousseau idealizes he diverges from Wordsworth. To the extent that Rousseau emphasizes the importance of wisdom and morality in representatives, Wordsworth concurs with him; but while the former postulates a divine inspiration for law, the latter argues for the enactment of law on the basis of his own particular idea of the general will.[83]

The foregoing evidence suggests that Wordsworth was only briefly, during his French trip, a disciple of Rousseau, that Rousseau generally was too idealistic for Wordsworth, and that he was supplanted by other, more particular writers, notably the seventeenth-century Republicans and the French thinkers more nearly contemporary with Wordsworth.

But before the latter are discussed, mention should be made of Rousseau's contemporaries and their impact upon Wordsworth's radical thought. Montesquieu may properly be considered first, not for chronological reasons alone but because *The Spirit of Laws* was second only to Rousseau's works as an influence upon English political thought. In many respects, it was more important to Wordsworth than anything Rousseau wrote – especially since Montesquieu often is obviously adopting and expanding the ideals of the English Republicans.

In this regard, Montesquieu would have been of particular interest to an Englishman because of his praise for the English constitution as it exists in theory. He marveled at the system of

[83] *Prose Works*, I, 12; Wordsworth quotes Rousseau directly in the "Letter to the Bishop of Llandaff" to support his contention that continued slavery makes men love that state. Wordsworth's reference is to Chapter One of the *Social Contract. Prose Works*, I, 9. For other comments on Wordsworth's debt to Rousseau, see Legouis, p. 227, and Melvin M. Rader, *Presiding Ideas in Wordsworth's Poetry*, "University of Washington Publications in Language and Literature", VIII, 2 (Seattle: University of Washington Press, 1931), pp. 197-198.

checks and balances, and singled out Harrington and Sidney for their theories about the corruption of power in the legislature.[84] Wordsworth may well have had Montesquieu as well as the Republicans in mind when he stated that political philosophers should always attempt to devise a system to keep the goals of the governors the same as those of the governed, and to restrain the power of the former.[85]

Also pertinent to Wordsworth's personal interests was Montesquieu's belief that a republic obligated a person to accept "public employment", for such acts were "attestations of virtue".[86] Such an idea was unusual, and it may have prompted Wordsworth's sudden involvement in the affairs of state not only upon his return to London but also during his final weeks in Paris in 1792.

With the Republicans, Montesquieu placed a heavy emphasis upon virtue: without virtue a free nation could not endure; Montesquieu's prime example in this regard was the English Commonwealth.[87] As has been shown, this emphasis was central to Wordsworth also. But the two share a refinement of this point not much emphasized in the English Republicans: to both, a republic required less force to maintain public tranquility than did a monarchy; one of their primary criticisms of the latter form of government is that its legal code is usually unduly severe.[88]

Yet Wordsworth made no direct use of the most distinctive facet of Montesquieu's political thought: that as the climate, the topography, and the customs of nations vary, so should their laws, indeed their very governments, change.[89] From here Montesquieu went on to apply his theory in a ludicrous manner to England,[90] so it is small wonder Wordsworth failed to adopt it. In fact, Wordsworth in effect inverted the theory by having the

[84] M. De Secondat, Baron de Montesquieu, *The Spirit of Laws*, Mr. Nugent, trans., 3rd ed., 2 vols. (London: Nourse and Vaillant, 1758), I, 215-231.
[85] *Prose Works*, I, 9.
[86] *The Spirit of Laws*, I, 97.
[87] *Ibid.*, I, 28-29, 48-49.
[88] *Ibid.*, I, 118-120; Wordsworth, *Prose Works*, I, 12-13.
[89] *The Spirit of Laws*, I, 9.
[90] *Ibid.*, I, 331-332.

form of government influencing the mind and customs of the people – and even the landscape (*Descriptive Sketches*, ll. 702-725, 756-759).[91]

Nevertheless, it must be admitted that Montesquieu probably first interested Wordsworth in the differences between peoples, not of different nations, but of different regions. Indeed, in Montesquieu will be found much of the same concept of people from mountain areas that Wordsworth expressed in *Descriptive Sketches* with regard to the Swiss and in *The Prelude* with regard to his humble associates in the North country. To Montesquieu, men in cold climates are more vigorous, braver, and stronger; men in free lands, which are most often mountainous regions, are usually pure and frugal; and, finally, "when a people have pure and regular manners, their laws become simple and natural".[92] Such an idealization of humble mountain life must have recalled to Wordsworth's mind his own childhood associates. Temporarily, it helped him to form a political ideal centered on the natural and the moral. Later, when he enunciated his enlarged philosophy, he was to use exactly the same ideals, and to connect them with exactly the same group of people. Here, then, is an important instance in which Wordsworth's later thought originated in his political speculations.

Helvétius and Holbach have long deserved comparison with Wordsworth since they were prime influences on the thought of Godwin. In fact, since Wordsworth was enunciating "Godwinian" elements before Godwin himself expressed them, it might be profitable to examine the latter's sources to see if they possibly were a direct influence on Wordsworth.

Thoroughly utilitarian as was Helvétius, he undoubtedly had little lasting effect upon Wordsworth. Despite his negation of the natural, however, his corresponding emphasis upon reason and education[93] would have attracted the radical Wordsworth in his youthful systematizing. Just as Helvétius denied the validity of

[91]   *Poetical Works*, I, 82-86.
[92]   *The Spirit of Laws*, I, 435, 316-321, 386, 58-61.
[93]   Claude-Adrien Helvétius, *De L'Esprit*, Albert Keim, ed., 4th ed. (Paris: Mercure de France, 1909), pp. 84-138.

the passions, so did Wordsworth repudiate the Bishop of Llandaff's false display of emotion over the death of Louis XVI.[94]
Yet Helvétius also found room for religion in society, a distinctive
viewpoint for a liberal thinker of his time, and one which Wordsworth would not have missed; for, as the next chapter will bring
out more fully, Wordsworth allied himself not with the extreme
atheistic radicals but with the moderate, religion-oriented reformers. His early adulation of the English Republicans indicates
that this was so even when he was in France. All in all, then,
Helvétius probably reinforced Wordsworth's Republican faith in
education and virtue, and gave him the faint utilitarian echoes
that appear in the "Letter," notably when Wordsworth enunciates
a belief in "stern necessity".[95]

If Wordsworth dipped into Diderot's *Encyclopédie*, as well he
might under Beaupuy's aegis, he most likely would have been
struck not by Diderot's own basic philosophy of the good life,
but by Holbach's expansion of it. Although the latter set out to
remove religion as a criterion in all human pursuits, an endeavor
that for many was his only claim to fame, he did reveal attributes
that would have appealed to Wordsworth, notably his emphasis
on science and a purely scientific approach to law. Again, had
Wordsworth gone farther and read Holbach's *Système de la
Nature*, he would have found this scientific systematizing extended
to the whole natural universe. Such an approach obviously appealed to the young Wordsworth. Like Coleridge, he always dis-
played a healthy interest in the sciences; but more important, his
attempts to analyze the passions of men, to equate character with
environment, even to analyze his own mental development, were
so many manifestations of his indebtedness to the scientific spirit
which Holbach and his English imitators imparted.

Wordsworth did not have to read Holbach, Helvétius, or even
Diderot to be influenced by them, for their thought pervaded the
French intellectual atmosphere of the time. Indeed, Wordsworth
echoes so few of their ideas, and in such vague terms, that he
most likely learned of most of the work of the *encyclopédists*

[94] *De L'Esprit*, p. 94; Wordsworth, *Prose Works*, I, 4-5.
[95] *Prose Works*, I, 6; see also *Poetical Works*, I, 78.

through secondary sources – Beaupuy, newspaper reports, the debaters in the Assembly. But the point to be stressed is that in all likelihood he was first influenced by these writers through sources other than Godwin's *Political Justice*.

A final source of ideas in Wordsworth's reading at this time is Condorcet and his predecessors in the realm of philosophical psychology, especially Condillac. Unlike Helvétius and Holbach, these thinkers regarded man as inherently good, but corrupted by the forces of tyranny and ignorance. *The Prelude* is a tribute to Wordsworth's faith in human nature, a faith that is confirmed in *Descriptive Sketches* (ll. 520-535). And both in this poem and in the "Letter to the Bishop of Llandaff", the excesses of the mob, perversions of the passions, and social injustices at large are seen as consequences of the interdependent states of slavery and ignorance.[96]

Moreover, by starting with a belief in the innate goodness of man, Condorcet and his predecessors evolved an optimistic philosophy heavily emphasizing reason and education; it culminated with the theory "that the perfectibility of man is truly indefinite".[97] In this regard, Condorcet heavily praised Turgot, Price, and Priestley for being "the first and the most brilliant apostles" of the concept.[98] Science, as applied to the various realms of existence, was to be the agent of this amelioration. Wordsworth likewise was an optimist in 1792-1793, believing in the ultimate victory of truth and liberty on earth; this is the concluding theme of *Descriptive Sketches* (ll. 774-809), and it is implicit throughout the "Letter". More particularly, in the poem it is "Love and Truth" who "compose the train" of Nature (and therefore of Liberty), just as to Condorcet freedom was dependent upon the attainment of truth through reason *and* an enlargement of the sensibilities.[99]

In the exaltation of both these qualities, truth and feeling, and

---

[96]   *Prose Works*, I, 10-11.
[97]   Antoine-Nicolas de Condorcet, *Sketch for a Historical Picture of the ... Progress of the Human Mind*, June Barraclough, trans. (London: Weidenfeld and Nicolson, 1955), p. 4.
[98]   *Ibid.*, p. 142.
[99]   *Ibid.*, pp. 173-201.

in the emphasis on the scientific spirit and perfectibility, Condorcet paralleled not only Wordsworth's thought but also that of the English Dissenters at large. Likewise, Condorcet's admiration for the notable Dissenters was shared by many Frenchmen of his time. That Wordsworth sought out the leading Dissenting publisher upon his return to England, and submitted a poem fully in keeping with the primary tenets of these Dissenters, is direct proof that he was aware of these intellectual cross-currents of his day. The French moderate school, led by Condorcet, undoubtedly appealed to Wordsworth more than any other group of thinkers, besides the English Dissenters, of his time.

It must be kept in mind, furthermore, that though *The Progress of the Human Mind* was published posthumously in 1795 (in both England and France), Condorcet made his opinions known both as a member of the Legislative Assembly from 1791 to 1792 and in his subsequent attempts to devise a permanent Constitution for the nation. (As a constitutionalist, Condorcet was heavily indebted to the English Republicans, so that again the one would have called Wordsworth's attention to the other). *The Progress of the Human Mind* was essentially a final statement of the author's ideals, which ideals Wordsworth may easily have noted either in the reports of political affairs while he was in Blois or Orléans, or in the Assembly itself while he was in Paris.

In fact, the Assembly, particularly its Girondin members, may be regarded as the third area of political influence upon him when he was in France. Beaupuy was probably a directing agent, first of all arousing Wordsworth's enthusiasm for political theory and reform (and no doubt by example giving him a high opinion of human nature), then leading him to the principal political works of the past, and incidentally communicating his moderate Girondist views. Then, from his reading, Wordsworth molded his scattered ideas and feelings into something approaching a system. And by his associations with the Assembly, he saw his literary interests applied to active politics. The fact that the Assembly was heavily dependent upon the same writers that appear to have influenced him merely bespeaks Wordsworth's awareness of the political climate of opinion, and reinforces the conjecture that these writers influenced him. Further, if he did have access to reports of the legislative sessions during the long months after Beaupuy had left, the Assembly then no doubt also helped to direct the course of Wordsworth's reading.

That Wordsworth sympathized primarily with the Girondins might be expected of him, in the light of his generally moderate views at this time and especially in the light of his indebtedness to Beaupuy, who was a follower of Brissot. Fortunately, the poet leaves no doubt about his familiarity with the prominent Girondins and about his admiration for their abilities: "Reflecting upon the fate of the greatest portion of the members of the constituent and legislative assemblies, we must necessarily be struck with a prodigious annihilation of human talents." [100] Years later, Wordsworth was more explicit in referring to his dedication to these men:

> I doubtless should have made a common cause
> With some who perish'd.
>
> (*The Prelude*, X, 195-196).

Generally speaking, of the two Revolutionary factions, the Girondins were the more literary in their inclinations. As H. T. Parker has noted, the debates and writings of the times are filled with references to classical political writers, Brissot especially being inspired by such ancients as Cicero and Sallust.[101] Here Wordsworth would have encountered one more area of mutual interest with the Girondins. Further, the ideals that they derived from the Roman writers were those which Wordsworth came to emphasize: "a simple life, frugality, industry, temperance, self-control, courage, integrity, and justice".[102] Whether it was the classics, the Girondins, or Wordsworth's personal experiences which led the poet to these same ideals may be debated; in all probability the last, as confirmed and elaborated by the other two, made the greatest imprint upon his mind.

These classical ideals are reminiscent of those of the English Republicans – notably virtue and truth – which again were shared in common by the Girondins and Wordsworth. Fink's study of

[100]   *Prose Works*, I, 23.
[101]   *The Cult of Antiquity*, pp. 11-21, 49-52.
[102]   *Ibid.*, p. 23.

the extent of the Republican impact upon the Revolution reveals that the Girondins were primarily responsible for the interest in the seventeenth-century writers, and that emphasis was centered on Harrington, especially through "a whole series of constitutional proposals which bear unmistakably the impress of the *Oceana*".[103] These proposals were presented to the Convention, formed in September, 1792, and thus they were being debated at the very time that Wordsworth was back in Paris.

Much evidence supports the contention that the debates of the Girondins now came to play a meaningful role in Wordsworth's development. Aside from the simple fact that he spent six weeks in Paris in the autumn of 1792, time enough to assimilate the central thought of the Girondins, he now had sufficient background to comprehend the extent of the Girondist indebtedness to the English Republicans. Further, by this time he would have been able to discern the vast differences between the Jacobins and the Girondins, both in methods and in aims. The distinctions between the two, it has been noted, did not become apparent to contemporaries on the scene until the two groups clashed head-on in the Convention; earlier, the separation might have been imperceptible to Wordsworth.[104]

More specifically, Wordsworth later stated to James Muirhead, the biographer of James Watt, that "I went over to Paris ... at the time of the revolution in 1792 or 1793, and so was *pretty hot in it*; but I found Mr. J. Watt there before me, and *quite* as warm in the same cause."[105] This James Watt was the son of the famous inventor. Together with Thomas Cooper he mingled freely in Revolutionary circles throughout 1792, the two becoming sufficiently notorious to be denounced by Burke in the House of Commons on March 4, 1793. The mere fact that Wordsworth fraternized with Watt indicates the extent of his interest in polit-

---

[103] "Wordsworth and the English Republican Tradition", pp. 107-109.

[104] Michael John Sydenham, *The Girondins* (London: Athlone Press, 1961), pp. 130-131.

[105] James Patrick Muirhead, *The Life of James Watt* (New York: Appleton, 1859), p. 376; Wordsworth in his old age was unsure of the date, understandably so, since he left France at the very end of 1792. There can be no doubt, however, that he is referring to his stay in Paris of the fall of 1792.

ical affairs, confirming the conjecture that his association with Beaupuy and his readings of the past summer had combined to make him a political enthusiast.

At the same time, his friendship with Watt and the consequent implications also point to the conclusion that the political conditions in Paris were another source of ideas for him. Watt himself could have supplied some of these, for he too was aware of the intellectual basis of the Revolution, as indicated in part by his carrying the bust of Algernon Sidney in a procession of April 15, 1792.[106] Two days before that, Cooper and Watt delivered a "discours" to the *Société des Amis de la Constitution*, in which they expressed their sympathy with the Revolutionaries in the face of *"un concert des puissances despotiques de l'Europe"* — [107] the same sympathy that Wordsworth showed in writing to Mathews in May, 1792.[108] To judge from their message, Cooper and Watt believed in the cause of humanity at large, regarding themselves as citizens of the world, at the same time that they acknowledged their ties to England. And amidst their vague and commonplace expressions of revolutionary faith may be found several beliefs that have clear lines of influence from Rousseau and the English Republicans.[109] Possibly Watt led Wordsworth to works the poet had missed during the summer; certainly he was to Wordsworth a kindred spirit, one who helped him to clarify his ideals.

More important, however, is Wordsworth's active participation in the Revolution during this fall of 1792. His sympathies were still with the Girondins, as suggested by his previously mentioned lament over their downfall and by *The Prelude*, where he describes his fear that the leaders of Paris, impious and fanatical, were striving to control the whole nation (X, 106-128). Yet Wordsworth's sentiments originally stemmed from his admiration for the Girondins, not from his antipathy for the Jacobins; *The Prelude*, after all, was written when the poet, looking back ten

[106]   Mrs. Moorman, p. 205.
[107]   *Discours ... prononcé à la société des amis de la constitution, séante à Paris, le 13 avril 1792* (Paris: Société des Amis de la Constitution, 1792), p. 2.
[108]   *Early Letters*, pp. 77-78.
[109]   Cooper and Watt, pp. 2-3.

years, could recall the Reign of Terror which the Jacobins ultimately precipitated. The fact is that Wordsworth shared several
ideas with the Jacobins in opposition to the Girondins.

One of the primary objects of the "Letter to the Bishop of
Llandaff", the conviction of Louis XVI, is the same as that which
occupied most of the attention of the Jacobins while Wordsworth
was in Paris.[110] The method in each instance is the same: those
who plead the cause of humanity in condemning the king's execution are themselves the inhumane, in their defense of the mon-
strous wrongs perpetuated by the monarch. Likewise, the heavy
emphasis Wordsworth places throughout the "Letter" on the trial
and death of the king was obviously occasioned by his first-hand
observation of the Jacobins' insistent clamor for the head of
Louis.

Another distinction between the Girondins and the Jacobins
is also important because of its bearing on Wordsworth's development. As the Parisian mob became more and more unruly, the
Girondins grew consistently more hesitant about reform; increasingly, at important crises, the Jacobins took up the cause of
humanity in opposition to the irresolute moderates.[111] It is not
hard to imagine which group Wordsworth sided with: he himself
continued to believe in reform since he continued to have faith
in man; the mob was a mob only because it lacked edification.
Thus the fierce dedication of the Jacobins to the cause of mankind must be added to the list of sources for Wordsworth's own
love of humanity.

Yet, if Wordsworth was an extremist, he was so only in his
emphasis on the humane. In all other respects, he was essentially
one with the Girondins. Above all this was so in their common
exaltation of the intellect and in their admiration of the English
Republicans. As was the case with Wordsworth's relationship
with Watt, the Girondins also may have led the poet to Republican works that had escaped him; and they surely helped to

[110] *Prose Works*, I, 4-5.
[111] Sydenham, p. 209. It is also worth noting that Watt and Cooper were
primarily associated with the Jacobins while they were in France. See Dumas
Malone, *The Public Life of Thomas Cooper, 1783-1839* (Columbia: University of South Carolina Press, 1961), pp. 34-44.

increase his adulation for his English predecessors. By themselves, they gave to Wordsworth a final political principle for him to take back to England: the right of the individual in the face of state oppression.[112] This was to be especially close to Wordsworth's heart when he returned to England and was confronted by the repressive measures of Pitt's war-time ministry.

These, then, were the sources of Wordsworth's political thought while he was in France: Beaupuy, his reading, his political associations in Paris. It is now necessary to decide, as explicitly as possible, the state of mind they produced in Wordsworth. From all that has been said, their most obvious and most important effect on Wordsworth was in making him a political enthusiast, a transformation that began in London in the spring of 1791 and culminated in Paris at the end of 1792. So heavy was the influence of political utopias on the poet that his political ideology came to be centered on the general to the exclusion of the specific; if the state as a whole were truly representative of the people, and if education were universalized, then all abuses, private and public, would ultimately be corrected. This attitude explains his continued refusal to get involved in the various reform agitations, for he saw that particular injustices were but small reflections of deeper maladies in men and in their societies. When he returned to England, he discovered renewed agitation for the abolition of the slave trade; but he could not get excited over the issue, for he was convinced that, "if France prosper'd",

> this most rotten branch of human shame,
> Object, as seem'd, of a superfluous pains
> Would fall together with its parent tree.
> <div align="right">(<i>The Prelude</i>, X, 202-227).</div>

The individual and his social realm were thus the prime objects of Wordsworth's attention during his republican career. With

---

[112] *Ibid.*, p. 210; Sydenham feels that the Girondins made one other important ideological contribution in their last days: their insistence on the rule of law. If Wordsworth was aware of this, it would have had no effect upon him. In part because of his unpleasant experiences with Lord Lonsdale, law was itself repressive to him; nature, not man, was from the first the only law-giver he acknowledged.

regard to the latter, he was unrelenting in his opposition to monarchy and to any form of government that vested authority in the
few, although he admitted that in times of tyranny and general
ignorance great men must assume dictatorial control in order to
lead their people to freedom and to knowledge (*The Prelude*, X,
177-189). Likewise, he acknowledged the need for representatives of the people, but these were to be only the most intelligent
and the most virtuous men of the nation.

More particularly, Wordsworth was already beginning to distinguish nations, and even smaller areas, according to the character of their inhabitants, and to correlate that character with the
government of the nation or with the topography of the area.
Though he was a citizen of the world insofar as he loved man
and freedom, he realized that his mind was indelibly marked as
that of an Englishman, indeed that of a Lake Country Englishman. Now that he was versed in Montesquieu, he could see that
his own character was the product of the place of his upbringing;
he became more aware of it, and began to recognize in its inhabitants those ideal qualities emphasized alike by the English
Republicans and by Montesquieu. The consequences of this
awareness were far-reaching, for not only did it result in Wordsworth's exaltation of the simple life in his mature poetry but it
also helped him to achieve his poetic style itself and his method
of organizing his poetry on the basis of "character".

By the time Wordsworth left France his political creed centered
on two ideals: the glory of England and the life of virtue. His
correspondence from France reveals that he was still essentially
an Englishman, as in his letter to Mathews of May 19, 1792:
"You have the happiness of being born in a free country, where
every road is open, where talents and industry are more liberally
rewarded than amongst any other nation of the Universe".[113]
Why, then, did he return to England reluctantly, feeling that he
would be "No better than an alien in the Land"? (*The Prelude*, X,
194). In the political context, the answer to this is obvious: Pitt's
ministry, in its hostility to reform and to revolutionary France
alike, was warping the character of the nation; to Wordsworth,

[113]   *Early Letters*, p. 77.

this was all the more criminal because of his love for his land and for its past.[114]

At the same time, Wordsworth's concern with the virtuous is evident throughout *Descriptive Sketches* and the "Letter to the Bishop of Llandaff", as has been fully indicated in the preceding discussion. Likewise, in *The Prelude* he makes it clear that, as a consequence of his association with Beaupuy, he came to use moral stature as the primary criterion in evaluating a nation or an individual (X, 144-176 are among the many illustrations of this).

Another significant aspect of Wordsworth's early career bears upon this also – his frequent references in his letters to becoming a clergyman. Even in France he wrote to Mathews to say that he intended to take orders, though he wanted to defer the occasion temporarily in favor of a literary career.[115] By this time Wordsworth was already well along in his incursion into political thought under Beaupuy's guidance; he may well have made a limited acquaintance with the English Republicans by now. Further, one of his primary criticisms of English life, both before he left England and in the "Letter to the Bishop of Llandaff" after his return, was the corruption of the Established Church. To the Republicans, a state church was an essential component of the government; above all, it was the primary agent in guiding the people to virtue and knowledge. Since Wordsworth was dedicated to these same goals, and since he was familiar with Republican thought, in all likelihood he was considering the life of a clergyman so that he could effect the reforms he deemed necessary in the English church, and so that he could himself be an agent of virtue and knowledge to mankind at large.

Such a philosophy presupposes a high faith in man, something Wordsworth developed by merging two radically different outlooks. From the English Republicans he adopted the concept that

---

[114] From the distance of ten years Wordsworth probably combined his hesitancy to leave France with his depression a few weeks later, in the spring of 1793, over England's declaration of war with France, possibly to the extent that he over-stated his description of his emotions on his return to England.

[115] *Early Letters*, p. 76; May 19, 1792.

man is noble because of his spiritual qualities, because of his relationship with God. On the other hand, the French thinkers of the late eighteenth century led Wordsworth to his exaltation of the powers of the mind. By combining these two, Wordsworth arrived at his own particular idea of perfectibility – one that stressed the cultivation of qualities already inherent in man, rather than the attainment of traits totally foreign to him (*The Prelude*, X, 663-675).

Parallel to this, Wordsworth began to evolve at this time his theory of the hero, a theory also expressed in such later poems as "The Happy Warrior"; despite the lapse of years, his central idea remained the same. Hero-worship is most evident in his attitude to Beaupuy, who is in fact a partial prototype for his later portrait of the ideal hero. But elsewhere in *The Prelude* Wordsworth tells of his belief in 1792 that all mankind could attain the level of the hero if they were led to that end by a man who had enlarged his view of humanity; the poet believed

> that the virtue of one paramount mind
> Would have abash'd those impious crests, have quell'd
> Outrage and bloody power, and in despite
> Of what the People were through ignorance
> And immaturity, and, in the teeth
> Of desperate opposition from without,
> Have clear'd a passage for just government,
> And left a solid birthright to the State,
> Redeem'd according to example given
> By ancient Lawgivers.
>
> (*The Prelude*, X, 177-189). [116]

Noteworthy here also is Wordsworth's consistent emphasis on virtue and learning as the means to man's enlargement.

---

[116] Ms. A of *The Prelude* (X, 179) contains the line: "Creed which ten shameful years have not annull'd" – Wordsworth's way of saying in 1804 that he still had faith in man despite Pitt's repression and the Jacobins' Reign of Terror. Later manuscripts delete the line, a fact often cited by those who dwell on the older Wordsworth's conservatism. A moment's consideration, however, would indicate that Wordsworth could hardly have kept adding years to the line as he revised the poem. Perhaps literalists would be satisfied with this line: "Creed which forty-seven years have not annull'd."

A frequent observation in Wordsworth scholarship is that
during his stay in France the poet turned from nature to man
and only later came back to his love for the former.[117] *The Prelude*
seems to support this idea:

> until not less
> Than three and twenty summers had been told
> Was man in my affections and regards
> Subordinate to her.
>
> (VIII, 482-485).

Two points must be set straight about this: Wordsworth's exaltation of man was necessary to his philosophical development; but
this substitution of man for nature in no way implies that he felt
any lessening in his regard for nature's power over man. When
he later came to reemphasize nature, he still continued his noble
faith in man. Similarly, throughout this early humanitarian period
Wordsworth acknowledges the role of nature in the life of man:
it appears in *Descriptive Sketches* and the "Letter to the Bishop
of Llandaff" alike.[118] Possibly during Wordsworth's months of
depression in 1794, when he was immersed in a totally mechanistic philosophy, he might have totally forgotten nature. But before that, nature and man were alike central to his thought.

The important, lasting contribution of Wordsworth's year in
France, then, was this extremely exalted ideal of man, one that
made ample reservation for the spiritual and for the natural.
Although it lacks any acknowledgement of the interpenetration of
the natural and the human, it is still a significant and necessary
foreshadowing of the philosophy of the mature Wordsworth.

---

[117] De Selincourt, *The Prelude*, p. 580; Garrod, p. 58.

[118] Hartman's idea that *Descriptive Sketches* "questions" nature is acceptable to me, although I feel his analysis is here inappropriately intellectu-
alized. Hartman goes on to say that "though Wordsworth is sure *that* Power
abides, he is no longer sure *where* it abides". The poem, he feels, "relates
the story of an Idea of Nature in search of a nature adequate to it". This,
in part, helps to explain Wordsworth's inability as yet to connect nature to
man. *Wordsworth's Poetry*, pp. 102-104. At the other extreme, Garrod over-
simplifies when he says this idea of nature "is derived obviously from the
system of Rousseau" and is a "naive" "return to Nature". *Wordsworth*, pp.
54-55.

In conclusion, a brief word should be added about *The Prelude*. Its account of Wordsworth's activities and of his state of mind during his year in France can be amply verified by such outside sources as letters, our knowledge of public events, his reading, and his writings of this time. His failure to mention the Annette Vallon episode should be taken as a sign that to him, at least, the affair was of little importance to his intellectual development; I think the above discussion has corroborated Wordsworth's supposition. Over all, the reliability of *The Prelude* has been demonstrated once again.

IV

LONDON, 1793: WORDSWORTH AND THE
DISSENTING TRADITION

By the end of 1792 Wordsworth had returned to England, and was staying with his brother Richard in London.[1] Only a few assured facts are known about his activities and associates during this London visit. *An Evening Walk* and *Descriptive Sketches* were published by Joseph Johnson shortly after the return from France, probably about the end of January, 1793. Sometime after the appearance on January 15, 1793, of the Bishop of Llandaff's attack on the execution of Louis XVI, Wordsworth hastily penned a strongly republican defense of France that condemned the Bishop above all for his acceptance of the *status quo*. This essay remained unprinted until 1876. Further, from *The Excursion* it is known that when in London he associated with a Mr. Nicholson, a Dissenter.[2] Here Wordsworth may be referring to any of three visits to London, those of 1791, 1793, or 1795; but the first two are most probable. Also in London "he saw Mr and Mrs Rawson",[3] Dissenters and distant relatives, in whose home Dorothy grew up while Wordsworth was at Hawkshead. All that can be said of his departure from the city is that it was between the middle of June and the first part of July, 1793.[4]

The Prelude is likewise niggardly in its information about this portion of the poet's career. He confesses that the slave trade

---

[1] The only evidence to support this is in a letter from Richard to Christopher Cookson: "William arrived back, he is with me." Mrs. Moorman, p. 211; Mrs. Moorman assumes that Wordsworth resided with his brother for the duration of his stay.

[2] *Poetical Works*, V, 373-376.

[3] *Early Letters*, p. 97.

[4] *Ibid.*, pp. 95, 97.

agitation failed to interest him; he tells of the months of inner turmoil that the war with France occasioned; he condemns the war and England's leadership, yet laments France's gradual tendency to extremism (X, 189-381). But, though he expands on his frame of mind, Wordsworth joins his family and early biographers in being reticent about the actual course of his second long sojourn in London.

Consequently, scholars have relied heavily upon conjecture in studying this year in Wordsworth's life, above all with regard to his biography, although his state of mind at the time has been much debated also. Some scholars have stated with disarming assurance that at this time he became a student of Godwin – even meeting him at Johnson's table.[5] To others, he is a disciple of different thinkers, ranging from the Republicans to Paine. The central weakness in all the early interpretations was that they refused to grant any connection between this portion of Wordsworth's career and his later philosophy. Legouis and Harper treat the young poet as a wayward boy, whose later philosophy was a reaction against his youthful sinning;[6] their successors have at least redressed these wrongs, if none too precisely. Ironically, however, both of these early scholars touched on important facets of the London years that would have supplied useful information about the poet had they only carried their investigations to a logical conclusion.

Although Legouis continues his chauvinistic love for Rousseau by regarding Wordsworth's "Letter to the Bishop of Llandaff" as intrinsically Rousseauistic, he does mention an element of the work that has escaped notice:

Though in respect of his ideas he is much nearer to Paine than to Mackintosh, Wordsworth nevertheless differs from the former in his sustained sobriety, his tone of almost religious fervour, and a restrain-

---

[5] Harper, I, 212.
[6] Legouis, p. 327; Harper, I, 140-141. Meyer is one of the few later scholars to express a belief in the interrelationship of Wordsworth's early politics and his later philosophy, pp. 110-112; but he fails to develop the idea.

ed manner of expressing himself which . . . indicates the puritan austerity of his temperament. [7]

All this is remarkably accurate, but Legouis would ascribe it merely to Wordsworth's "temperament". It seems more likely that this "puritan austerity" can be traced both to Wordsworth's childhood years in the North of England and to his various readings and friendships of the early 1790's.

Harper likewise skirts a significant area of conjecture without ever entering it. He starts with a fact that cannot be disputed – that Wordsworth was connected with Joseph Johnson – and then enquires briefly into possible associations that resulted from it; his conclusion is that

Wordsworth's connection with the English 'Jacobins', with the most extreme element opposed to the war and actively agitating in favour of making England a republic, was much closer than has been generally admitted. [8]

Nor can this be disputed, as the early poems and letters, and the "Letter to the Bishop of Llandaff", amply prove; but Harper's idea does not follow from his own evidence. Actually, his error is a common one: to fail to differentiate between the various groups of liberal thinkers and to regard them all as radical *sans-culottes*; he simply did not go far enough into the Johnson circle. Garrod makes the same mistake: "Johnson's press was a good deal employed by the heretics of the time, political and religious." [9] As the subsequent discussion will reveal, this is merely a cruelly unfair and ignorant acceptance of the anti-reform propaganda of Pitt's government.

Inattention to Johnson and his circle has continued up to the present. At most, scholars have been willing to say only that Johnson was a possible introduction to other liberals – essentially

---

[7]   Legouis, p. 232. Albert Venn Dicey at once contradicts and concurs with Legouis when he says that the "Apology" is less radical than is often suggested and that it is marked by the language of moderation. *The Statesmanship of Wordsworth, An Essay* (Oxford: Clarendon, 1917), p. 66.

[8]   Harper, I, 211-212.

[9]   Garrod, p. 57. Read, *Wordsworth*, p. 83, employs the same slanted phrasing; he describes Johnson as "a radical free-thinker, whose house was a rendezvous of English republicans".

the point Harper made years ago; but no new names have been added to the list of possibilities, and no new insights into Wordsworth have accrued.[10] Usually, however, scholars have simply ignored Johnson and the implications of Wordsworth's publication at Johnson's press.

Todd's failures here are especially flagrant. He indiscriminately paints Johnson as a mere radical; he hypothesizes that Wordsworth may have met Godwin and his circle at Johnson's, despite the fact that this connection which Harper first suggested has been disproved ever since the emergence of Godwin's diary several years ago;[11] and he involves himself in the controversy over whether Paine or Godwin most influenced the "Letter to the Bishop of Llandaff", a debate current in the 1930's, but long since resolved by the negation of both possible influences.[12]

Between their preoccupation with Godwin and their indifference to Wordsworth's known associations, it is small wonder Wordsworthians have found the poet's stay in London an enigma. Godwin's influence on the "Letter to the Bishop of Llandaff" was first seriously supported in 1932 by C. W. Roberts, who concludes that Wordsworth's defense of the Revolution was written at the earliest after May, 1793 – time enough to allow for Wordsworth's assimilation of Godwin's thought.[13] Meyer and Fink together have totally exploded the theory, the one by a negative argument that shows Godwin's thought was merely an amalgamation of current ideas, the other by his convincing study of the use Wordsworth made of the English Republicans in his pamphlet.[14] Yet the myth persists – not just in claiming that Godwin was the origin of the

---

[10] Meyer, pp. 93-94; Moorman, pp. 218-219; Todd, pp. 55-56.

[11] The diary was first made public in 1952, after its owner, Lord Abinger, kindly permitted Professor Newman I. White of Duke University to have it microfilmed.

[12] Todd, pp. 55-56, 60-61.

[13] Charles W. Roberts, "The Influence of Godwin on Wordsworth's Letter to the Bishop of Llandaff", *Studies in Philology*, XXIX (1932), 590-591. Paine's influence on the "Letter to the Bishop of Llandaff" has been discussed by Edward Niles Hooker, "Wordsworth's Letter to the Bishop of Llandaff", *Studies in Philology*, XXVIII (1931), 522-531.

[14] Meyer, p. 134; Fink, pp. 110-111 and note; see also Fink's review of Todd, *Modern Philology*, LVI (1958), 138.

thought of the "Letter", but also in regarding him as the primary youthful influence on Wordsworth.[15]

The many lesser misinterpretations consequent upon the over-emphasis of Godwin and the neglect of Johnson are too numerous to enumerate. Suffice it to say that the following discussion not only represents a reevaluation of Wordsworth's frame of mind and of his associations but also offers many incidental corrections of accepted hypotheses about his career at this time.

The Prelude is explicit about one thing – that during the whole of 1793 Wordsworth was both aware of the political situation and highly moved by it emotionally (X, 189-361). Two events of this time especially weighed upon him, the war with France, which began in February, and the ensuing Reign of Terror in that country, resulting in the persecution of the Girondins. By these developments Wordsworth's two central ideals were shaken, for the war represented England's refusal to acknowledge her own tradition of political enlightenment, which Wordsworth knew to be central to Girondist theory; while the Reign of Terror indi-cated the final negation of that tradition as the Girondins had hoped to apply it to France. In fact, the memory of the Revolu-tion continued to be an important agent in Wordsworth's devel-opment for several years; *The Prelude* makes this clear by its emphasis, for not only are two books given to the poet's residence in France, but the following three books

are given up almost entirely to 'reflections on the French Revolution', as they occurred to Wordsworth at the time . . . or to reflections on his own reactions to the political events, particularly the outbreak of war, and on the inward condition of his mind and spirit which were thrown by these events into a severe and prolonged state of crisis and suffering. [16]

The political atmosphere which confronted Wordsworth on his return from France was little different from that of his earlier months in London, except for the conditions that resulted from the outbreak of war. Although petitions for Parliamentary reform

---

[15] Cole and Postgate, p. 140, and Hayden, p. 7, exemplify this common over-simplification on the part of Wordsworth scholars and intellectual historians alike.
[16] Mrs. Moorman, p. 220.

and motions to abolish the slave trade continued to appear before Commons, the primary issue of Wordsworth's second spring in London was the war itself. The Foxites greeted the declaration of war with a storm of opposition, but as time went on their minority votes diminished more and more, while the Ministry began to add to its side increasing numbers of the Opposition.[17] And out of Parliament the reform societies, as active as before, if not more so because of the war, were beginning to feel the first effects of Pitt's repressive measures. Despite enormous popular demonstrations, the government turned a deaf ear to pleas for peace and for reform. By May even *Political Justice* was being threatened with prosecution, and then followed the notorious prosecution in Scotland of Muir and Palmer. Whether these acts were genuinely motivated by fears for the national safety, or whether they were simply part of a clever minister's attempt to exploit the situation, the result was that the nation at large fell gradually prey to a witch-hunt dedicated to the complete removal of all Revolutionary sympathy and reform agitation. No attempt was made to distinguish between dangerous radicals and more moderate liberals.

All this meant that every political liberal was subject to suspicion, if indeed he was not made to fear for his very well-being. At the least, political theorists suffered from a wholly alien climate of opinion. Such was certainly the case with Wordsworth. In the "Letter to the Bishop of Llandaff", he alludes to the Birmingham riots that two years before had resulted in the destruction of Priestley's laboratory – a subject long out of the news except among those who regarded the incident as typical of the general hostility even to sane reform and to all forms of enquiry; moreover, Wordsworth joins with those disgruntled reformers who saw governmental machinations behind all popular outbursts against liberals:

Left to the quiet exercise of their own judgment, do you think that the people would have thought it necessary to set fire to the house of the philosophic Priestley, and to hunt down his life like that of a traitor or a parricide? [18]

[17]   *Parliamentary Debates*, XXX (1792-1794), 344-925.
[18]   *Prose Works*, I, 10.

Even more noteworthy than this is the way Wordsworth associates himself throughout the "Letter" with the liberals in their state of oppression:

> The friends of Liberty congratulate themselves upon the odium under which they are at present labouring, as the causes which have produced it have obliged so many of her false adherents to disclaim with officious earnestness any desire to promote her interests; nor are they disheartened by the diminution which their body is supposed already to have sustained. [19]

The knowledge of the reformers' attitudes that Wordsworth here reveals and his sympathy for them are indications of his dedication to their cause; but more important, his undertaking to speak authoritatively for them suggests that he numbers himself among their ranks.

If Wordsworth actually did associate with political liberals, however, their various circles must be differentiated, for they varied markedly in their methods and in their objectives. In general terms, there were at least three types of left-wing thinkers: the reformers, the philosophic radicals, and the liberal Dissenters. Most numerous were the reformers, who were represented in Parliament primarily by Fox. They numbered the vast majority of the various reform societies in their ranks. Briefly, they were dedicated to Parliamentary reform and to the correction of social and economic abuses. Like all other liberals, they opposed the war with France; but they were, as a rule, not inordinately attached to the ideals of the French Revolution, nor were they necessarily hostile to monarchy or to the British Constitution. In fact, their method for attaining the reform of abuses was entirely constitutional, for all their petitions and reform proposals were presented directly to Parliament.[20]

Wordsworth admired Fox and the cause he stood for, as his letter of 1801 to Fox attests,[21] and he was sympathetic to re-

---

[19]   *Ibid.*, pp. 22-23.
[20]   On the reform societies, see Maccoby, pp. 47-62. See also: Cole and Postgate, p. 130; Walter Phelps Hall, *British Radicalism, 1791-1797* (New York: Columbia University Press, 1912), pp. 159-178; Watson, *The Reign of George the Third*, p. 324.
[21]   *Early Letters*, pp. 312-315.

formers in general. But *The Prelude*, while suggesting this, also makes it clear that he was little interested in reform agitation (X, 204-227). Similarly, the "Letter to the Bishop of Llandaff" does reveal his belief in the reform of Parliament and of the penal code;[22] yet the primary intent of the work is not to espouse the alleviation of social abuses, but to attack monarchy for its effect on public morality and education. Nor is there any indication that Wordsworth ever knew any reform proponents personally. Although Godwin associated with many of the reformers, Wordsworth evidently was not in his company when reformers were present; and the poet's name appears in none of the lists of those who attended the various meetings of the reform societies.[23]

At the opposite pole were the philosophic radicals, men wholly dedicated to the utter destruction of all monarchies and to the universal establishment of democracy. Included among them in various ways were Paine, Godwin, Holcroft, and Thelwall. They differed among themselves as to the best method of overthrowing monarchy – revolution or gradual constitutional evolution. But their differences are not so important as the ideals they held in common, especially the ability of democratic government to perfect the human condition. Paine's *Rights of Man* and *Age of Reason* generally typify these more extreme liberals to the extent that Paine emphasizes reason and natural rights and uncompromisingly opposes tradition and the British constitution. Also, implicit in the thought of most of the radicals was a deistic, mechanical concept of the universe – of both man and nature; they looked back to the French thinkers of the mid-century as their guides.[24]

As others have pointed out, the thought of the "Letter to the Bishop of Llandaff" has many similarities to the ideas of the

[22] *Prose Works*, I, 12-13, 22.
[23] Godwin's Diary; *The Morning Chronicle*, which closely followed the activities of the reformers; *Whig Club, Instituted in May 1784* (London, Barr, 1792).
[24] Godwin's debt to these writers was openly acknowledged; but they were likewise influential on Paine and Holcroft. See Thomas Holcroft, *The Life of Thomas Holcroft*, Elbridge Colby, ed., 2 vols. (London: Constable, 1925), II, 33n.

radicals, notably Paine;[25] but Paine's ideas, like those of Godwin, were common to the time, so that there is no way of proving that Paine influenced Wordsworth directly. All that can be concluded is that Wordsworth's "Letter" does in part belong with other works of the extremists, insofar as it is indebted to Holbach and Helvétius and their necessitarian philosophy, and particularly to the extent that it defends regicide and violent revolution. But the "Letter's" greater debt to the English Republicans and its heavy emphasis on virtue and education must not be forgotten, for at these points Wordsworth tends to differ from the radicals contemporary with him.

Further, when Wordsworth first arrived back in England, the liberal, literary intellectuals were only just beginning to divide into moderates and extremists. During his previous visit to London, he would have seen Dissenters working actively with men who were later to become notorious revolutionaries. Brand-Hollis, a prominent Dissenting leader, worked with Godwin and Paine on *The Rights of Man*,[26] while Johnson himself later undertook to publish the work, until he became fearful that it might lead to prosecution.[27] But an even surer indication of this unity among the intellectual liberals is Godwin's diary, which is a daily account of its author's activities during these very years, helpfully listing not only those in attendance at each gathering but also the year in which Godwin met each of his acquaintances. It is an invaluable source of information about radical groups during the 1790's. Pertinent here is the fact that, until Godwin began to seclude himself to write *Political Justice*, his associates numbered Whig politicians, radical theorists, and Dissenters; at Johnson's, at the Hollises', or at the various tavern meetings, Holcroft, Paine, and Thelwall mingled freely with such Dissenters as Fawcett, Kippis, Price, and Priestley, and with many of Fox's supporters in Parliament. But in 1793, such displays of unanimity began to cease: the extremists appeared less and less in the company of the Dis-

---

[25]   Hooker, "Wordsworth's Letter to the Bishop of Llandaff", 522-531.
[26]   *Life of Holcroft*, II, 33.
[27]   Alexander Gilchrist, *Life of William Blake* (London: J. M. Dent, 1942), pp. 78-82; interestingly, Blake, Godwin, Holcroft, Paine, and Mary Wollstonecraft all frequented Johnson's shop in the early 1790's.

senters, while Godwin himself tended to associate henceforth with only two Dissenters, Fawcett and Robinson, his publisher.

Two factors undoubtedly lay behind this gradual fragmentation: the course of the Revolution, and the increasing hostility of the government to radical activity. Moderates were alike repelled by the Jacobin excesses and hesitant to appear as enemies of the English constitution. In this regard, Wordsworth upon his return was decidedly an extremist, for the "Letter to the Bishop of Llandaff", besides defending every undertaking of the French revolutionaries, also is outspoken in its advocacy of violent revolution and its opposition to all forms of monarchy. But when mere regicide blossomed into mass murder, Wordsworth turned away from the Revolution, in contrast to such die-hards as Paine and Thelwall (The Prelude, X, 346-381). Henceforth, Wordsworth found that he had more in common with the moderates, who silently lamented the course of events both in England and in France, than with certain extremists who attempted to excuse every sort of atrocity in the name of their ideals. Proof that at the least Wordsworth noticed this change in others is supplied by The Excursion:

> History, . . . will tell
> How rapidly the zealots of the cause
> Disbanded – or in hostile ranks appeared;
> Some, tired of honest service; these, outdone,
> Disgusted therefore, or appalled, by aims
> Of fiercer zealots — so confusion reigned,
> And the more faithful were compelled to exclaim,
> As Brutus did to Virtue, 'Liberty,
> I worshipped thee, and find thee but a Shade!'

Although the Solitary is speaking here, the emphatic tone and the choice of words indicate that Wordsworth's own views are being expressed; after all the Solitary was himself a "fiercer zealot". When in the succeeding lines the narrative pose is fully resumed, the Solitary confesses his own subsequent moral decay:

> when the simply good
> In timid selfishness withdrew, I sought
> Other support, not scrupulous whence it came.[28]

[28]   *Poetical Works*, V, 102-103.

The self-criticism is not as important as the comment on the "simply good"; is it the Solitary or Wordsworth who is condemning them for "timid selfishness"? Since this part of the poem is primarily concerned with the Solitary's inability to understand humble virtues, the poet is certainly implying that those who were blind partisans of the Revolution and of reason eventually lost sight of the beauty of simple morality, and even misinterpreted the motives of those less extreme.

In fact, the text of the "Letter to the Bishop of Llandaff" may possibly reveal this transformation in Wordsworth's outlook, for at the beginning Wordsworth's tone is that of a vehement revolutionary, bent on universal democracy at all costs. By the end of the work, his emphasis is on virtue and public happiness; his attitude is that of a moderate, patiently awaiting in an alien atmosphere the time of mankind's release from slavery and ignorance. Herein lies an important objection to the claim for Godwin's influence upon the "Letter to the Bishop of Llandaff"; if Wordsworth's account in *The Prelude* of his revulsion from the terrorism in France is accepted, the essay must have been written before February, 1793, the month *Political Justice* appeared.[29]

Indeed, the principles of Godwin's book in large part represent the difference between the Dissenters and the philosophic radicals, for Godwin's system reflects his Dissenting background only in its emphasis on education; its negation of the emotions and its empirical materialism that attempts to account for all causality were diametrically opposite to Dissenting ideals. Probably this disparity explains Godwin's gradual withdrawal from the circles of Johnson and the Hollises; certainly the book clarified for the first time the ideological differences between the two liberal extremes.[30] Thus by the spring of 1793 Wordsworth could hardly have been a follower of Godwin when he was a devotee of the English Republicans, a believer in virtue and intuitive perception, and a sympathizer with the Dissenting ideals.

There can be no doubt that at some time Wordsworth was

[29]   *Godwin's Diary.*
[30]   See, for example, *The Analytical Review*, XVI (1793), 121-130, 388-404, for an expression of Dissenting objections to Godwin's philosophy.

dedicated to Godwin's concept of necessity: "'Throw aside your books of chemistry', said Wordsworth to a young man, a student in the Temple, 'and read Godwin on Necessity'".[31] But when was this? Again the structure of *The Prelude* is of assistance. Through line 657 of Book X Wordsworth's account is strictly chronological; he describes his experiences of 1793 in London and on the Isle of Wight, during which his mind was torn between France and England, and he reaches the time in the summer of 1794 when he heard of the death of Robespierre (July 28). Then he suddenly reverts to the beginning of his year in France, when he "was led to take an eager part/ In arguments of civil polity" (X, 660-661); he proceeds then to recount his studies in the "management/ Of Nations" (686-687), and his coincidental high hopes for mankind, followed by his fall "out of the pale of love" when "Britain opposed the Liberties of France" (760-761). At this point Wordsworth describes his lapse into Godwinian necessitarianism, when

> the Philosophy
> That promised to abstract the hopes of man
> Out of his feelings, to be fix'd thenceforth
> For ever in a purer element
> Found ready welcome.
>   (X, 807-811).

This passage clearly cannot refer to the period when Wordsworth was in London and writing the "Letter to the Bishop of Llandaff"; the break in the chronology of his account indicates that, for it stresses the importance of Wordsworth's succumbing to Godwin (it being, in effect, the final crisis before the poet arrived at his own philosophy), it emphasizes the political origin of most of Wordsworth's ideas during these years, and it indicates that his conversion to Godwin took place *after* the death of Robespierre. Hence, when he states that this conversion was partly brought about because the French had now "become Oppressors in their turn" (X, 792), he is not referring to the early warfare of 1793, or to the later invasion of Switzerland, but to

---

[31]   William Hazlitt, *The Spirit of the Age, The Complete Works of William Hazlitt*, P. P. Howe, ed., 21 vols. (London: Dent, 1932), XI, 17.

the French attacks on neighboring countries in the fall of 1794.[32] This is all the more evident when it is noted that *none* of his work before late 1794 manifests any of the ideas that are specifically Godwin's.

The implication behind all this is that, if in early 1793 Wordsworth retained his radical sympathies and yet was alien to the reformers and to the atheistic political philosophers, he was consequently closest in spirit to the Dissenting circles. There is much that points to this: besides his brother Richard, all of his known associates in the spring of 1793 were Dissenters, and his thought of that time has many striking similarities to Dissenting ideas. This is not to say, nor is any of the following evidence meant to suggest, that Wordsworth was ever a Dissenter in the religious sense; he may have sympathized with their plight without believing in their theology. Further, he did not mingle with the Dissenters to the point that he became prominently identified with them (or with any other political group, for that matter). This is suggested both by his being completely disregarded in the political literature of a time when name-dropping was a common practice, and more particularly by the failure of the *Critical Review* to single out his political position (its primary method of determining the worth of a work) in its reviews of *An Evening Walk* and of *Descriptive Sketches.*[33] Nevertheless, an investigation of Wordsworth's connections with Dissenters and their thought will shed light on the state of his mind in 1793, and reveal as well yet another formative influence on his thinking.

The Dissenters varied greatly from one congregation to another in their political and religious thought, as might be expected of a tradition that encompassed Baptists, Independents, Presbyterians, and Unitarians. One cliché about the Dissenters needs to be qualified. It is common to describe them as middle-class businessmen, conservative in their politics and decidedly unintellec-

---

[32]   De Selincourt is the only Wordsworth scholar to agree exactly with this dating of the poet's Godwinian period, though his method of arriving at this conclusion is historical, and is not dependent either upon the narrative structure of *The Prelude* or upon the poet's mental development as it is indicated in his works. *The Prelude*, pp. 604-605.

[33]   *Critical Review*, VII (1793), 347-348, 472-474.

tual in their outlook. While such may be said of the vast majority
of Dissenters – particularly the Baptist and Independent congregations – there was in the late eighteenth century a vocal minority that espoused liberal principles and agitated for the abolition
of the Test and Corporation Acts, as well as for other reforms.
These liberal Dissenters were frequently either former Anglicans
or Presbyterians who had been converted to the Socinian or Arian
movements that began to gain ground from about 1770 on.
Wordsworth thus grew up in the very years that a decided turn
towards Unitarianism was sweeping the established church and
its dissent alike, in all parts of England; in London he would
have been surrounded by this controversy between traditional
Dissenters and the Unitarians. In the early 1790's particularly a
great number of works appeared defending Unitarian theology
and explaining their authors' conversion to the movement. Among
the more prominent converts, both clerical and lay, were William
Frend, Theophilus Lindsey (who was a graduate of Wordsworth's
college, St. John's, and was also a friend of Joseph Johnson),
Thomas Palmer, and Gilbert Wakefield.

Although they were not all Unitarians, the liberal Dissenters
were in general agreement about the political and social issues of
their time. Like the reformers, they were loyal Englishmen who
sought reform through constitutional means; but at the same time
they were usually professional men not workingmen, and they
were in the 1790's more of an oppressed minority than the reformers. Like the philosophic radicals, the liberal Dissenters
looked to the tradition of Locke and were thus inclined to a
mechanical view of the universe; but they were less extreme than
the radicals, both in politics and in their espousal of the mechanical. In effect, they looked upon Locke and the Glorious
Revolution as the culmination of the seventeenth-century Republican tradition, whereas the radicals saw Locke as the fountain-
head of the French Enlightenment and what they hoped would
be an equivalent English development.

Something of the toleration and the lack of doctrinal absolutism typical of the liberal Dissenters is revealed in John Aikin's
"Memoir of Gilbert Wakefield". Aikin points out that although

Wakefield had "dissented" from Anglican doctrine and worship, he nevertheless

> was far from uniting with any particular class of those who are usually denominated *dissenters*. He had an insuperable repugnance to their mode of performing divine service; and he held in no high estimation the theological and philosophical knowledge which it has been the principal object of their seminaries of education to communicate. [34]

Independent-minded as Wakefield was, he nevertheless can be called a Unitarian and he was a close associate of many liberal Dissenters, including both Aikin and Joseph Johnson.

The manner in which Wordsworth was introduced to liberal Dissenting circles is unknown, but it is obvious from his known acquaintances that in some way he was indeed introduced to them. His two poems appeared by February, 1793; hence, if the normal time is allowed for negotiations between author and publisher, Wordsworth must have been introduced to Johnson's circle as early as January, 1793, within a month after his return to England. Also, he was acquainted with another Dissenting family then in London, his distant relatives the Rawsons, who could have been his means of meeting other Dissenters. At the very least, Dorothy's description of their encounter reveals that they were favorably impressed with one another: "Ever since he saw Mr and Mrs Rawson in London he has wished for an opportunity of accepting their very pressing invitation to their house." [35]

The extent of Wordsworth's familiarity with Dissenters is more

---

[34] Lucy Aikin, *Memoir of John Aikin* (Philadelphia: Abraham Small, 1824), pp. 453-454. For the point of view of the "orthodox" Dissenters towards the Unitarian movement, see David Bogue and James Bennett, *History of Dissenters, From the Revolution in 1688, to the Year 1808*; 4 vols. (London: Printed for the authors, 1808-1812), IV, 311-326. This early work reflects a doctrinaire view of the Dissenting tradition, the Unitarians being presented as apostates to the cause. The authors are consistently condescending to Priestley, for example. See IV, 379-383.

[35] *Early Letters*, p. 97. Dorothy Wordsworth to Jane Pollard, July 10, 1793. Mrs. Moorman, p. 214n, notes that the Rawsons were Unitarians, but she ascribes no other significance to the fact than that they thus would have been "less likely to disapprove of William's political views than Mr. Cookson".

clearly defined in the Fenwick note to *The Excursion*, where he mentions that his portrait of the Solitary was based largely on

a Mr. Fawcett, a preacher at a dissenting meeting-house at the Old Jewry. It happened to me several times to be one of his congregation through my connection with Mr. Nicholson of Cateaton Street, Strand, who . . . used often to invite me to dine with him on Sundays; and I took that opportunity (Mr. N. being a Dissenter) of going to hear Fawcett, who was an able and eloquent man. [36]

By 1793, Fawcett had become a noted preacher, attracting " 'the largest and most genteel London audience that ever assembled in a dissenting place of worship' ".[37] Yet, judging from the Fenwick note and from the portrait of Fawcett as the Solitary in *The Excursion*, Wordsworth's later opinion of Fawcett was not favorable:

He published a Poem on War, which had a good deal of merit, and made me think more about him than I should otherwise have done. But his Christianity was probably never very deeply rooted; and, like many others in those times of like shewy talents, he had not strength of character to withstand the effects of the French Revolution, and of the wild and lax opinions which had done so much towards producing it, and far more in carrying it forward in its extremes. [38]

Wordsworth's later conservatism may explain in part his adverse opinion of the man. More important, however, his criticism of Fawcett is exactly what the clergyman's colleagues would have said of him. He was one of the few Dissenting clerics who refused to lessen their zeal for the Revolution as it became more and more extreme; and Godwin's diary suggests that he grew farther apart from the Dissenters who professed moderation, since he, Godwin, Holcroft, and Thelwall were constant companions as the year progressed.[39]

Later, Wordsworth mistakenly believed that Fawcett sank into "habits of intemperance" that "hastened his death",[40] a mistake

---

[36]   *Poetical Works*, V, 374-375.
[37]   *DNB*, XVIII, 260-261.
[38]   *Poetical Works*, V, 375.
[39]   Godwin's Diary; see especially entries from June 21, 1793, to the end of the year.
[40]   *Poetical Works*, V, 375; the same error was made by Wordsworth at the time of Fawcett's death: "I was sorry to see from the Papers that your

which he would not have made if he had had any continuing
interest in the man, and which would have heightened his antagonism to him. Nevertheless, despite his extremism in certain
areas, Fawcett was still a Dissenter, and he may well have influenced the young Wordsworth. Arthur Beatty has argued that
the former's *The Art of War* was a source for Wordsworth,[41] and
a similar case may be made for his *Sermons* (1795) and *Poems*
(1798) – both of which Wordsworth could have come across
earlier in other forms.

Strong circumstantial evidence connects Wordsworth with a
number of other prominent Dissenters at this time. Two in particular may be noted, Thomas Cooper and Thomas Christie.
Cooper's activities with Wordsworth in France have already been
mentioned in Chapter Three. He was an avowed Unitarian and
a disciple of Priestley, if more extreme in his views and inflammatory in their expression than his master. He did, however,
eventually turn against the Revolution.[42] Cooper was in London
in the spring of 1793, associating with Samuel Rogers and other
young Dissenters of an intellectual, literary, liberal cast.[43] Since
Wordsworth had much in common with Cooper and his friends,
he possibly renewed his acquaintance with Cooper at this time
and so became further involved in Dissenting circles through him.

Thomas Christie was also in France at the same time as Wordsworth. While there he was busy writing a reply to Burke and "a
Sketch of the new Constitution of France", both of which were

---

Friend poor Fawcett was dead; not so much that he was dead but to think
of the manner in which he had sent himself off before his time." WW to
Hazlitt, March 5, 1804; *Early Letters*, p. 447. M. Ray Adams was the first
to correct Wordsworth's mistake. *Studies in the Literary Backgrounds of
English Radicalism* (Lancaster, Pa.: Franklin and Marshall College, 1947),
pp. 191-226.

[41]   *Joseph Fawcett: The Art of War; Its Relation to the Early Development
of William Wordsworth* (Madison: University of Wisconsin Press, 1918).

[42]   Malone, *The Public Life of Thomas Cooper, 1783-1839*, pp. 53-72.
Malone notes that Cooper thought "the works of Milton, Harrington, and
Sydney as both less profound and less popular than those of Paine, Sieyès,
Barlow, Oswald, and Mirabeau" (p. 47n), a view that would have run
counter to that of most Dissenters.

[43]   P. W. Clayden, *The Early Life of Samuel Rogers* (London: Smith, Elder,
1887), p. 265.

published by Johnson.[44] There is no proof that Wordsworth met Christie in France, but this is a distinct possibility for few Englishmen were then in the country. In any event, Christie was a member of Johnson's circle, being co-founder with him of the *Analytical Review*, and Wordsworth could well have met him through Johnson. Christie was a liberal, a well-known author in his day, and a zealous Unitarian.

As was stated in Chapter II, Wordsworth may have been introduced to Holborn in 1791, at which time he possibly learned of the Dissenting community. When he returned in 1793 he stayed with his brother at Staple Inn, and in 1795 he again chose to reside in Holborn, for he then lived with Montagu at Lincoln's Inn.[45] Although coincidence must not be ruled out, Wordsworth would hardly have concentrated his activities in this area because it was the legal center of London. He may well have decided to stay in Holborn during his 1793 and 1795 visits to the city because it was the center of the publishing trade and because it was also the home of those whose ideals and interests he shared, in addition to economic reasons.

It is worth noting, however, that even in the Lake Country, seemingly so remote from the world of liberal intellectuals in London, Wordsworth as a young boy would have been surrounded by Dissenters, particularly Presbyterians – the very group that was most influenced by the Unitarian movements that swept the country as he was growing up. Sparsely populated Westmoreland contained but a handful of such congregations, but the other counties Wordsworth would have known well – Cumberland, Lancashire, and even Yorkshire – numbered a great many Dissenting chapels. The latter two, in fact, each contained over a hundred such congregations.[46] It would be difficult to discover to what extent the North country farmers Wordsworth so much admired had turned to Dissent, but evidently some such mass conversion had taken place. If so, Wordsworth's admiration of

[44] John Nichols, *Literary Anecdotes of the Eighteenth Century*, 10 vols. (London: Printed for the Author, 1812-1815), IX, 389-390.
[45] Mrs. Moorman, pp. 211, 260.
[46] Bogue and Bennett, *History of Dissenters*, IV, 327-328.

these men for their rugged simplicity, their honesty, and their dedication to work may be seen as another link with Dissent. We may recall Legouis' perception of a "Puritan austerity" in Wordsworth,[47] certainly a prominent aspect not only of the man but also of his poetry. It seems likely that this characteristic can be traced to Wordsworth's rustic upbringing and to his various connections with Dissent – and not to any influence of the Methodist movement, as has occasionally been asserted.[48]

The most significant piece of evidence connecting Wordsworth with the Dissenters, however, is his choice of Johnson as his publisher. Johnson was regarded in his day as the father of the book trade [49] (although other booksellers were more popular with buyers, so that financial gain may be ruled out as the poet's motive for deciding on Johnson), and he was the publisher of most of the contemporary writers who are now remembered with any favor. But if Johnson is at all recalled today, he is dismissed as the first publisher of Wordsworth who incidentally also published the works of Cowper and Priestley, and, excepting Paine's, most of the replies to Burke's *Reflections*. Only Fink has suggested a possible intellectual connection between Johnson and the poet: that, if he had not already done so in France, then at the publisher's table he must surely have been introduced to the thought of the seventeenth-century Republicans.[50]

---

[47] Legouis, p. 232.

[48] See, for example, F. C. Gill, *The Romantic Movement and Methodism* (London: The Epworth Press, 1937), pp. 163-168.

[49] Charles Knight, *Shadows of the Old Booksellers* (London: Bell and Daldy, 1865), pp. 272-276; see also John Aikin's obituary article on Johnson in the *Gentleman's Magazine*, CVI (1809), 1167-1168; *DNB*, XXX, 21-22; Phyllis G. Mann, "Death of a London Bookseller", *Keats-Shelley Memorial Bulletin*, 15 (1964), 8-12; and Kenneth Neill Cameron, ed., *Shelley and His Circle, 1773-1822*, 2 vols. (Cambridge: Harvard University Press, 1961), I, 66-74. Eleanor Nicholes has commented that Johnson "provides an excellent example of a phenomenon too often neglected in the history of ideas, the impact of a pioneering publisher on the intellectual life of his time. His imprints show a remarkable range: novels, translations, poetry, textbooks, medical, scientific, and political works. The list reveals a liberality of mind, a belief in the free congress of ideas." *Ibid.*, I, 68n. This acknowledgment suggests that Johnson is beginning to receive some of the recognition he so justly deserves.

[50] Fink, pp. 110-111; Professor Fink merely notes that Milton and Sidney

But other facets of Johnson's character, ideals, and requirements bear significantly on Wordsworth's development. In the first place, Johnson clearly enforced specific demands of any work before he would publish it, demands of which any writer would have been well aware if he thought of submitting a work to him. The number of his publications was small, at least in comparison with such houses as Cadell, Dodsley, Longman, Rivington, and Robinson – all immensely successful publishers. Johnson, in contrast, obviously sought out works that would be enduring and ignored the temptation of popularity.[51] Especially was this so with regard to literature: poetry he published infrequently; fiction at best rarely; and contemporary drama almost never. That which he did accept was almost invariably devoid of the excesses of the time, particularly sentimentalism and gothicism. Instead, the literary productions from Johnson's house had to have an intellectual quality that made them both original and incisive. If in theme they coincided with Johnson's views on religion and on politics, all the better; seldom were views contrary to Johnson's expressed in works that he issued. Above all, any work, whether literary or otherwise, had to manifest an inherently noble view of man and an emphasis on virtue as an active principle of life.

Equally small were the number of writers Johnson published and the number of topics with which he seems to have been concerned. Chief among his interests was the cause of the Dissenters; but the paramount issue of the time for them, the repeal of the Corporation and Test Acts, quickly disappeared with the advent

---

were highly admired in Johnson's group, and then defends this in a footnote which mentions the facts that Thelwall named a son after Sidney and edited Moyle, and that Johnson published editions of Milton and Sidney in 1791 and 1795 respectively. Aside from the fact that Thelwall cannot be regarded as a member of Johnson's coterie, there is the further simple objection that Fink does not go far enough to show the extent of the Republican influence on the Dissenters; in most respects, the political ideals of the two groups were identical.

[51] *The Modern Catalogue of Books* (London: Bent, 1803) is the most complete publishing history of the 1790's of those which indicate the publisher. *The Critical* and *Monthly* reviews are the best supplemental sources.

of the war with France. In Parliament, where a long series of attempts to obtain repeal had been made in previous years, not a single motion to that effect was made in the session of the spring of 1793. The same trend is seen in the works that Johnson issued; whereas from 1788 to 1792 many of his publications were on this very question, from 1793 onward the emphasis shifted to a larger frame of reference – in general terms, the application of an enlightened view of humanity to the social and political realms. This is very important, for though Wordsworth sympathized with the plight of the Dissenters,[52] he would have placed the Corporation and Test controversy in the same category as that over the slave trade: when more essential failings were remedied, then these abuses would of necessity be corrected. In effect, then, the philosophical tendency of Wordsworth and of the Dissenting writers was the same, for they both had turned to a deeper realm out of a growing realization of the inefficacy of isolated reform measures; and for both that deeper realm was human nature.

Likewise in the area of speculative politics, although Johnson had once at least permitted his press to be a voice for the extremists, by the time Pitt's repressive measures began to appear he had broken his connection with them. In earlier years he had published works by Joel Barlow and other extremists; Godwin and Paine had frequented his shop. But by 1793, as was in part suggested by the previous discussion of the gradual break between Godwin and Johnson's circle, he was no longer publishing their works or associating with them.[53] Again, this parallels Wordsworth's development as it has been discussed.

Here, then, were Wordsworth's central interests at the time – human nature and politics – being given the primary emphasis by one publisher. Moreover, the few remaining subjects on which Johnson published books were all subsidiary interests of Wordsworth; besides literature as such, they included education, science, and travel.

The truly convincing point, however, is that almost every con-

---

[52]   *Prose Works*, I, 10, 22-23.
[53]   Godwin's Diary; John Knowles, *The Life and Writings of Henry Fuseli*, 3 vols. (London: Colburn and Bentley, 1831), I, 161.

temporary work ever accepted as a significant influence on the young Wordsworth was published by Johnson; likewise, of the earlier works that were important in the poet's development, virtually all were reissued by Johnson at some time. These facts are all the more significant when it is kept in mind that Johnson published but a small fraction of the works that appeared in the 1790's. In political thought, he published English Republicans and French writers alike, as well as contemporary theorists (Barlow and Wollstonecraft) and reformers (Cartwright, Cooper, and Wyvill). All the works of Priestley, political, scientific, and theological, came from Johnson's press. More striking, however, is the fact that Hartley's psychological works were republished by Johnson, probably thus bringing them to Wordsworth's attention, for Hartley's ideas soon after began to appear in his writings.[54] Further, the list of Johnson's publications includes Bartram's *Travels*, a work that heavily influenced Wordsworth from 1793 onwards. And finally, there are Johnson's poets – Cowper, Darwin, and even Coleridge, among others – these being among the few poets of the 1790's whom Wordsworth admired. Also worth noticing are Milton, whose works were republished by Johnson, and three minor poets, John Aikin, George Dyer, and Joseph Fawcett, whose works contain several interesting parallels to that of Wordsworth.

On the surface, then, Johnson's tastes and ideals were such as would have appealed to the young Wordsworth; the subjects he emphasized were those in which the poet was interested; his writers included almost all those which influenced him. That a personal connection existed between the publisher and the poet cannot be doubted. From all accounts, Johnson was famed as a kindly and fair man of high principles, revealed particularly by his liberality toward Cowper on the publication of *The Task*,

---

[54]   In 1791 Johnson published a translation of a German book by Pistorius which could have first made Wordsworth interested in Hartley: *Notes and Additions to Dr. Hartley's Observations on Man ... To which is prefixed, A Sketch of the Life and Character of Dr. Hartley*. For Hartley's influence on Wordsworth, see Arthur Beatty, *William Wordsworth: His Doctrine and Art in their Historical Relations*, 2nd ed. (Madison: University of Wisconsin Press, 1927), pp. 97-127.

which was an unexpected success.[55] Most likely Wordsworth knew of the esteem in which the publisher was held by his associates, and shared that opinion. In the spring of 1794 he referred to Johnson as "my publisher",[56] bespeaking his continued intellectual affinity with the man; it is worth noting that until the fall of that year he remained steadfast to the same ideals he shared with Johnson in 1793.

Finally, another distinctive characteristic of Johnson was that he surrounded himself with his writers; on Tuesday evenings the various ministers, poets, politicians, and scientists in his circle would gather at his home to exchange ideas. It is impossible to prove that Wordsworth attended any of these sessions; he may well have been invited once Johnson became aware of his political principles and his literary potentialities. But it can be said with assurance that Wordsworth was aware of this group, that he sympathized with its ideals,[57] and that it helped to direct the course of his development for the next year.

Of Johnson's associates, probably the closest to him was Henry Fuseli, the painter, who actually lived with Johnson for a number of years. As Tuveson has noted, Fuseli "deliberately cut himself off from the romantic movement" in art and turned to Burke. He attacked the extravagance of contemporary descriptive poetry, yet his own work reveals an interest in "the non-rational side of experience".[58] Johnson's friendship with Fuseli, as well as his continuing use of a kindred painter, William Blake, as an illustrator for his publications, is significant, for it suggests a side to these liberal Dissenters that needs to be emphasized. As much of the subsequent discussion will show, they were not necessarily believers in an arid, mechanical universe. They followed Locke

[55]   *Gentleman's Magazine*, CVI (1809), 1167-1168. Frank Arthur Mumby, *Publishing and Bookselling*, rev. ed. (London: Jonathan Cape, 1954), pp. 200-203.
[56]   *Early Letters*, p. 120.
[57]   This is best revealed at the end of the "Letter", where Wordsworth is particularly vehement in his admiration for those Englishmen remaining faithful to the cause of humanity. *Prose Works*, I, 22-23.
[58]   Ernest Lee Tuveson, *The Imagination as a Means of Grace; Locke and the Aesthetics of Romanticism* (Berkeley and Los Angeles: University of California Press, 1960), pp. 175-179.

and found order in the known universe, but many of them were also deeply interested in the unknown within us and beyond us, just as were Blake, Wordsworth, and Coleridge – all of whom had early and lasting connections with the Dissenting world.

Among Johnson's many other acquaintances were Mary Wollstonecraft (who assisted him for a number of years in his publishing work), Richard Price, Joseph Priestley, and John Aikin (all of them eminent Dissenting ministers), the young Hazlitt, and for a time William Godwin. Moreover, several liberal Anglicans frequented Johnson's shop. Most notable were Samuel Parr and Richard Porson, who fully shared his ideals in morality and politics.[59] Hence, whether Wordsworth was personally familiar with these men or whether he only knew their writings, the presence of their ideas in his own work points to the conclusion that Johnson and any other literary Dissenters the poet met were important agents in introducing him to a new area of intellectual enquiry.[60]

In its rudiments Dissenting thought was little removed from the philosophy which Wordsworth brought back with him from France – the most essential reason why he can be identified, in thought or in action, primarily with them and not with other radical groups. On the most elementary level, he shared with the Dissenters a love for England and its past; and, like the poet, they too looked mainly to the seventeenth century: "It was their constant purpose to appear as the makers of the Glorious Revolution, as pure Whigs in Church and State, ruling in apostolic succession after Sidney and Locke."[61] All of them were deeply conscious of their literary, political, and scientific heritage from the seventeenth century.

---

[59] For Parr, see Leslie Stephen's article in the *DNB*, XLIII, 356-364; see also M. L. Clarke, *Richard Porson* (Cambridge: University Press, 1937), pp. 41-44 especially.

[60] In the ensuing discussion of the thought of the Dissenters, all the writers can in some way be related to Johnson; in all but a few cases the specific works referred to were published by him. Yet those that came from other houses still perfectly typify Dissenting thought.

[61] Lincoln, *English Dissent*, p. 8.

But besides their mutual bond in history, they regarded themselves as aliens in their native land. The Dissenters were dedicated to their country's welfare, desirous only of disseminating virtue and knowledge among their fellowmen. Consequently, when the ministry savagely attacked all liberal thought, indiscriminately grouping the Dissenters with the "enemies of the Constitution" and repressing all reform agitation, they were made to feel the futility of their cause. As was shown, when Wordsworth returned to England he too felt like an alien; and he similarly soon became conscious of the spirit of persecution that overshadowed all liberal thought – a fact which explains his failure to publish his "Letter to the Bishop of Llandaff". And most important of all, he was aware that others suffered with him in feeling the ingratitude of a nation for those who merely wished it well.[62]

As to specific political principles, he again would have found the Dissenters to be most compatible with his own moderation. Both detested England's part in the war with France – not only because it was a symbol of the nation's hostility to freedom, but also because of its devastating effects on the economic and moral status of the lower classes. *The Prelude* is a testimony of the poet's hatred of the war for the former reason, and his corresponding bitterness towards Pitt for sending the fleet into "unworthy service" at "The unhappy counsel of a few weak Men" (X, 276-307). More specific details are given in "Guilt and Sorrow", the first draft of which was written in 1793 and 1794, while he still held the political principles of his return to England and before he turned to extreme rationalism. The "Advertisement" to the poem reveals that, just before he began writing, the desolate landscape of Salisbury plain and the thought of Druidic rituals caused him to reflect on the "calamities, principally those consequent upon war, to which, more than other classes of men, the poor are

---

[62] *Prose Works*, I, 22-23. The political climate that Wordsworth is here talking about is best illustrated by its effect on Priestley, a man of high moral principles and a sincere love for his nation, who was forced to flee to America to escape the wrath of mob and ministry alike. One of the many other indications of this climate is noted in the *Morning Post*, January 1, 1794, which describes how the sermons throughout the country on this fast day inflamed people against Dissenters.

subject".[63] The poem itself centers on a soldier's widow, who with her children had accompanied her husband to America, only to see them all perish as a result of the war; she is now devoid both of moral fiber and of material possessions. The earliest versions made it evident that the primary object of Wordsworth's attention was warfare itself:

> Say, rulers of the nations, from the sword
> Can aught but murder, pain, and tears proceed?
> Oh, what can war but endless war still breed?

At the same time he attacks the repressive acts that follow in the course of war, and even more he condemns laws that are over severe:

> Must Law with its own scourge
> Still torture crimes that grew a monstrous band
> Formed by his care, and still his victims urge
> With voice that breathes despair to death's tremendous
> verge? [64]

Although the war with France provoked the hostility of all liberals, many of them were motivated only by their radical love for the Revolution. The Dissenters, however, founded their opposition on the principles that war in general was unchristian and that it was harmful to public morality and to the material welfare of the poor.[65] Years later this attitude became widespread, but at the start of the war it was peculiar to the Dissenters. Even Samuel Parr, an intimate associate of Priestley's circle but usually hesitant to accept innovation, was a strong opponent of the war and an equally strong advocate of poor law reform.[66]

Parr, however, was no more hesitant about constitutional reform than any of the Dissenters. By 1793, Englishmen had become so sensitive about their constitution that even the most innocent proposal was received with suspicion; Dissenting advo-

[63]   *Poetical Works*, I, 95.
[64]   *Ibid.*, I, 340, notes: from Ms. I of "Guilt and Sorrow", stanzas 57-58.
[65]   Gilbert Wakefield, *The Spirit of Christianity, compared with the Spirit of the Times in Great Britain*, 3rd ed. (London: Kearsley, 1794), pp. 10-14.
[66]   Adams, *Studies of Radicalism*, pp. 270, 288, 293; Fawcett's *The Art of War* is a characteristic Dissenting protest against war.

cates of change were heard infrequently, and those who did speak out concentrated wholly on the duration of Parliaments and on the extent of representation.[67]

Such moderation is found in all aspects of Dissenting political thought, from the practical to the theoretical. Repeatedly, they stand by two absolute ideals – morality and their nation – thus paralleling Wordsworth's emphasis in "Guilt and Sorrow" and in *The Prelude*, where he tells of the shock to his "moral nature" that the war with France occasioned, because it was a sign of his own country's essential corruption (X, 235). The objections of the Dissenters to Godwin and Paine particularly show Wordsworth's affinity with them in this regard. The *Analytical Review*, published by Johnson and a reliable index of Dissenting thought, was full of praise for Godwin's *Political Justice*; but near the end of the review it made several important qualifications:

His morality is bold and imperious: if in any instance it be either impracticable or inconsistent, it seems to be in his doctrine of sincerity – . . . we are sorry to add, that we observed one or two insinuations, with respect to public worship and a future state, which we scruple not to pronounce highly offensive and improper. [68]

Such moral and theological qualifications, besides being typical of the publisher and his associates, were the very objections Wordsworth would have had to Godwin, especially since he consistently placed heavy emphasis on the religious elements of government and of private life.

Even more marked is the difference between Paine and the moderates, who from the very first revealed open hostility to *The Rights of Man*. Christopher Wyvill's *Defense of Dr. Price* illustrates both this and the Dissenters' insistence on their patriotism;

[67]   William Frend's *Peace and Union*, 2nd ed. (Cambridge: Robinsons, 1793), typifies the new caution among reformers; see especially pp. 9-10. But the Dissenters always were more aware of their ties to England than were the rest of the liberals. Priestley's letter to the National Assembly (1792), while acknowledging "the common cause of liberty, and the rights of men", quickly adds that such a view is not inconsistent with his duties to his own country. See Anne Holt, *A Life of Joseph Priestley* (London: Oxford University Press, 1931), pp. 176-177.
[68]   *Analytical Review*, XVI (1793), 404.

in his very Preface Wyvill notes that Paine is not among those he defends, for the latter's "avowed purpose is, not to reform or amend the System of our Government, but to overthrow and destroy it".[69] Priestley himself later attacked Paine's *Age of Reason* on much the same theological grounds and he was seconded enthusiastically by Johnson's magazine.[70]

Moderation and morality in politics were thus central to the outlook of the Dissenters and Wordsworth alike. But both also appealed to a higher authority than the arena of politics: human happiness and well-being were still the primary ideals in life; and if a government failed to supply them, then the people were justified in revolting. Indeed, the right of revolution, at least in the abstract, was one of the most important precedents that the seventeenth century supplied its intellectual descendents. Christie's reply to Burke centers on this very point, and is couched in language that closely resembles Wordsworth's "Letter to the Bishop of Llandaff":

There is something that I hold to be greater and dearer than the British or any Constitution: that is, *The Rights of Man*, founded on the great principles of eternal justice and reason. It is from these rights that all particular Constitutions derive their authority, ... Men should recollect, that if the period could arrive, when The Rights of Man were no longer acknowledged or appealed to by nations, the British Constitution would rest solely on the basis of mere *power*. [71]

Further on, Christie admits that evils accompany revolutions, but to him this is no excuse for accepting the *status quo*; to illustrate his point, he makes an analogy with the tearing down of an old house: it is inconvenient while only a pile of rubble remains of

---

[69]   The Rev. Christopher Wyvill, *A Defence of Dr. Price, and the Reformers of England* (London: Johnson, 1792), Preface.

[70]   Priestley, *An Answer to Mr. Paine's Age of Reason* (London: Johnson, 1795); *Analytical Review*, XXI (1795), 630-636; also significant is the *Analytical's* treatment of *The Rights of Man*, for while the review was totally in agreement with Paine's reply to Burke, it did relegate the book to the summary section at the end of the issue. IX (1791), 312-320. See also Gilbert Wakefield, *A Reply to the Second Part of The Age of Reason* (London: Symonds, 1795), and his *Examination of the Age of Reason* (London: Kearsley, 1794).

[71]   Thomas Christie, *Letters on the Revolution of France* (London: Johnson, 1791), p. 16.

your home, but it is necessary.[72] Wordsworth likewise appeals to the rights of man and distinguishes between power and natural rights; he too condemns Bishop Watson for regarding representation as perfect. Above all, he repeatedly states that confusion and tyranny are inevitable consequences of revolution before order and genuine liberty appear.[73]

With regard to political heritage, Wordsworth has been shown to be a disciple of the seventeenth century; "a Republican" he called himself in the "Letter to the Bishop of Llandaff", a direct acknowledgement of the conversion to the English Republicans that he experienced in France. Upon his return, he would have discovered that among the radicals the Dissenters particularly were conscious of an English liberal tradition; the extremists turned instead to Rousseau and his associates. Moreover, in contrast to the Girondins, who looked to the theorists of the Commonwealth, Wordsworth shared with the Dissenters an awareness that the Glorious Revolution was fully a part of that tradition: "Our English forefathers at the time of the Revolution set us an example how to act on similar lines; if we are plagued with a grievous Tyrant, rise and destroy him." [74] Ever since the centenary celebration of 1788, the Glorious Revolution had been a reminder to liberal Dissenters that their ancestors had given them a precedent for political agitation. In fact, Burke's *Reflections* was occasioned by Price's sermon celebrating the English revolution, in which he asserted that 1688 had established "The right to resist power when abused. ... The right to chuse our governors; to cashier them for misconduct; and to frame a government for ourselves." [75] This attitude appears often in Dissenting works, particularly the emphasis upon the right of the people to choose their own leaders.

As to the Republican theorists themselves, the Dissenters were

[72]   *Ibid.*, pp. 117-148.
[73]   *Prose Works*, I, 5-6, 10-11, 14.
[74]   *Middle Years*, II, 753.
[75]   Quoted in Carl B. Cone, *Torchbearer of Freedom. The Influence of Richard Price on Eighteenth Century Thought* (Lexington: University of Kentucky Press, 1952), p. 182; see also Capel Lofft, *Remarks on the Letter of Burke* (London: Johnson, 1790), pp. 8-9, 78-79.

as fervent in their admiration for them as were the Girondins. Thomas Hollis, who flourished in the middle of the century, was an especially avid lover of the Republicans, and brought out editions of Locke, Nedham, Neville, and Sidney.[76] His heir, Thomas Brand-Hollis, helped to continue the tradition; in his library Mackintosh "found he was indebted to the works of Milton, Sidney and Locke".[77]

That Hollis did in fact help to perpetuate the memory of the Republicans is obvious; hardly a Dissenting work of the 1790's failed to contain some laudatory comment upon Harrington, Milton, or Sidney.[78] In addition, the liberals emphasized the fact that the Republicans were their countrymen; whereas the French merely admired the thought of the seventeenth-century theorists, their English successors habitually looked upon them pridefully, dwelling on their contribution to the nation's constitutional theory. They were particularly conscious of the fact that the Republicans, no less than they themselves, labored in the cause of freedom in the face of every kind of oppression. Wordsworth's awareness of this situation has been noted; and he too was comforted by recalling the seventeenth-century Republicans. Indeed, it is possibly significant that he first did this after his London sojourn of 1793:

> So Virtue, fallen on times to gloom consigned,
> Makes round her path the light she cannot find, . . .
> Acknowledging though round her Danger lurk,

---

[76]   Lincoln, pp. 35-36.

[77]   *Public Characters of 1808*; quoted in Adams, *Studies of English Radicalism*, p. 156.

[78]   Among the many illustrations of this are John Cartwright, *An Appeal, . . . on the Subject of the English Constitution*, 2nd ed. (London: Printed for the Author, 1799), *passim*; Thomas Cooper, *A Reply to Mr. Burke's Invective against Mr. Cooper*, 2nd. ed. (London: Johnson, 1792), p. 83; George Dyer, *Memoirs of the Life and Writings of Robert Robinson* (London: Robinsons, 1796), pp. 222-223; Price, sermon of November 4, 1789, quoted in Cone, p. 181; Wakefield, *Spirit of Christianity*, pp. 39-40, and *passim*. With regard to Dyer, attention may be called to Lamb's essay, "Oxford in the Vacation", where he is described on his walk: "at that moment, reader, he is on Mount Tabor – or Parnassus – or co-sphered with Plato – or, with Harrington, framing 'immortal commonwealths' – devising some plan of amelioration to thy country, or thy species."

> And Fear, no night in which she cannot work.
> In dangerous night so Milton worked alone
> Cheared by a secret lustre all his own
> That with the deepening darkness clearer shone. [79]

Beyond the realm of political theory, the Dissenters would have been favorably regarded by Wordsworth for their attitudes toward education and public morality. As the previous quotation reveals, his emphasis is on the ethical; "Virtue", in fact, may be both an expression of the poet's personal ideal and a description of those he knew to be unjustly persecuted for their opinions. From his experiences with Beaupuy and with Girondist sympathizers in Paris, Wordsworth had arrived at a moderate liberalism that stressed the consistent maintenance of high principles in personal conduct. He did not have to go far to decide that any government which impeded the attainment of that ideal was unworthy, or to realize that war and economic distress worked against popular morality. "Guilt and Sorrow" is essentially a commentary to that effect, and the inculcation of morality and knowledge was the prime object of the magazine the poet and Mathews projected early in 1794, a review indicatively entitled *The Philanthropist*.[80] Many of the Dissenters did more than just advocate public morality; in contrast with many of the members of Parliament they were often noted for their upright character. Especially was this so of Price and Priestley, so that when in the "Letter to the Bishop of Llandaff", in referring to the perverting influences of the government on the populace, Wordsworth singles out the burning of Priestley's house, he is turning to what for him would have been the most prominent contemporary example of persecuted virtue.[81] In addition, having known and loved as noble

---

[79]   *An Evening Walk*, insert of 1794 between ll. 398-399, *Poetical Works*, I, 35. Ever after Wordsworth seems to have associated persecuted virtue and love of liberty with Milton. Of the concluding lines to "Guilt and Sorrow", which deal with war and oppression, de Selincourt notes: "The concluding stanzas of MS. 1 are far more inspired by Milton's great political utterances in prose and verse than by Godwin." *Poetical Works*, I, 340-341. See also *The Prelude*, I, 185-219.

[80]   *Early Letters*, pp. 125-129. See also *An Evening Walk*, insertion of 1794 after B, l. 155, *Poetical Works*, I, 16; *The Prelude*, X, 228-361, 430-440.

[81]   *Prose Works*, I, 10.

a man as Beaupuy, he likely reserved his respect for those who
most nearly approached the Frenchman. Yet the Dissenters were
to him more than just the symbols of beleaguered virtue; he would
have found in their moral principles an intellectual affinity that
he had not known since his days with Beaupuy.

These Dissenters were neither cut-and-dried worshippers at the
altar of reason nor religious dogmatists. The *Analytical Review*
well indicates this in a review of Price's *Discourse on the Love of
our Country*; the praise says as much of Dissenting ideals as it
does of Price: "This sermon breathes the animated sentiments of
ardent virtue in a simple, unaffected, nay even negligent style;
yet, . . . many passages occur which are truly eloquent – the heart
speaks to the heart in an unequivocal language." [82] Virtue, simplicity, and sensibility; where else in the 1790's would Wordsworth have found these three ideals conjoined with political
liberalism? Indeed, add to these his high philosophy of man,
which he also shared with the Dissenters, and the result will be
the essential elements of his thought of 1793.

Again, like Wordsworth the Dissenters placed the responsibility
for general morality on the government; the extent of public
virtue and happiness was to both the final index of the value of
the state. To Priestley "the happiness of the whole community is
the ultimate end of government", [83] by which he may be taken to
mean economic and spiritual well-being. To Dyer the good government was that which kept the magistrates just "and the whole
nation virtuous and happy – no other government is good". [84]
Price, too, regarded the state as existing for a moral purpose; in
effect, it should be an example to the people, and it can be judged
in moral terms [85] – something Wordsworth did frequently.

Education, however, was an essential means in assisting the

[82]   *Analytical Review*, V (1789), 471-475.
[83]   *An Essay on the First Principles of Government* (London: Dodsley, . . .
Cadell, . . . and Johnson, 1768), p. 59.
[84]   *The Complaints of the Poor People of England*, 2nd ed. (London: Ridgway, 1793), pp. 3-6.
[85]   Lincoln, p. 116; see also the sermons of Fawcett, delivered at the Dissenting meetinghouse in the Old Jewry, for further emphasis on the role of
the community in morals. *Sermons*, 2 vols. (London: Johnson, 1795), II,
237-238, and *passim*.

state to that end, an inevitable qualification of the Dissenters both because of their debt to the seventeenth-century Republicans and because of their acceptance of Locke's educational theory, especially that devolving from the concept of the *tabula rasa*.[86] The Dissenting academies were the tangible consequences of this doctrine, schools that were noted for their standards at a time when many, Wordsworth among them, were criticizing Oxford and Cambridge for their lack of scholarly distinction. This is not to say that the emphasis was placed on higher education; quite the contrary, for universal virtue was held to be impossible without a system of nation-wide education on the lower levels. Within the Dissenting ranks opinion varied as to the government's role in formal instruction; but to all of them knowledge was a prerequisite for virtue. Hence pleas for a comprehensive system of educating the poor were common.[87]

In the realm of education, the Dissenters were the most persistent and the most vociferous agitators for universal education and for the abolition of the test at Oxford and Cambridge. In both instances they were of interest to Wordsworth. The attack in *The Prelude* on the religious atmosphere at Cambridge varies little from the condemnation the Dissenters heaped on the university, particularly when William Frend was deprived of his fellowship in 1793 for his Unitarian tendencies.[88] Moreover, the clamor had been heard earlier, both in London in 1791 and at Cambridge while Wordsworth was there. The leading opponent of exclusion at Cambridge was Robert Robinson, minister of the Dissenting chapel there; although he was dead by the time Wordsworth came to be interested in educational reform, his cause was continued by his disciple in this regard, George Dyer.[89] Dyer was especially close to Wordsworth in his attitude about exclusion, for he argued that education was a natural right, and he attacked

[86]   *Ibid.*, p. 116.
[87]   Cooper, *Reply to Burke*, pp. 76-77; Dyer, *Complaints*, pp. 16-21, and *Life of Robinson*, pp. 224-225; Priestley, *First Principles*, pp. 64-71.
[88]   Wakefield, *Spirit of Christianity*, pp. 16-19; compare with *The Prelude*, III, 407-459.
[89]   Dyer, *Life of Robinson*, pp. 472-477.

the universities for their aristocratic tendencies and for their intolerance – exactly the points which the poet made.[90]

As to universal education, Wordsworth too placed a heavy emphasis on the malign influence of ignorance on popular morality; this was one of the most enduring of his interests, for it appears in the "Letter to the Bishop of Llandaff", in the *Lyrical Ballads*, and in the poems and letters of his old age. Further, he clearly evaluated the state in terms of the extent of education and the consequent general morality. Like Dyer, he early came to believe that hereditary preferment and artificial distinctions of rank occasioned "the corruption of the public opinion".[91] On the other hand, if a government permitted total representation (the same political reform that the Dissenters were seen to desire in 1793), then, since "it would no longer be their interest to keep the mass of the nation in ignorance, a moderate portion of useful knowledge would be universally disseminated".[92] In confirmation of his concern with this point, the description of his London career in *The Prelude* also contains an attack on the "reservoir of guilt/And ignorance" for which he held the governments of the world responsible (X, 430-440).

The following passage in *The Prelude* is particularly suggestive of Dissenting educational ideals and of their actual practice in their academies:

> yet I,
> Methinks, could shape the image of a Place
> Which with its aspect should have bent me down
> To instantaneous service, should at once
> Have made me pay to science and to arts
> And written lore, acknowledg'd my liege Lord,
> A homage, frankly offer'd up, like that
> Which I had paid to Nature. Toil and pains
> In this recess which I have bodied forth
> Should spread from heart to heart; and stately groves,
> Majestic edifices, should not want

[90] *Inquiry into ... the Thirty-nine Articles*, Johnson, 1792; quoted in Adams, *Studies of English Radicalism*, pp. 240-243. Compare *The Prelude*, III, 380-491, 614-643.
[91] *Prose Works*, I, 10-11.
[92] *Ibid.*, I, 11-12.

> A corresponding dignity within.
> The congregating temper, which pervades
> Our unripe years, not wasted, should be made
> To minister to works of high attempt,
> Which the enthusiast would perform with love;
> Youth should be aw'd, possess'd, as with a sense
> Religious, of what holy joy there is
> In knowledge, if it be sincerely sought
> For its own sake, in glory, and in praise,
> If but by labour won, and to endure.
> The passing Day should learn to put aside
> Her trappings here, should strip them off, abash'd
> Before antiquity, and stedfast truth,
> And strong book-mindedness; and over all
> Should be a healthy, sound simplicity,
> A seemly plainness, name it as you will,
> Republican or pious.
>
> (*The Prelude*, III, 380-407).

Here are a number of parallels with Dissenting ideals: the co-emphasis of science and the arts, the *enthusiasm* for learning, the insistence on the dignity and the religious purity of learning, the equal stress on hard work and pleasure, the historical sense, and above all the way in which he insists upon "a healthy, sound simplicity"; "Republican or pious" would suggest hostility both to Establishment excesses and to radical extremes and again indicates a Dissenting moderation.

But though the Dissenters obtained Wordsworth's admiration and interest for their political moderation, their love of the Republicans, and their principles of education and morality – all of which he shared with them – he would have been above all grateful to find a group that shared his philosophy of man. The previous chapter has delineated his gradual evolution of an extremely high and noble concept of humanity. Much that he encountered in London upon his return would have been antagonistic to it; Pitt's repressive measures were indications that the government, and the major part of the nation, had no faith whatsoever in human nature. Such a faith was implicit, however, in every Dissenting principle, whether it concerned education, government, or religion. Price again was the leading spokesman in this regard; as his biographer summarizes his philosophy,

it was God's plan for man to attain the perfect life on earth. This perfect life was the free life. Since God wanted man to be free, He bestowed upon him the capacity for enjoying liberty, and gave to him dignity of personality, individuality, a conscience, free will, and intelligence. Thus endowed, man was an autonomous moral agent able to choose the right course and therefore to act virtuously. This moral freedom is the basis for all other freedoms, of which political and religious are the most important. [93]

Herein is the typical Dissenting juxtaposition of every major realm of human endeavor, molded together to form one coherent belief in God's scheme; most important, behind it is an extremely exalted view of mankind, grounded in the concept of a relative yet universal "Inward Light".

Intelligence and morality were the two facets of human life that were usually singled out as signs of man's superiority. To Priestley, for example, man's higher intellect made him capable of "unbounded improvement" and enabled him to achieve moral status; but it was the responsibility of the government to be the agent of this process.[94] Hence the Dissenters combined a belief in the intellect, or *reason*, and a belief in perfectibility, with morality, and with sensibility, for that matter. It is at this most essential point that Wordsworth is one with them, in opposition to such philosophers as Godwin who negated the emotions and the spiritual aspects of life.

Therefore it is no surprise that Wordsworth announced in the opening of his "Letter to the Bishop of Llandaff" that he undertook the work only because Bishop Watson was the author of a work attacking the French Revolution. Watson had for years been a staunch advocate in the Lords of repealing the Corporation and Test Acts; he was a hero to the Dissenters and an apostate to his fellow bishops:

The names of levelling prelate, bishop of the Dissenters, ... were looked upon by your friends — perhaps by yourself — as an acknow-

---

[93]   Cone, p. 2. See also Lincoln, pp. 101-102; Fawcett, *Sermons*, II, 85-117 especially: "On the Respect that is due to all Men."
[94]   Priestley, *First Principles*, pp. 2-9.

ledgment of your possessing an enlarged and philosophical mind; . . .

On opening your Appendix, your admirers will naturally expect to find an impartial statement of the grievances which harass this Nation, and a sagacious inquiry into the proper modes of redress. They will be disappointed. [95]

Obviously, Wordsworth shared that disappointment. Yet he was probably not especially sensitive on the issue of the Test Acts. His knowledge of the Dissenters' esteem for Watson and his reaction to the Bishop's about-face, a reaction that was strong enough to occasion a lengthy political pamphlet, can be best explained by assuming that he was familiar with the thought of these people, and he admired them for it.

If there were no supporting evidence, it would be fallacious to assume that Wordsworth's respect for the Dissenters was a sure indication that they influenced him. And it is doubtful that they had any noteworthy original effect on him in the realms of his political thought, his love for the Republicans, his emphasis on morality and education, and his faith in man; to this extent, they were most likely kindred spirits who helped him to clarify his principles and to dedicate himself to them with greater conviction. But other elements of Wordsworth's thought appeared for the first time after his 1793 visit to London and these in every case were also important aspects of Dissenting philosophy. The following discussion of the Dissenting influence on Wordsworth is not meant to be all inclusive. Other specific instances of their impact on him will appear in later chapters. I intend the next few pages as a broad and frequently tentative outline of their influence.

For many Dissenters, science was almost as fascinating as religion and politics. The subject was a primary component of their heritage, for they looked to the time of Locke and Newton as their guide in everything.[96] Johnson's intense concern with the subject has been noted, and further indication is supplied by

[95] *Prose Works*, I, 4.
[96] Locke has already been mentioned; an example of the concern with Newton is Robert Young's *An Examination of . . . the First Book of Sir Isaac Newton's Principia* (London: Johnson, 1788).

Priestley, who likewise divided his attention among the realms of politics, religion, and science. In all three areas he was a recognized authority, but to his country at large he was primarily a scientist – the role in which Wordsworth referred to him in the "Letter to the Bishop of Llandaff".[97] And in this regard Priestley was fully a disciple of Locke, since he began with a mechanistic and necessitarian position and evolved an interpretation of the universe that encompassed both human morality and physical properties.[98] Hence Priestley and his associates went much farther than such predecessors as Holbach in their attempts to apply science to every realm of human experience, for the later scientists made room in their discipline for the moral and spiritual. Erasmus Darwin may be regarded as part of this tendency, insofar as he attempted to correlate science and poetry.

It cannot be said that the Dissenters led Wordsworth to science. It was one of his favorite subjects at Hawkshead and at Cambridge, and while he was in France he likely familiarized himself with the efforts of the *encyclopédists* to apply science to the social aspects of life. As he was steeped in the tradition of Locke and Newton, he surely would have been interested in Priestley's attempts to apply their systems to other areas. Especially would he have wanted a philosophy of science that took into account the emotions and the moral sense. By finding this, he was able to reconcile his necessitarian rationalism with the poetic, which he did soon thereafter when he turned to the works of Hartley, a Lockean who applied a mechanical philosophy to psychology, and to the poetry of Darwin.

Most important, however, is the fact that Wordsworth's discovery of the Dissenting expansion of science led him to a larger view of the universe, one that remained with him permanently although he eventually de-emphasized the means to that enlarged vision. But it is seen in his poetry almost immediately, significantly in an insertion in *An Evening Walk*; he contrasts those who are indifferent to nature with

[97] *Prose Works*, I, 10.
[98] Lincoln, pp. 151-181.

> those to whom the harmonious doors
> Of Science have unbarred celestial stores,
> To whom a burning energy has given
> That other eye which darts through earth and heaven,
> Roams through all space and [   ] unconfined,
> Explores the illimitable tracts of mind,
> And piercing the profound of time can see
> Whatever man has been and man may be.
>
> (1794 insertion after 1. 127). [99]

This perfectly illustrates his attempt to identify the realm of the intuition with science. Moreover, the wording is distinctly Newtonian and mechanistic, while the concluding lines show his awareness of the applications of science to the mind (Hartley) and to the future (Condorcet).

H. W. Piper has suggested a connection between Unitarian thought and Wordsworth in terms of "a doctrine of life in natural objects . . . which first appeared in his poetry in 1794". Unlike Newton's God, he points out, "the newer doctrine stressed an independent life and sensibility in every organized form of being, . . . and this opened the way for the possibility, . . . of a moral relationship between man and natural objects".[100] As Piper indicates, this idea of "life in natural objects" appears in Wordsworth's additions to *An Evening Walk* particularly. It is not unlikely that these revisions were prompted by his association with Unitarian Dissenters, notably Priestley. As an enthusiast of science, Wordsworth like Coleridge would have been fully aware of Priestley's ideas, since he was the foremost English scientist of his day.

---

[99]   *Poetical Works*, I, 12 (corrected); this passage may be compared to the "Lines, written . . . at Hawkshead", in which Wordsworth alludes to science enthusiastically but without imparting to it all the powers here elaborated. *Ibid.*, I, 259-261.

[100]   H. W. Piper, *The Active Universe: Pantheism and the Concept of Imagination in the English Romantic Poets* (London: The Athlone Press, 1962), pp. 71-72. Piper adduces a number of connections between Wordsworth and various Unitarians, though he too feels that Wordsworth never became a follower of the movement. He also notes certain "contacts between the members of the Lunar Society and Wordsworth and Coleridge" – these members being Darwin, Priestley, Cooper, Watt, Beddoes, and Davy – "almost every one" of whom "was a Unitarian, a radical and a scientist". *Ibid.*, pp. 63-72, 26-27.

While Piper acknowledges a Newtonian influence on Wordsworth, he nevertheless feels that

Wordsworth's conception of the Life in nature as well as out of it goes beyond Newton's conception to the point of contradicting its central assumption, the inertness of matter, ... Newton's conception of the relationship finds God in nature, but it stresses His transcendence and virtually excludes the immanence stressed by Wordsworth and Coleridge. Matter itself remains inert and mechanical, and there is no room here for Wordsworth's 'moral life' in natural objects. [101]

We may accept this differentiation while at the same time noting that the Dissenters likewise tended to adapt the Newtonian worldview, at times finding immanence (or at least vitality) in nature and consistently making room for the moral in nature. As Basil Willey says of Priestley, the scientist's aim was to

remove from 'matter' the odium attaching to it from its supposed sluggishness, solidity, and the like. Once this is done, the distinction between matter and 'spirit' ceases to be important, and 'matter' will no longer seem incompatible with 'thought' or 'sensation' .... [Matter] is not inert, for powers of attraction and repulsion are inherent in it, and are the true causes of its so-called 'solidity' and 'resistance'. [102]

This concept of the vitality of nature, which was further emphasized and developed by such later Dissenters as Fawcett, is thus a significant parallel to Wordsworth's own mental development away from his Newtonian heritage.

Willey elsewhere relates Wordsworth to the seventeenth-century natural philosophers:

In so far as it was the abstract world-picture (the world as 'machine') of the seventeenth century natural philosophers which had exploded the mythologies, Wordsworth may be said to have owed to them (as well as to his own temperament) his root-assumption that truth could only be achieved by 'making verse deal boldly with substantial things.' [103]

In the broad terms of intellectual history, Willey's assertion is

[101]   *Ibid.*, pp. 10-11.
[102]   Basil Willey, *The Eighteenth Century Background* (New York: Columbia University Press, 1940), pp. 174-175.
[103]   Willey, *The Seventeenth Century Background* (London: Chatto and Windus, 1934), p. 298.

acceptable; but in specific terms of direct influence, the world of Dissenting thought would seem to be a more direct origin of Wordsworth's emphasis on the dispassionate search for truth in an atmosphere of free enquiry and his insistence on the particular in poetry.

The young Wordsworth thus belonged to the Locke-Newton tradition of English materialism, but as it had evolved along humanitarian, religious, and scientific lines among the Dissenters. It would seem clear, then, that the so-called "historical sense" that he developed sometime in the 1790's was in large part influenced by the Dissenters' traditionalism. Certainly the Dissenters can be granted a larger place in bringing Wordsworth to a sense of the past than can Burke, although the latter has been claimed as the poet's primary source.[104] While Wordsworth later changed his opinion of Burke, the fact remains that he was utterly opposed to everything Burke stood for in the 1790's (including the appeal to tradition as a means of maintaining the *status quo*; as late as 1804 his letters reveal hostility to Burke, and the lines of *The Prelude* that praise him were not added until 1820 or after.[105] Thus his interest in the Whig Revolution, in tradition, and in "the organic nature of the life of man in a political society" came about long before his conversion to Burke's position; the most likely source of that interest is English Dissent.

A further point militates against Burke's influence on the young Wordsworth: his thorough-going empiricism in every matter from aesthetics to politics. While the Dissenters were grounded in the same tradition of Locke and Newton, by the late eighteenth century certain indications of a new direction became apparent: a revival of interest in Platonism. This revival may be seen throughout Johnson's circle. His close friend Fuseli reflects it in his paintings, as does of course Blake, who, if not literally a member of Johnson's group, at least worked closely with him over a number of years. The most central figure in this revival was

---

[104] Dicey, *Statesmanship of Wordsworth*, pp. 14-15; Willard L. Sperry, *Wordsworth's Anti-climax* (Cambridge: Harvard University Press, 1935), p. 68.
[105] *Early Letters*, p. 491; *The Prelude*, p. 565 (de Selincourt's notes).

Thomas Taylor, son of a Dissenting minister and the associate of many Dissenting intellectuals, particularly the prominent Thomas Brand-Hollis, who "was one of Taylor's intimate friends".[106] Taylor took upon himself the task of reasserting Platonism in the late eighteenth century, and he published a long series of works, both translations and interpretations, to make the practical eighteenth century English mind interested in Plato. Significantly, his most important works were published between 1793 (a year in which three of his works appeared) and 1804.[107] These were, of course, the very years that Wordsworth was most in touch with the London Dissenting intellectuals, and these books would have been the subject of much of their attention. Among the other members of Johnson's circle who associated with Taylor were Mary Wollstonecraft, Capel Lofft, and Gilbert Wakefield. On the periphery of this group was Richard Porson, perhaps the greatest classicist of the time, who attacked Taylor's writings in the liberal *Morning Chronicle* for their faulty knowledge of Greek.[108] Johnson himself reflects this trend in his publications as well as in his friendships, for he published a number of works that reveal the new tendency either directly or implicitly; among these might be noted the works of Frank Sayers and Joseph Fawcett.

Fawcett's *Sermons* are an especially revealing example of the way in which the Dissenting empirical tradition came to be colored by the revival of Platonism. In his first sermon, "On the Omnipresence of God", Fawcett emphasizes not only the scope of the Deity's presence, but also the active nature of that presence:

The Creator ... is himself the great principle of universal vitality. ...
He is the great spring and impulse that actuates all things. He is himself the attracting power that holds the particles of all bodies

---

[106]   Quoted in George M. Harper, *The Neoplatonism of William Blake* (Chapel Hill: The University of North Carolina Press, 1961), pp. 28-29.
[107]   *Ibid.*, pp. 272-273. Wordsworth in fact owned a copy of one of Taylor's 1793 publications: *The Cratylus, Phaedo, Parmenides and Timaeus of Plato. Ibid.*, pp. 287-288.
[108]   John Selby Watson, *The Life of Richard Porson* (London: Longman, Green, Longman, and Roberts, 1861), pp. 198-209.

together, and combines all bodies into the beautiful systems we see them compose. He is himself the living soul that inhabits, and animates every living thing; that propels every drop through every vein; that produces every pulsation of every artery, every motion of every limb, every action of every organ, throughout the whole animal kingdom. Every operating principle, through the whole compass of things, is God, the moment willing, God, the moment acting. He is the life of the world: at once the maker, the inspector, and the mover of all things. [109]

Here we again have the typical Dissenting synthesis of the apparently opposing realms of religion and science. And just as in science the Dissenters emphasized the ability of that discipline to unify and enlarge our mental faculties, so in religion the perspective, though grounded in empirical perception, ultimately transcends the material.

Here we are at the heart of Wordsworth's belief in the late 1790's, this point of view first becoming noticeably apparent in *The Borderers* and then being expanded and developed in *Lyrical Ballads*. In fact, Fawcett's *Sermons*, published in 1795, may well have had a direct impact on Wordsworth's play, which was written the following year, for it parallels Fawcett's thought in many places, both in the above-noted transcendental tendencies and in such other ways as the enquiry into the nature of evil and into the causes and consequences of poverty. Certainly we may detect Fawcett's influence on *Lyrical Ballads*, notably in the most Platonic poem of the volume, "Tintern Abbey". The following lines are very reminiscent of the above passage from Fawcett, particularly in Wordsworth's repetition of the phrase "living soul":

> that serene and blessed mood,
> In which the affections gently lead us on, –
> Until, the breath of this corporeal frame
> And even the motion of our human blood
> Almost suspended, we are laid asleep
> In body, and become a living soul:
> While with an eye made quiet by the power
> Of harmony, and the deep power of joy,
> We see into the life of things.

(41-49)

[109] Fawcett, *Sermons*, I, 32-33. See also I, 2, 35; II, 172, for other instances of Fawcett's Platonism.

Thus, while the Dissenters paralleled Wordsworth in their empirical premises, they also like him were working their way to a point of view that transcended the material. That such English Romantics as Coleridge and Hazlitt should evolve an idealistic philosophy *through* their early Dissenting thought and that later an American "Dissenter", Emerson, should likewise evolve a transcendental philosophy from his earlier material perspective, would suggest that for Unitarian Dissenters at least the movement towards Platonism was no mere reaction from materialism. Their particular brand of empiricism, involving as it did the notion of the "Inward Light", contained the seeds of the Platonic revival. I think it likely that these seeds were also implanted in the young Wordsworth when he associated with the London Dissenters and that they later bore fruit in *Lyrical Ballads*.

Similarly, although Wordsworth already had a philosophy grounded on moral principles when he first discovered Dissenting thought, he still found much there that was new to him. While he had for some time objected to certain features of the Anglican church, he still contemplated taking orders upon his arrival back in England – implying that he accepted its essential doctrines. Yet in 1793 he began to attend the Old Jewry meetinghouse; and in the "Letter to the Bishop of Llandaff" he expresses deep bitterness that the "servility" of the Anglican clergy should make them "the advocates of slavery civil and religious", a fact "which has prejudiced many people against religion itself".[110]

It can only be conjectured how far he turned from his church in 1793; but turn from it he did, as Coleridge indicated in May, 1796, when he called Wordsworth "a Republican & at least a *Semi*-atheist".[111] His objection to the Church was political in origin; the extent of his youthful radicalism makes this understandable, and his criticism of Anglican clerics proves it. Further, this objection is exactly that which the Dissenters put forth: that the Church of England, in the 1790's at least, manifested too

---

[110]   *Prose Works*, I, 3-4.
[111]   *Collected Letters of Samuel Taylor Coleridge*, Earl Leslie Griggs, ed., 4 vols. (Oxford: Clarendon Press, 1956-1959), I, 215-216.

many of the excesses of the state itself; it reflected too much of the dissolute absolutism of the government.[112]

Further, Wordsworth was no doubt influenced by the consistent attempts of the Dissenters to interrelate religion and politics, and by their consequent insistence that religious liberty was essential to a free nation.[113] Wakefield, for example, argued that true Christianity inevitably meant the abolition of all distinctions and all forms of exclusion and slavery,[114] while Priestley addressed himself to the French, admonishing them for incautiously deriding religion. Comparing religion to chemistry, he pointed out that that field was not discarded because it was once overloaded with false ideas: "Neither, then, ought we to discard every thing that bears the name of religion, because we have exploded superstition and priestcraft."[115] Of all the radicals, only the Dissenters consistently made this application of religion to republicanism; Wordsworth's renewed emphasis on the religious in 1793 and 1794, while he still retained his radical principles, must have been largely indebted to these defenders of the Christian spirit of liberty. Even in *The Excursion*, he has the Wanderer reply to the Solitary's attack on man and religion by alluding to the various ancient religions, wherein full social freedom was allowed (IV, 575-670; it is worth noting that these lines once again make heavy use of Milton).

Anyone familiar with him knows that Wordsworth was extremely interested in the poor and sympathetic to their plight. Nevertheless, his was not a simple sociological concern asking what to do with them. As the narrative portrayals in "Guilt and Sorrow" and in many other poems attest, he regarded extreme poverty as inconsistent with a truly natural and religious society. It was offensive not only on material grounds but for spiritual reasons as well, since it occasioned immorality and ignorance,

---

[112]   John Aikin, *The Spirit of the Constitution and that of the Church of England, Compared* (London: Johnson, 1790), p. 3.
[113]   Andrew Kippis, *An Address Delivered at the Interment of the late Rev. Dr. Richard Price* (London: Cadell, 1791), pp. 13-14.
[114]   Wakefield, *Spirit of Christianity*, pp. 39-40.
[115]   Joseph Priestley, *Letters to the Philosophers and Politicians of France* (London: Johnson, 1793), p. 3.

and since it implied that the state was irreligious and indifferent to the poor.

There were many programs for the poor in Wordsworth's time, yet most of them merely centered on material improvement and on enforced educational and religious discipline, to be carried out through the establishment of "houses of industry".[116] Wordsworth was a staunch foe of such schemes, and of all proposals that failed to take into account the fact that the poor were human beings. Dyer's point of view would have gratified him:

if I love and pity the poor, I also respect them. . . . Great wealth and extreme poverty are evils in governments, and the effects of public injustice. But the orders of rich and poor, within certain limits, are beneficial; mutual wants produce mutual obligations and mutual advantages. . . . The prosperity and the wealth of nations depend on the poor. [117]

This perfectly parallels Wordsworth's argument both in "Guilt and Sorrow" and in *Lyrical Ballads*, where it is only extreme wealth or poverty that corrupts. And time and again he insists that a nation's well-being depends on its poorer classes.[118]

Further, the Dissenters argued in behalf of the rights of the poor – not abstract rights that reason dictated, but their rights as the creatures of God. John Aikin, for example, claimed that the poor man's rights were his comforts, these being his wife and children, property, freedom, and "social and convivial enjoyments".[119] Fawcett makes a similar case in his *Sermons*:

The lordly oppressor of the rustic neighbourhood, the little tyrant of the poor man's fields, has been ever in habits of looking upon them that have no riches, as having no rights; as beings beneath his notice; without claims to justice; as no more than dust, whom he may walk over without doing them wrong; . . . in regarding mankind in the humblest classes of life, we have to reflect, not only that they

---

[116] Typical in this regard is Thomas Ruggles, *The History of the Poor*, 2 vols. (London: Deighton, 1793-1794).

[117] Dyer, *Complaints*, p. 2. John Aikin attacks workhouses in a letter to the *Gentleman's Magazine*, 58 (Jan. 1788), 40-41.

[118] See, for example, "The Old Cumberland Beggar" and its Fenwick note, *Poetical Works*, IV, 234-240, 445-446; also *Early Letters*, pp. 313-314.

[119] Aikin, "Humane Thoughts on the Rights and Comforts of the Poor", *Gentleman's Magazine*, 58 (1788), 40-41.

are the creatures of God, but that they have received from him the same nature as ourselves. . . .

In the sight of him who thus considers all mankind, a crime of how enormous a nature, of what frightful magnitude, must the oppression and the destruction of any of these appear. [120]

Generally in his *Sermons* Fawcett glorifies the humble life, suggesting that virtue may more often be found with poverty than with wealth – and with virtue contentment.

This same bias towards poverty pervades Wordsworth's poetry. Not only does he implicitly argue for the rights of the poor, he also finds in them an inherent nobility that is clearly religious in its connotations. In the spring of 1794, a year after hearing Fawcett's sermons and mingling with the London Dissenting world, he composed the first version of "Guilt and Sorrow" (then entitled "Salisbury Plain"). Here, in the story of "The Female Vagrant", he initially glorifies her humble life, and then describes how she and her father have been oppressed:

> the walk of private life
> [Is] Unblessed by Justice and the kindly train
> Of Peace and truth, while Injury and strife
> Outrage and deadly Hate usurp their reign. [121]

In effect, they were deprived of the very rights Aikin demands for the poor.

Likewise, to the Dissenters war was just one of many symbols of the government's acceptance of the *status quo*, and of its indifference to the welfare of the nation at large – an indifference that reflected its failure to acknowledge the spiritual and the

[120] Fawcett, *Sermons*, I, 50-54; see also his sermon entitled "Poverty with Virtue more eligible than Wealth without", I, 255-275. The Dissenters have frequently been dismissed as Puritanical and materialistic businessmen for whom poverty was a sin. But these passages from Aikin and Fawcett, which typify their circle, show that such assertions do not apply to the intellectual Dissenters of late eighteenth-century London, at least. In fact, Johnson himself was one of the very few members of his circle who could be called a businessman – and he was anything but piously indifferent to the unfortunate.
[121] *Poetical Works*, I, 339. For ms. 1 in general see both I, 94-118, and I, 330-341.

emotional in man.[122] This attitude clarifies several aspects of Wordsworth's thought, among them his continued admiration for Fox, whom he praised for manifesting "a constant predominance of sensibility of heart". Indeed, his attack on the ministry in his letter to Fox is perfectly in keeping with the outlook of the Dissenters:

It appears to me that the most calamitous effect, which has followed the measures which have lately been pursued in this country, is a rapid decay of the domestic affections among the lower orders of society. This effect the present Rulers of this country are not conscious of, or they disregard it. [123]

The poet's attitude towards the *status quo* was also a probable consequence of his associations with Dissenters. Unlike the extremists, they were concerned only with a consistent but moderate amelioration of the human condition, not just in politics, but in education, religion, and the social aspects of life; they were most harsh, however, with those who insisted that the constitution had been perfected. Wordsworth shows exactly this prejudice, especially in his denunciation of Bishop Watson for being blind to corruption and for stating that the constitution was perfect.[124] Later, he summed up this period of his life by saying "In Britain, ruled a panic dread of change" (*The Excursion*, III, 827). The process having been started for him by the Dissenters, it was an easy step for Wordsworth to apply this condemnation of the *status quo* to one other realm – poetry.

That a number of Dissenting poets anticipated Wordsworth's poetic innovations is apparent, and it is likely that at least some of these poets directly influenced Wordsworth's development. Johnson's literary interests and his apparent distaste for contemporary literary excesses have already been noted, and these may have been an indirect influence in shaping Wordsworth's taste. As we have seen, Johnson was the publisher of Darwin and Cowper, two poets who significantly influenced Wordsworth by

---

[122] Christie, *Letters on the French Revolution*, pp. 36-37; Priestley, *Essay on First Principles*, p. 144.
[123] *Early Letters*, p. 313.
[124] *Prose Works*, I, 20-21.

applying poetry to science (*The Temple of Nature*)[125] and to politics ("Address to the Bastille" in Book V of *The Task*). Also from Johnson's press came the poetry of John Aikin, George Dyer, and Joseph Fawcett, all Dissenters and all sharing traits in common and with Wordsworth. Each of the four is concerned with liberty, and each is addicted to emotional portraits of women with babes in their arms, the innocent victims of an unfeeling society. While the three Dissenting poets are by no means Wordsworth's equals in poetic talent, like him they do not succumb to sentimentalism; in each case behind their emotional appeal is a clear socio-economic thesis, either in attacking war and repression on England's part or in glorifying a life of freedom, virtue, and intellect. While Wordsworth ultimately universalized his poetry and expanded its scope by excising references to party and to his political motivation, it is important to note that he started from exactly the same position as that of Aikin, Dyer, and Fawcett: at the heart of most of the poems in *Lyrical Ballads* is a political and social statement.

Although little direct evidence can be adduced to connect Wordsworth with the poetry of these Dissenters, he can be linked to it in other ways. His attendance at Fawcett's sermons has already been noted. In addition, Arthur Beatty has made a case for Fawcett's *Art of War* as "representative" of a class of poetry that undoubtedly left its impress on Wordsworth. Beatty points out that such poems were "written for the most part by members of the Wordsworth group, . . . and between 1790 and 1798",[126] a statement that can be qualified to the extent that many of these "Wordsworthians" were in fact liberal Dissenters. No specific evidence connects Aikin and Wordsworth, although the former was a prominent writer in the 1790's whose works were also published by Johnson and who from 1792 to 1798 resided in

---

[125]   Christopher Wordsworth records that his brother's poetry was admired by Darwin, another indication of the intellectual affinity between Wordsworth and the Dissenters. *Social Life in the English Universities*, p. 589. Darwin's conjectured political influence on him is discussed by Garrod, pp. 55-56.
[126]   Arthur Beatty, *Joseph Fawcett: The Art of War*, p. 234.

London, where he was at the center of the Dissenting intellectual circles.[127] In the case of Dyer, much of whose poetry was published by Johnson, he and Wordsworth associated frequently in the mid-1790's, from at least early 1795 on.[128] A brief discussion of these poets will illustrate how they reflect the application of Dissenting thought to poetry, and how Wordsworth, following their lead, carried poetry one step farther.

Fawcett particularly shows the extent to which Wordsworth's mental development was paralleled by other thinkers who were aware of the political events of their time. Before the Revolution, his works were totally in the gothic and the sentimental tradition; afterwards, he became an enthusiast for political theory, and his poetry began to indict social abuses. As his lecture notes reveal, his ideology, which originated in his reading of the Roman republicans, was strikingly similar to Wordsworth's:

Choose a good government: virtue the consequence. Institutions and circumstances of society produce virtue or vices. Liberty and good laws make good men. [129]

Both Aikin and Fawcett emphasize the moral responsibility of states for the well-being of their subjects; each resorts to narrative poetry to show how the government, usually by involving the nation in war, can bring economic disaster to the lower classes, and ultimately occasion widespread degeneration. Fawcett, for example, tells the story of a war widow who is refused relief and who subsequently kills her child on a street in Liverpool.[130] Aikin in some ways goes beyond mere social criticism, particularly by placing the natural beside the rational:

> The first rights of Nature when tyrants invade,
> And Freedom and Justice aloud call for aid,
> Unmov'd at the voice shall I stupidly stand,
> Or raise in the conflict a timorous hand?

[127] Lucy Aikin, *Memoir of John Aikin, M.D.*, pp. 90, 122-123.
[128] Godwin's Diary.
[129] Charles Cestre, *John Thelwall: A Pioneer of Democracy and Social Reform in England During the French Revolution* (London: Sonnenschein, 1906), pp. 24-26, 57-58.
[130] Fawcett, "War Elegy", *Poems* (London: Johnson, 1798), pp. 247-251.

> O never must cold-hearted Selfishness know
> The noble delights of a generous glow. [131]

The moral implications here are apparent, as is the emphasis on emotional sympathy. These poets, then, attempted to introduce humanitarianism into poetry – exactly what Wordsworth began to do in "Guilt and Sorrow".

Aikin's poetic principles are revealed in "An Essay on the Application of Natural History to Poetry", as described by his daughter:

It begins with taking notice of the frequent complaint of the general insipidity of modern poetry; ... Novelty of subject, he pronounces to be the present requisite, and he recommends that it should be sought among 'the grand and beautiful objects which nature every where profusely throws around us; and which, though the most obvious store of new materials to the poet, is that which of all others he has most sparingly touched.' ... he proceeds to offer examples of ... the vagueness and indistinctness, and sometimes the inconsistency and absurdity, which the neglect of the study of actual nature had introduced into poetical description. ... the 'false representations of nature which ancient error or fable first introduced, but which the poets of every age have adopted' ... are at length condemned; on the principle, that 'nothing can be really beautiful which has not truth for its basis,' and on the further consideration of 'the boundless variety of genuine beauties, ... which nature liberally scatters around us,' and of 'the danger of suffering falsehood and error habitually to intrude even in matters of the slightest importance.' [132]

The abiding Dissenting obsession with truth is thus Aikin's central concern, this truth to be achieved by the poet's being accurate in his natural description and by his avoiding inexact imagery. We may recall at this point Wordsworth's Priestleyan concern with the "substantial" in poetry, as well as his delight in the variety of nature, much as Aikin expresses it above, and his emphasis on novelty.

Many of the same values are inherent in Fawcett's poetry. His long poem "Change", for example, is a study in contrasts between

---

[131]   John Aikin, "Counter-Remonstrance", *Poems* (London: Johnson, 1791), pp. vi-vii; see also "A Winter Piece", pp. 20-21.
[132]   Lucy Aikin, *Memoir of John Aikin*, pp. 24-25.

the varied and fluctuating physical world and the static world of the spirit. While superficially the poem may seem to adopt a melancholic pose, a genuine world-weariness reminiscent of Wordsworth's work of the mid-1790's animates his despair. Perhaps most significant, however, Fawcett's depression leads him to a vision of a perfect state, where truth is paramount. His vision is conveyed through typical Romantic light imagery:

> Of moral science, lamp to love and peace,
> The lucid crescent of his vision shines, whose
>   bright increase
> Shall lose its horns in plenitude of light,
> And reach a glorious fall, that ne'er shall
>   wave to night. [133]

Similarly, Dyer, in such poems as "The Union of Poetry and Philosophy" and "Union of Painting and Poetry", advocates the extension of poetry to spheres heretofore ignored, the latter poem again leading to a pictorial concern with detail and accuracy of imagery, and the former insisting on the intellectual substance of poetry:

> And ye wise critics, who have shap'd the rules
> That guide our taste, and fix our wav'ring schools,
> Say, what is Genius? Truth's harmonic light:
> And what is Judgement but the rule of right. [134]

Other elements of Dissenting thought may be found expressed by these three poets. As one instance, Aikin wrote a poem entitled "Ode on the Genius of a Commonwealth", which expresses the writer's concept of the ideal government for England – one embodying all the reforms sought by the Dissenters and bearing unmistakable signs of seventeenth-century Republicanism. In a note to the poem, Aikin states: "By *Commonwealth*, the writer understands every form of government, in which the basis of legislative power is laid in the great body of the people." [135] This

[133]   Fawcett, *Poems*, p. 101.
[134]   Dyer, "Union of Poetry and Philosophy", *Gentleman's Magazine*, 71 (1801), 1029-1030; "Union of Painting and Poetry", *Ibid.*, 74 (1804), 159-160.
[135]   Aikin, *Poems*, pp. 63-68.

definition may be paralleled to Aikin's satirical "Remarks on the Charge of Jacobinism", in which he claims that a good Jacobin should "hold that a majority may be lawfully governed by a minority, upon the pretext of the public good" and should "pay no regard to the will of the nation", whereas *Republicanism*, the spirit of which is, in fact, the very essence of every thing free in political constitutions, is not *Jacobinism*, but the very reverse".[136] This clear-cut distinction between English Republicanism and later French extremism is commonplace among the Dissenters; equally typical is the fact that ideals such as these should appear verbatim in poetry. Aikin concludes his ode with an apostrophe to the republican ideal:

> Great Guardian of collected Man!
> Sole object of the Patriot's care!
> Thy form sublime let Briton's scan,
> And fix their gen'rous passions there:
> Forgot each petty, selfish end,
> To THEE let ev'ry thought extend:
> Be THINE the public trust, the ruling part:
> Let Kings command the knee, but THOU possess
> the heart.

Beyond the political ideals and the willingness to make room for the emotions, what needs to be stressed here is Aikin's insistence on overcoming narrowness, on enlarging one's faculties. As we have seen, the emphasis on the "whole" view characterizes the Dissenters in their scientific and philosophic pursuits; here it is found also as a political (and literary) requisite. On all four counts they may be paralleled with Wordsworth.

Aikin, Dyer, and Fawcett did not necessarily have a direct influence on Wordsworth, for many Dissenting poets manifest the same characteristics. These three simply reveal the Dissenting approach to poetry at its most characteristic, particularly in their attempts to relate the various areas of intellectual enquiry to poetry. It can be said, however, that from his associations with Dissent, whether the political moralists or the poets (and we may number Cowper and Darwin among the Dissenting poets, in prac-

---

[136] *Memoir of John Aikin*, pp. 320-321.

tice at least), Wordsworth came to realize that poetry could be more meaningful, and that it could be made more pertinent to his fellowmen, than were the works of most writers in his day. This recognition, in effect, represents the beginning of his revolt against most of the poetry of the eighteenth century.[137]

His revolt, of course, was manifested in his style as well as in his thought; but here, too, his awakening of 1793 was the origin of his revolutionary theory of versification. The decision to write in the language of the "common man" has obvious political overtones, but that decision was not original to Wordsworth. The Dissenters, in the first place, stressed simplicity in every human endeavor, and they likewise insisted that all distinctions between men be abolished, especially aristocratic appellations. Typically, this emphasis was applied to their literary methods. The praise in the *Analytical Review* for Price's "simple, unaffected, nay even negligent style" has already been noted.[138] Dyer's biography of Robinson, published in 1796, makes it clear that this was a quality the Dissenters consciously cultivated as a symbol of their ideals. Seen in this perspective, Wordsworth's later off-hand remark that Dyer's book was the best biography in English[139] becomes an important insight into the origin of his theory of poetic diction.

Dyer's Preface is essentially a defense of his language, which he makes clear is derived from his love of liberty:

The language of equality is adopted in this volume: it is the language of truth and soberness. ... Such names only are used as distinguish the sex, except where patents, degrees, and the like, give an appropriate and determinate appellation. The truth is, those artificial distinctions, that originated in tyranny, and are perpetuated by custom, lie at the bottom of many serious evils that exist in society: they are commensurate with such as proceed from the accumulation of property. [140]

Artificiality, custom, and tyranny were all anathema to Words-

---

[137]   The "revolutionary" tendency of Wordsworth's style in his poems of 1793 was not missed by the *Monthly Review*, which censured them for their daring figures of speech in particular. *Monthly Review*, XII (1793), 216-218.
[138]   *Analytical Review*, V (1789), 471-475.
[139]   H. C. Robinson, *Correspondence*, I, 40.
[140]   Dyer, *Life of Robinson*, pp. vii-viii.

worth; excess property was attacked in the "Letter to the Bishop of Llandaff" and in his later poems as well. In other words, he continued to share these beliefs with Dyer for some time, so that his subsequent application of Dyer's principles to poetry was possibly prompted by this book.

Later in his Preface, Dyer describes his style in a little more detail:

My language, . . . will appear naked and unadorned, and my periods will want the harmony, that accompanies a great name. Among writers I appear, as a native of Botany Bay, or Otaheite, among civilised nations. France has emancipated mankind from these attempts at false greatness. By bursting the bars, which imprison truth, she has aggrandised her species. [141]

Here again, the Revolution is applied to style, a style that has many of the qualities of the poet's. He and Dyer became close associates, and they admired each other's works. Unfortunately there is no record when they first met, although Dyer, interestingly enough, changed his own poetic style as a result of reading *Lyrical Ballads*.

A parallel aspect of style is the frequent Dissenting insistence that the language of poetry is not fundamentally different from the language of prose — an understandable position in the light of the Dissenters' emphasis on simplicity and on direct expression of theme. Beatty has noted William Enfield's role in the debate over the subject, Enfield writing to the *Monthly Magazine* as "Enquirer" in defense of the position that Wordsworth later adopted in *Lyrical Ballads*.[142] Enfield was a prominent Dissenting minister and educator whose works, on a wide variety of subjects, were published by Johnson.

In yet another area of poetry may the Dissenters have influenced Wordsworth: Aikin, Fawcett, and their fellow poets used narratives to comment on the plight of the poor. Moreover, the *Analytical Review*, while generally praising *Descriptive Sketches*, found fault with it for its lack of any narrative thread.[143] If

[141]   *Ibid.*, p. ix.
[142]   Beatty, *William Wordsworth: His Doctrine and Art*, pp. 55, 56n.
[143]   *Analytical Review*, XV (1793), 294-297.

Wordsworth was indeed aware of the intellectual endeavors of the Dissenters, and if he respected Johnson's critical judgments – both of which are highly probable – then his immediate conversion to narrative poetry in "Guilt and Sorrow" can be regarded as a result of his Dissenting connections.

It is possible also that his recurrent use of America for the setting of his poems originated in his associations with these same people. References to America are relatively infrequent in political literature of the 1790's, no doubt partially because Paine had become disenchanted with the nation and also because it was not sufficiently republican for the extremists, France having replaced it in their hopes for a land of absolute equality. But to the Dissenters America was still a land of religious as well as political freedom; Price for years remained in touch with such patriots as Franklin and Washington, while Priestley (along with a number of others, including Wordsworth's early associate, Cooper) even emigrated to America when he had become disillusioned with England. Generally, in both politics and religion there was a constant interchange between English Dissenters and their friends in the new nation.

Wordsworth undoubtedly shared their interest. His choice of reading reveals his fascination with the land, while his use of it for settings would indicate that he associated it with his own Lake Country, with the important reservation that America had political freedom as well as natural liberty.

In sum, English Dissent may be said to have directed Wordsworth towards a nobler view of man, a greater sense of tradition, a fuller awareness of the role of nature in human life, more respect for science, and a deeper understanding of the potentialities of literary expression than he had possessed previously. While the full consequences of this influence did not appear for some time, we may detect a change in Wordsworth's writings after the spring of 1793. The immediate results of his Dissenting associations would thus be a moderating of his political thought and a turning away from his conventional early verse towards a poetic idiom that was more personal, more substantial, and better expressive of his ideology.

There remains one important question: why, since the Dissenters were so central to his intellectual development, did Wordsworth so seldom acknowledge them in such sources as his letters, the Fenwick notes, and *The Prelude*? Actually, very few of Wordsworth's early letters are extant, and in these there are a surprisingly large number of references to Dissent, if not acknowledgments of Dissenting influence. The Fenwick notes, written in his Anglican and conservative old age, may be dismissed as unreliable sources of information about his liberal and unorthodox early manhood. *The Prelude* is the key here, for in Dissent as in his liberalism, the poem's essential truthfulness must be defended against the frequent charges that Wordsworth either distorted the facts or else omitted that which was unsavory.

Six reasons may be listed for Wordsworth's failure to give credit to his Dissenting connections in the poem (and incidentally in his letters):

1) I feel he tended to associate the Dissenters with London intellectual circles in general; his account of his visits to the city are thus a telescoped (and as almost always in the poem, generalized) description. Then, too, his 1791 account serves as a summary of all his visits to London, so that his later experiences tend to get slighted.

2) Even today, the Dissenters are only with difficulty distinguished from other liberal circles. Socially, at least during Wordsworth's 1793 stay in the city, they still mingled with those of other political viewpoints. Even ten years later, Wordsworth may have been too close in time to this earlier influence to discern it.

3) Much of the Dissenting influence on him was a reinforcement of his earlier views or of that which was innately his already. For Wordsworth, it would have been difficult to tell where confirmation ceased and direct, original influence began.

4) Similarly, in many instances the Dissenters acted simply as intermediaries, leading Wordsworth to various other writers and traditions which then became the active influence on him.

5) The consequences of his associations with Dissenters appeared only gradually over a number of years. That is, the Dis-

senters *directed* him towards certain positions; but he did not immediately arrive at them in every instance.

6) Perhaps as important as any of the above (and partially accountable for all of them), these intellectual Dissenters were not self-righteous Puritans who wore their religion on their sleeves; we have seen that humility and tolerance of the opinions of others were among their ideals. Wordsworth thus could well have mingled with many of these men without knowing (or without being fully conscious) that they were Dissenters. He never refers to Johnson, for example, as a Dissenter, though he mentions his name several times in his letters.

At any rate, it is worth noting that when *Lyrical Ballads* appeared, the *Analytical Review* gave the volume its most enthusiastic reception. Only "The Ancient Mariner" was objected to, as might have been expected. The "Advertisement", containing the outlines of Wordsworth's poetic theory, was praised for being "sensible", while most of the poems were singled out for their simplicity. Further, after quoting the whole of "Goody Blake", the reviewer commended the poet for not using an indiscriminate amount of pity, for not, in other words, lapsing into sentimental excesses.[144] All of this is very meaningful praise, since it shows how closely Wordsworth was adhering to the poetic restrictions of the Dissenters, in opposition to the accepted taste of the day. Above all, it indicates that a central portion of their philosophy was retained by the poet and eventually evolved into the basic premises of *Lyrical Ballads*.

[144] *Analytical Review*, XXVIII (1798), 583-587.

V

TOWARDS INTELLECTUAL CRISIS, 1793-1794

At the prompting of his relatives, Wordsworth was anxiously seeking a means of supporting himself by the early summer of 1793. Not having decided on a career, he was debating between teaching and authorship. Ultimately he found that he could effectively combine the two careers.

In spite of this apparent vacillation, he had attained by now a philosophy of life which he held with great conviction. In its outlines, it shows the influence of his year in France and of his association with the Dissenters as well. Neither mechanistic nor sensualistic, it was centered instead on his belief in the natural goodness of man, and on his moral perfectibility; the church and the state were responsible for helping mankind to achieve perfection. Hence politics and morality should be closely interwoven, a requirement Wordsworth first began to stress during his republican days in France. He was, then, a moderate liberal, seeking reform – moral, as well as economic and political – through the constitution and through the inevitable processes of time.

His state of mind in the summer of 1793 can only be inferred vaguely from *The Prelude* and from circumstantial evidence. Surely his separation from Annette, the hostility of most of his family, his poverty, the continued high-handedness of Lord Lonsdale, and the political developments in France and England all combined to dishearten the young reformer who had dedicated himself to the amelioration of humanity. Yet he was not necessarily driven to the depths of despair, nor did he bitterly resign his hopes of mankind, as Darbishire, Harper, Hartman, and Todd suppose.[1] In fact, the next year of Wordsworth's life may be regarded as the period when he was actively seeking to apply and to communicate his philosophy of man in some tangible way. His activities and his writings during this time exemplify both that philosophy and that quest; they reveal further that each was directly owing to his development in France and to his association with the Dissenters.

His leave-taking from the city, far from being a sign of a revulsion from London life or from his acquaintances there, was the simple consequence of financial necessity; he had to go wherever opportunity took him. It is not known how many futile attempts he made to obtain a job. He had hopes "of being engaged as tutor to Lord Belmore's son",[2] but they were soon dispelled. Then a former schoolmate, William Calvert, reappeared in the poet's life and suggested that the two of them tour the west of England, a proposal which Wordsworth readily accepted. After spending a month on the Isle of Wight (*The Prelude*, X, 298), the two young men proceeded across Salisbury Plain until Calvert's carriage overturned in a ditch. Calvert continued on his horse, leaving the poet to walk to the home of his friend Jones in Denbighshire, which he reached by the end of August.[3]

Wordsworth's continued friendship with Jones is one of the enigmas of his career, for the two had little in common, as Mrs. Moorman amply shows.[4] How long the poet remained in Wales with his friend is not known. At Christmas, 1793, he was in Whitehaven, but his whereabouts between September and December are a mystery. Most likely he spent much of the time with Jones – the Wordsworth circle was accustomed to long visits – and then toured the west country for the remainder of the fall.

One alternative is that Wordsworth made a hasty visit to Paris – a story that originated with Carlyle, who claimed that the poet in his old age told of witnessing the execution of the Giron-

---

[1] Helen Darbishire, *The Poet Wordsworth* (Oxford: Clarendon Press, 1950), p. 26; Harper, I, 206-210; Hartman, pp. 116-117; Todd, pp. 63-64.
[2] *Early Letters*, p. 103.
[3] *Ibid.*, p. 109.
[4] Mrs. Moorman, pp. 130-131.

din Gorsas in Paris on October 7, 1793.[5] This is difficult to accept. Wordsworth would have had to journey across England, cross the Channel in time of war, and then remain undetected as an enemy alien. Moreover, there is no plausible motive for the trip; the political affairs in France were no longer attractive to him, and if Annette were his object, why was he in Paris? The episode may well be merely the result of a lapse of memory on the part of Wordsworth in telling the story or of Carlyle in recounting it. No reference to such a trip appears in the letters or in *The Prelude*.

At any rate, early in 1794 he and Dorothy were staying together at the Rawsons', the first meeting of brother and sister in four years. Fairchild notes that Dorothy had "happily associated" with Unitarians at Halifax and Norwich and that Wordsworth joined her at the former place in 1794, when he "was warmly received by a circle of cultivated, liberal folk whom he found much more congenial than Canon Cookson".[6] Once again, we find Wordsworth turning to Unitarian circles for intellectual stimulation. In April, 1794, the two moved into the first of their many homes, Windy Brow, near Keswick, which had been put at their disposal by the generous William Calvert. Six weeks later they traveled to Whitehaven to stay with the wife of their cousin John Wordsworth, after which Dorothy departed to visit other relatives and the poet returned to Windy Brow. Until the early part of 1795 he cared for the ailing Raisley Calvert, who had matched his brother's munificence by offering to share his income with Wordsworth and by bequeathing a large portion of his estate to him.[7] That the young poet should have won the favor of the Calverts is additional proof of his dedication to the cause of humanity in 1793 and 1794. He later wrote that Raisley Calvert left him the legacy "from a confidence on his part that I had powers and attainments which might be of use to mankind".[8] Calvert would not have known that he was thus assisting the

[5] *Ibid.*, pp. 238-242, presents a detailed and impartial analysis of this conjectured episode.
[6] *Religious Trends in English Poetry*, III, 156.
[7] *Early Letters*, pp. 126-127, 129-140.
[8] *Ibid.*, p. 546.

development of a great poet, but he would have been able to recognize a dedicated humanitarian and a determined spirit who promised to fulfill his ideals.

Undoubtedly heartened by the Calverts' faith in him, Wordsworth returned to poetry; indeed, the last months of 1793 and the spring of 1794 were his most fruitful creative period up to that time. His poetry now had a motivating force, the good of humanity, and he directed all his energies toward that end. From his walk on Salisbury Plain came the first version of "Guilt and Sorrow", which he wrote while staying with Jones. Then followed several lengthy additions to *An Evening Walk* and *Descriptive Sketches*, as well as early versions of some of the poems in *Lyrical Ballads* and of certain passages in *The Prelude*. Despite all this, and a number of revealing letters to Mathews, his state of mind during this period is the most controversial subject of his early career. Especially is this so with regard to the conception of "Guilt and Sorrow", the first version of which Wordsworth entitled "Salisbury Plain".

To many scholars, this poem is yet another manifestation of Wordsworth's continuing obsession with Godwin.[9] Just as common is the idea that it reflects his mental turmoil of the time — a "morbid condition", as Todd calls it.[10] To Campbell and Mueschke, the poem may be divided into two parts, one of them in the tradition of sentimental poetry and the other essentially belonging to the gothic school.[11] Harper has rightly challenged the second half of this interpretation, noting that the poem is designed to arouse pity, not terror, and that it is too slow-moving and matter-of-fact to excite any sort of supernatural fear.[12] Hartman over-ingeniously finds in the poem "a horror of the horizontal".[13] On the other hand, to the poet's latest biographer,

[9] See especially Harper, I, 256, and Hayden, p. 83; in reply, see Meyer, p. 134, and Schneider, pp. 214-215.
[10] Todd, p. 63; see also Hayden, pp. 103-104, and Meyer, pp. 135-137.
[11] "Guilt and Sorrow: A Study in the Genesis of Wordsworth's Aesthetic". *Modern Philology*, XXIII (1926), 293-306.
[12] "Wordsworth's Guilt and Sorrow", *Review of English Studies*, III (1927), 71-73.
[13] Hartman, p. 119.

"Guilt and Sorrow" represents his return to nature; Mrs. Moorman intelligently observes that he excised the visionary part of the poem from its published version and added it to *The Prelude,* tacit proof of his realization that his experience on Salisbury Plain which occasioned the poem was highly poetic.[14]

In fact, it was, as he must have known, a turning point in his career. Mrs. Moorman's interpretation is basically the same as that of Garrod: "some time shortly after August 1793 . . . Wordsworth first began to view Man and Nature in inter-connexion".[15] It almost goes without saying that this is poles apart from Godwinism, and from psychological abnormality, for that matter. A detailed analysis of Wordsworth's thought in late 1793, as indicated by his poetry of this time, will show that Garrod and Mrs. Moorman are essentially correct: the poet at that time began to relate his humanitarian ideology to real life, as symbolized by nature.[16] He did share the current views of all liberals by accepting necessitarianism and by lamenting the war with France, but his thought was not Godwinian and his mental state was not "morbid".

In the first place, many of Godwin's ideas had repeatedly appeared in other writers of his day; although the poet clearly believed in reason, necessity, and perfectibility, he could have found these ideals in a host of other places, among them the works of Priestley. Further, "Guilt and Sorrow" can hardly reflect Wordsworth's own supposed inner turmoil since he was attempting to write an impartial, realistic account of the effects

---

[14] Mrs. Moorman, pp. 232-234. See also Enid Welsford, *Salisbury Plain: A Study in the Development of Wordsworth's Mind and Art* (New York: Barnes and Noble, 1966). Miss Welsford's study of the several versions of this episode supports my case in two central ways: in asserting the essential continuity of Wordsworth's work (and thus showing the significance of his early poems) and in noting that the first version of "Salisbury Plain" (1793) is characterized by "expectant hopefulness", as opposed to the 1795 version. See especially p. 25.

[15] Garrod, p. 79.

[16] Bateson, p. 109, makes much the same point: "From now on, Wordsworth determined, he would be the poet of humble life." However, Hartman asserts that "the active presence of human figures [in "Salisbury Plain"] . . . constitutes an advance over *Descriptive Sketches.* Wordsworth invents for the first time a human machinery to express what is an essentially non-human landscape feeling." P. 124.

of war on the lower classes; he was following the advice of the *Analytical Review* and making his poetry more impersonal through the inclusion of a narrative thread. Similarly, he would not have adopted the gothic and sentimental poses that he abhorred unless he wanted to use those modes for some special purpose; unlike most of the writers of the 1790's, he did not use them as ends in themselves. The 1793 manuscript of the poem contains the story of "the Female vagrant" and several long descriptions of Salisbury Plain, the story being "sentimental" and the description "gothic", but neither goes to the extremes that were common in the 1790's in poetry and fiction.[17] The gothic elements are meant to reinforce Wordsworth's indictment of society, the "guilt" of the poem. He was not seeking fear as an end in itself; rather he was attempting to show the frightful consequences of social corruption – effects that even nature could manifest. In a sense, an enlightened civilization should have overcome what Wordsworth might have called its "gothic elements", gothicism in literature being equivalent to corruption in life.

In the story of the woman, on the other hand, "sorrow" is the center of attention. But unlike a truly sentimental work, the poem is designed to reform, to show that only if men develop their "social passions" will mankind be perfected and all abuses be removed. Wordsworth here belongs to the humanitarian school that in his time, at least, was primarily composed of Dissenters, not to the sentimental school of feeling for feeling's sake.

Above all else, the poem attacks war – not merely that against France, although the "Advertisement" reveals that the sight of the fleet at Portsmouth in 1793 occasioned the poem, but war in general. In fact, Wordsworth repeatedly had the American Revolution in mind when adverting to the evils of warfare. The female vagrant had sailed with her husband, upon his induction into the army, to the "western world", where her children as well as her husband perished.[18] He noted in 1842 that, when he wrote the poem, "The American war was still fresh in memory".[19] In the

---

[17] *Poetical Works*, I, 94-127, 330-341.
[18] *Ibid.*, I, 110-111.
[19] *Ibid.*, I, 94.

previous chapter, the Dissenters have been seen to oppose war for economic and moral reasons; their animosity to England's conflict with France was motivated by more than just their sympathy with the Revolution. Likewise, they were largely responsible, in conjunction with Fox's group, for keeping the American war "fresh in memory". Price and Priestley, along with other Dissenters, had been among the most vociferous and publicized defenders of the colonies. The economic and moral overtones of "Guilt and Sorrow" and its references to the American Revolution thus suggest that the poet was still dedicated to the Dissenting principles he met earlier in the year.

Specifically republican ideals also recur throughout the poem. The woman is a victim of the oppression of a rich landowner, a condemnation of the outmoded and unrealistic legal code that could permit such conditions. Further, Wordsworth refers to the republican ideal of national self-determination; in a catalogue of the empires of the world, he notes the way in which colonies lose their natural beauty by being conquered, while the citizens of the home country "drink/The dregs of Wretchedness".[20] Continued also from Wordsworth's first acquaintance with radicalism is the emphasis on Milton; to quote again from de Selincourt: "The concluding stanzas of MS. 1 are far more inspired by Milton's great political utterances in prose and verse than by Godwin."[21] The best indication of Wordsworth's sense of intellectual kinship with Milton is that time and again, when he arrives at climactic situations in his poetry, he borrows from his predecessor's works to add vigor and emphasis.

In regard to religion and society, the poem again shows its author's affinity with the Dissenters. The focus is entirely on the lower classes, suggesting not only the economic ill-effects of war but also its harmful moral influence upon the poor; the woman had once been virtuous, having been born "by Derwent's side",

[20] *Ibid.*, I, 339. In this enumeration of the empires of the world, Wordsworth gets as far as India, at which point the manuscript is torn away; it is obvious that he was just beginning to deal with the British Empire, and the fact his account is missing may well indicate the severity of his judgment.
[21] *Ibid.*, I, 341.

but war and injustice in general had led her to depravity,[22] all of which is fully in keeping with the point of view of Dyer and other Dissenters. Similarly, in its attack on corrupt institutions, "Guilt and Sorrow" repeatedly refers to the predominance of "superstition" in the world, the very phrase the Dissenters used when condemning the political connections of the Anglican Church:

> Heroes of Truth, pursue your march, uptear
> The oppressors' dungeon from its deepest base;
> High o'er the towers of Pride undaunted rear
> Resistless in your might th' Herculean mace
> Of Reason, let foul Error's monster race
> Dragged from their dens start at the light with pain
> And die! pursue your toils till not a trace
> Be left on earth of Superstition's reign
> Save that eternal pile which frowns on Sarum's plain. [23]

Here is a clear correlation of political and religious corruption. The "Heroes of Truth" to Wordsworth were those who actively opposed oppression and superstition, not abstract theorists; it must be remembered that Godwin was not the sole advocate of reason and that such thinkers as Priestley connected the rational with the religious. A complete list of the poet's heroes would include not only Beaupuy and many Dissenters, but also the reformers and patriots of the past who likewise worked for the cause of man, particularly Gustavus I of Denmark, Milton and his fellow Republicans, Mithridates, Sertorius and his followers, and Wallace (see *The Prelude*, I, 157-219), all "natural Heroes" – and national ones.

Moreover, although the poet shared the prevailing faith in the ability of reason to perfect man, he carefully insisted upon the value of the emotions; "Guilt and Sorrow" reveals this as well as the earlier works. As a matter of fact, the seemingly extraneous scene in which the traveler and the vagrant come upon a father cruelly beating his child was added to the later MS. 2 simply to make that point. The narratives of the two main characters illustrate the occasions for economic and moral degradation, so that

---

[22] *Ibid.*, I, 106-118.
[23] *Ibid.*, I, 340-341 (corrected from ms.); see also I, 339-340.

their appeal is essentially to reason: remove the cause and the effect will disappear. But the episode illustrates that reason is not enough, and that compassion must accompany the workings of the rational mind. This point is implicit in the poem from the very first, as in the original version of the third stanza:

> The thoughts which bow the kindly spirit down,
> And break the springs of joy, their deadly weight
> Derive from memory of pleasures flown,
> Which haunts us in some sad reverse of fate,
> Or from the reflection on the state
> Of those who on the couch of Affluence rest,
> By laughing Fortune's sparkling cup elate,
> While we of comfort reft, by pain depressed,
> No other pillow know than Penury's iron breast. [24]

The theme of property is one that the poet shared with most Dissenters and with such contemporary thinkers as Godwin, Paine, and Wollstonecraft. But there is something else here – sensibility, a tacit acknowledgment of the feelings both as inevitable and as worthwhile.

The apprenticeship that Wordsworth served under Beaupuy, the English Republicans, the Girondins, and the Dissenters lies behind the whole of "Guilt and Sorrow". As far as his philosophy is concerned, the poem represents no new beliefs; he merely applied his thought of the spring of 1793 to the natural universe at large, and he attempted to express those views in poetry.

A lesser poem that probably owes its inception to the summer excursion of 1793 helps to confirm this interpretation of Wordsworth's development. "How Sweet to Walk along the Woody Steep" contrasts the tranquil beauty of nature with the implications of the fleet lying at anchor close by; at the sound of the "sunset cannon"

> The star of life appears to set in blood,
> And ocean shudders in offended mood,
> Deepening with moral gloom his angry flood. [25]

[24]   Ibid., I, 335 (corrected); see I, 119-121, for the child-beating episode.
[25]   Ibid., I, 307-308; de Selincourt (I, 374) dates this 1795-1797, after the poet's "Godwinian" period, because it appears in a notebook with other poems of that period. However, sketchy as the poem is, yet so vivid and

Once again, beside the condemnation of war is a clear statement in behalf of the natural and the religious. The obvious implication is that the poet's despair with the human condition was lightened by his faith in certain ideals — ideals which he shared with the Dissenters particularly.[26]

Although the poems and letters of the spring of 1794 reveal that Wordsworth had read *Political Justice* and was beginning to adopt part of Godwin's philosophy, the poet remained primarily a humanitarian republican dedicated to the enlightenment of man by means of poetry. On the surface, this is difficult to reconcile with the account in *The Prelude*:

> Through months, through years, long after the last beat
> Of those atrocities . . .
> I scarcely had one night of quiet sleep
> Such ghastly visions had I of despair
> And tyranny, and implements of death,
> And long orations which in dreams I pleaded
> Before unjust Tribunals, with . . . a sense
> Of treachery and desertion in the place
> The holiest that I knew of, my own soul.
> (X, 371-381).

Although Wordsworth is mainly referring here to the Terror in France, he also has in mind the systematic repression of English radicals that by 1794 had assumed the proportions of a witch-hunt. His preoccupation with the subject is indicated by the repeated references in his letters of 1794 to the various trials and to the tyranny of the government; Dorothy, in writing to Richard, proves that the political climate did indeed affect her favorite

---

firsthand in description, it is probably the impulsive jottings that Wordsworth scribbled down in 1793 while on his tour. Moreover, its bitterness is closer in spirit to the works of 1793 than to the poems of the later period, especially the account of the same episode in *The Prelude* (X, 291-307). The facts that he later worked on the poem and that in theme it parallels his subsequent works are mute testimony to the essential continuity of his thought from 1793 to 1798.

[26] "The Convict" (*Ibid.*, I, 312-314), though probably written later, may also have been prompted by the experiences of this summer. The poem is discussed in Chapter VI.

brother: "I think I can answer for William's caution about expressing his political opinions. He is very cautious and seems well aware of the dangers of a contrary conduct." [27] His opinions were not as extreme as were those of many radicals, but he still had good reason to fear the government's wrath.

Nevertheless, there is no direct indication that he underwent any crucial period of doubt in 1793 or early 1794. He was, after all, financially solvent for almost the first time in his life; he and Dorothy had been reunited, achieving their long-sought ideal of living together in the country; most of all, he had his noble ideals, and, consequent to them, he had finally found the career for which he was destined. The fact that this was one of his most fruitful creative periods testifies to his continued affirmative dedication.

In all probability, then, *The Prelude* must be taken literally, not figuratively: his dreams were tormented by the thought of the cruelty and criminality of the governments of the world, but his wakeful life was uplifted by his idealism and by his communion with nature. Following the description in *The Prelude* of his horrible nightmares is an account of the consolations that redeemed his nightly depression. He compares himself to "ancient Prophets", who walked in the conviction that they knew the true and the virtuous, while all about them in society was corrupted:

> So did some portions of that spirit fall
> On me, to uphold me through those evil times,
> And in their rage and dog-day heat I found
> Something to glory in, as just and fit,
> And in the order of sublimest laws; . . .
> I felt a kind of sympathy with power,
> Motions rais'd up within me, nevertheless,
> Which had relationship to highest things.
> (X, 402-430).

The passage as a whole is a testimony in behalf of the natural, the spiritual, and the virtuous; more particularly, it confirms the theory that Wordsworth in 1793 and throughout much of 1794 first guided his life according to the principles which he adopted

---

[27] *Early Letters*, p. 121; see also pp. 119, 124-126, 135, 137.

from the English Republicans and from the Dissenters and which he later enunciated more fully in *Lyrical Ballads*.[28]

It should be stressed, then, that Wordsworth's "ghastly visions of despair" do not refer to the monumental crisis of late 1794 and 1795. This earlier period of torment may be termed a political not a metaphysical dilemma, the very reverse of his later crisis.

In the spring of 1794 Wordsworth concentrated especially on the interdependent ideals of political reform and the dissemination of moral principles among mankind. The continued injection of his specific beliefs into his poetry indicates this, as does his penchant for tutoring those around him. Early in the year, at Windy Brow, Dorothy was his student, not only in French, in which the poet was then proficient, but also in Italian. He was possibly renewing his study of that language for the same reason that had prompted his trip to France – to become more familiar with the political thinkers of other nations; later that year he included Machiavelli and Beccaria in a brief list of important advocates of liberty.[29]

The most distinctive manifestation of his emphasis on general edification, however, is the plan for a miscellany that he and William Mathews hoped to publish, the result of the renewal of correspondence between the two young men. The title, at Wordsworth's suggestion, was to be "The Philanthropist" – in itself a sign of the poet's social concern. Moreover, his letters to Mathews which pertain to the scheme contain explicit avowals of his radical philosophy.

From the first, he dwells on the political situation and on ethical principles:

Of each others political sentiments we ought not to be ignorant; and here at the very threshold I solemnly affirm that in no writings of mine will I ever admit of any sentiment which can have the least tendency to induce my readers to suppose that the doctrines which are now enforced by banishment, imprisonment, ... are other than

[28] Mrs. Moorman, p. 248, is one of the few scholars who do not read too much into *The Prelude*; she, too, believes that his frame of mind at the time was more optimistic than has traditionally been thought.
[29] *Early Letters*, pp. 111-118, 125.

pregnant with every species of misery. . . . I am of that odious class of
men called democrats, and of that class I shall for ever continue.
In a work like that of which we are speaking, it will be impossible
. . . not to inculcate principles of government and forms of social
order of one kind or another. . . . Besides essays on morals and
politics I think I could communicate critical remarks upon poetry, . . .
upon the arts of painting, gardening, and other subjects of amusement.
But I should principally wish our attention to be fixed upon life and
manners, and to make our publication a vehicle of sound and exalted
Morality. [30]

Especially worth noting is Wordsworth's insistence that the magazine should focus on morality and politics, as well as the fact
that he regards himself as qualified to write on the subjects; evidently he had thought a great deal about them. Further, the inculcation of a "sound and exalted Morality" was a goal he shared
with the Dissenters; in this same letter he notes that "except one
or two of the reviews", all the current miscellanies "appear to be
written to maintain the existence of prejudice and to disseminate
error".[31] Of the many current miscellanies, almost all were mouthpieces for Pitt's ministry and the establishment. In all likelihood,
paramount among the exceptions which Wordsworth was thinking
of was the *Analytical Review*.

Nevertheless, uppermost in his mind here were the continued
repressive measures of the ministry; he must have been following
the successive trials and banishments with ever-increasing alarm
and disgust. In the country as he was, he would have been far
more conscious of his non-conformity than had he been in the
city. His belligerence here and elsewhere was certainly owing to
the fact that he was surrounded by hostility, both from his family
and from his rural associates – all of whom would have indeed
referred to radicals as "that odious class of men".

As the year progressed, his feeling of alienation increased. Out
of touch with those who were sympathetic with his ideals and
surrounded primarily by reactionaries, he gradually became more
extreme in his views. In Parliament, the once-clamorous Foxites
were beginning to lose heart, their numbers considerably weaken-

[30]   *Ibid.*, p. 119.
[31]   *Ibid.*

ed by those who had gone over to the side of the ministry. The nation as a whole feared an invasion from France and rebellion from within, making Pitt insist upon stronger security measures; the culmination was the suspension of the Habeas Corpus Act in the spring of 1794.[32] England was becoming a totally hostile land to the young liberal.

Nor was Wordsworth alone in this despair. It is apparent that the events of the summer and fall of 1794 represented a crushing blow to the hopes of many liberals. Their faith had sustained them through adversity until then, but English repression combined with French aggression destroyed that faith. John Binns records that after the treason trials of late 1794 even such extremists as Hardy, Horne Tooke, Thelwall, Holcroft, and Godwin ceased to attend the meetings of the various political societies.[33] Other liberals were also depressed by the turn of events, among them being John Aikin, Thomas Cooper, and Joseph Ritson; Aikin's mood of late 1794 is particularly reminiscent of that of Wordsworth.[34]

In late May his brother Richard wrote to Wordsworth, urging that he "be cautious in writing or expressing your political opinions. By the suspension of the Habeas Corpus Acts the Ministers have great powers." Dorothy's reply has already been noted: "He is very cautious and seems well aware of the dangers of a contrary conduct."[35] No doubt he was "well aware" of these dangers – aware and repelled. He was separated from the tempering influence of the Dissenters; he was dismayed at the course of the French Revolution, as Robespierre continued to bathe the nation in blood; and he became increasingly antagonistic and despairing about his own land. All these factors combined to effect his gradual departure from moderate republicanism; he was slowly repudiating the natural and succumbing to Godwinian materialism.

[32] Watson, pp. 357-360.
[33] *Recollections of the Life of John Binns* (Philadelphia: by the author, 1854), p. 43.
[34] Lucy Aikin, *John Aikin*, p. 103 ff.; Malone, *Cooper*, p. 53 ff.; Bertrand H. Bronson, *Joseph Ritson, Scholar-at-arms*, 2 vols. (Berkeley: University of California Press, 1938), I, 161.
[35] *Early Letters*, p. 121 and n.

A more extreme radicalism is apparent in his next letter to Mathews, dated June, 1794:

I disapprove of monarchical and aristocratical governments, however modified. Hereditary distinctions and privileged orders of every species I think must necessarily counteract the progress of human improvement: hence it follows that I am not amongst the admirers of the British constitution. Now, there are two causes which appear to me to be accomplishing the subversion of this constitution; first, the infatuation profligacy and extravagance of men in power, and secondly, the changes of opinion respecting matters of Government which within these few years have rapidly taken place in the minds of speculative men. [36]

In some ways, little of this is new to the poet. With the Dissenters, he had long deplored the existence of artificial distinctions between men, the moral failings of England's leaders, and the increasing acceptance of the *status quo* among political thinkers, by Burke and Pitt as well as by Bishop Watson – all apostates from the cause of reform. Likewise he had before this enunciated a faith in man's perfectibility. The hostility to the constitution, however, is something he had never revealed before. Yet Wordsworth qualifies; he does not object to the principles of the institution, but to the way they have been "subverted" by immorality and complacency – all of which bears out the contention that his moderation had been shaken mainly by the course of political events.

He goes on to insist that he favors only gradual reform:

The destruction of those institutions which I condemn appears to me to be hastening on too rapidly. I recoil from the bare idea of a revolution; . . .
After this need I add that I am a determined enemy to every species of violence? [37]

He is, in other words, a devotee of reason. It is obvious that by now he had read *Political Justice*, for many references to Godwin's ideas appear in this letter. Godwin, too, abhorred violence and exalted reason; like him, Wordsworth expresses a belief in

[36] *Ibid.*, pp. 123-124.
[37] *Ibid.*, p. 124.

"those rules of political justice, from which the farther any government deviates the more effectually must it defeat the object for which government was ordained". They both condemn "inflammatory addresses to the passions of men".[38]

Nevertheless, Godwin's place in the poet's development at this stage can be overemphasized. The central part of his philosophy still consisted of the ideals he adopted in France and in London – virtue and education. After noting that "the multitude walk in darkness", he proceeds to outline the prospectus of the miscellany as he envisions it, emphasizing these same principles:

each number should open with the topic of general politics; ... next should follow essays upon morals and manners, and institutions whether social or political. These several departments entirely for such as read for instruction; next should come essays partly for instruction and partly for amusement, such as biographical papers exhibiting the characters and opinions of eminent men, particularly those distinguished for their exertions in the cause of liberty, as Turgot, as Milton, Sydney, Machiavel, Beccaria, ... It would perhaps be advisable that these should, as much as possible, form a series exhibiting the advancement of the human mind in moral knowledge, ... Next should come a review of those publications which are particularly characterized for inculcating recommendations of benevolence and philanthropy. Some poetry we should have. For this part of our plan we ought to have no dependence on original communications, the trash which infests the magazines strongly impresses the justice of this remark; from *new* poetical publications of merit and such *old* ones as are not generally known the pages allotted to verse may generally be filled. [39]

The emphasis on the virtuous is the most noticeable indication of his essential separation from Godwin. Moreover, Wordsworth's heroes are certainly not those of Godwin; instead of Rousseau or Helvétius, he singles out Italian and seventeenth-century English political thinkers and patriots. Even "the advancement of the human mind in moral knowledge" is a subject which first interested him in France, while his disapproval of contemporary poetry was something he shared with the Dissenters.

---

[38]   *Ibid.*, pp. 124-125; see C. W. Roberts, "Wordsworth, 'The Philanthropist', and 'Political Justice' ", *Studies in Philology*, XXXI (1934), 84-91.
[39]   *Ibid.*, pp. 125-126.

As a matter of fact, he was actually aware that the principles of their miscellany would appeal to the Dissenters:

The dissenters, in general are not rich but in every town of any size there are some who would receive a work like ours with pleasure.

This, he realized, would be in marked contrast to members of the Church of England,[40] an institution repeatedly censured in this series of letters – further evidence that he was temporarily repudiating the church of his birth.

Meanwhile, he continued writing poetry during the spring of 1794, primarily in the form of additions to the two works which Johnson had published in the previous year. Some of these insertions have already been adduced as proof of the impact of the Dissenters upon him, notably in the realms of ethics and science. But their predominant theme is an affirmation of nature's power, a theme expressed in far more heartfelt terms than any of his previous works possessed; the influence of Dorothy and Windy Brow is evident in them, as in these lines added to *An Evening Walk*:

A heart that vibrates evermore, awake
To feeling for all forms that Life can take,
That wider still its sympathy extends
And sees not any line where being ends;
Sees sense, through Nature's rudest forms betrayed,
Tremble obscure in fountain rock and shade,
And while a secret power those forms endears
Their social accents never vainly hears. [41]

Meyer has even gone to the extent of saying that the transcendental qualities here help to refute those who overemphasize Coleridge's influence on Wordsworth.[42] At this juncture it is merely necessary to emphasize that transcendental overtones do exist in these lines, as well as an avowal in behalf of sensibility. The same qualities are apparent in the two lengthy passages that were inserted into *Descriptive Sketches*.[43]

[40] *Ibid.*, p. 126.
[41] *Poetical Works*, I, 10.
[42] Meyer, p. 167; see also Piper, pp. 72-79.
[43] *Poetical Works*, I, 66-67.

Ironically, these additions reveal that the poet was adopting the transcendental philosophy he had met in the London Dissenting world at the very time that he was beginning to succumb to Godwinism; that he could do so is understandable: each point of view presupposes that the mind is capable of systematizing human nature and the physical universe. But as yet his grasp was firmly on the powers of nature. He refers to a friend with him, probably Dorothy, whose mind is awake "To Nature's impulse", in contrast to the masses who are indifferent to it; later he concludes that

> From love of Nature love of Virtue flows
> And hand in hand with Virtue Pleasure goes. [44]

In addition, these insertions also show his attitude toward the political situation. To this period belong the previously quoted lines that compare the poet's feelings to Milton's desolation in knowing that virtue has "fallen on times to gloom consigned". In a similar passage, he again refers to a former period of oppression, tacitly comparing the land Rome subjugated to the Lake Country under Pitt's domination:

> What bards, in strains more faint at every close,
> Pour griefs which once the troubled winds scarce bore
> To meet the languid battle's dying roar,
> When Freedom here beheld the bird of Rome
> O'er her last barrier shake his deepest gloom,
> And sighs from every fountain shade and cave
> Wept the last remnant of the great and brave? [45]

The thought that adverse political conditions can silence a poet – even one dedicated to liberty – was doubtless crossing Wordsworth's mind often in 1794; by the end of the year his fears were borne out, and he was unable to find inspiration.

At this point, *The Prelude* helps to clarify Wordsworth's development. After noting that nature consoled him in the dark days of 1793 and 1794, he proceeds directly to the time when he first heard of the death of Robespierre – presumably in mid-August,

---

[44] *Ibid.*, I, 12-13, 16.
[45] *Ibid.*, I, 36.

1794. The news brought back his faith in France; he enthusiastically reaffirmed his republican principles. But then he began to
be incautious, blithely condemning all manifestations of conservatism in government:

> in the People was my trust
> And in the virtues which mine eyes had seen,
> And to the ultimate repose of things
> I look'd with unabated confidence.
>
> *(The Prelude,* X, 441-657).

This was his frame of mind in the summer of 1794, the poet
heartened in his idealism but dangerously ready to advocate the
most ill-advised reform.

Following this, the poem reverts to his first days in France,
tracing briefly his gradual political development. Wordsworth is
obviously preparing the reader for a crucial turning point – namely
his horrible period of doubt and depression when he turned to a
mechanical philosophy. The agents for this are evident also. No
sooner had Robespierre's death rekindled his hopes than the
French became "Oppressors in their turn", changing "a war of
self-defence/ For one of conquest, losing sight of all/ Which they
had struggled for" *(The Prelude,* X, 792-797).[46]

Likewise, in England the liberals had increasing cause for
bitterness in late 1794. The war had led to consecutive disasters,
while the government still leagued itself with those nations responsible for the partition of Poland; and finally the infamous
treason trials were held in the fall in Edinburgh and in London.[47]
Wordsworth fully shared this bitterness:

> Our Shepherds (this say merely) at that time
> Thirsted to make the guardian Crook of Law
> A tool of Murder; they who ruled the State, . . .
>   leagu'd
> Their strength perfidiously, to undermine
> Justice, and make an end of Liberty.
>
> *(The Prelude,* X, 646-657).

---

[46] De Selincourt, pp. 604-605, proves conclusively that Wordsworth is here
referring to the French campaigns of the fall of 1794.
[47] Maccoby, *English Radicalism,* pp. 83-87.

The same attitude is apparent in a letter to Mathews of November 7, 1794: "I cannot . . . abet in the smallest degree the measures pursued by the present ministry. They are already so deeply advanced in iniquity that like Macbeth they cannot retreat."[48] Instead of being disillusioned, however, he became a hardened extremist, and, as *The Prelude* implies, he adopted the necessitarianism of Godwin.

It is no wonder, then, that Wordsworth's muse was silent for the remainder of the year. Godwin's mathematically precise, dry, and unemotional philosophy was the antithesis of the natural and spiritual idealism that first inspired the poet. Yet he repudiated that idealism, thanks primarily to external political conditions:

I begin to wish much to be in town; cataracts and mountains, are good occasional society, but they will not do for constant companions; . . . This is a country for poetry it is true; but the muse is not to be won but by the sacrifice of time, and time I have not to spare. [49]

In the same letter, he also announces his defection from their plan for a miscellany, in effect turning from nature and humanitarianism at the same time. At the first opportunity, namely the death of Raisley Calvert, he departed for London and sought out the company of William Godwin.

---

[48] *Early Letters*, p. 135; Wordsworth also condemned Pitt's handling of the Polish situation, p. 128, and rejoiced at the acquittal of the defendants in the treason trials, p. 137.

[49] *Ibid.*, p. 136; Wordsworth to Mathews, November 7, 1794.

VI.

LONDON AND RACEDOWN, 1795-1797:
DISSENT VS. RATIONALISM

Wordsworth's frame of mind as he set out for London in the early part of 1795 is suggested by the last letter he wrote to Mathews from the country. It was begun in late December of the previous year, the poet at that time expressing fears for Calvert's life and noting that he has "a most melancholy office of it". When he concluded the letter on January 7, he was even more down-hearted: "I have lately undergone much uneasiness of mind; but I have had sufficient *time* on my hands to write a folio Vol:!"[1]

Calvert's impending death surely was in large part the occasion for the poet's mood. But, if *The Prelude* is to be trusted, the primary source of his melancholy was the conflict in his mind between his republican idealism and mechanical necessitarianism, a system that was then sweeping the land:

> This was the time when all things tending fast
> To depravation, the Philosophy
> That promised to abstract the hopes of man
> Out of his feelings, to be fix'd thenceforth
> For ever in a purer element
> Found ready welcome. Tempting region that
> For Zeal to enter and refresh herself,
> Where passions had the privilege to work,
> And never hear the sound of their own names;
> But, speaking more in charity, the dream
> Was flattering to the young ingenuous mind
> Pleas'd with extremes, and not the least with that
> Which makes the human Reason's naked self
> The object of its fervour.

> *(The Prelude*, X, 806-819).

[1] *Early Letters*, pp. 136-139.

The work primarily responsible for this exaltation of reason was *Political Justice*, and from every account it did indeed find "ready welcome". Although Coleridge had his reservations, Southey became an avid Godwinian; Crabb Robinson claimed that the book "directed the whole course of my life"; and Hazlitt later declared that, in the light of it, "Tom Paine was considered for the time as a Tom Fool to him; Paley an old woman; Edmund Burke a flashy sophist."[2] It is interesting that most of these young men discovered Godwin in 1794, the same time that Wordsworth had become a convert, more than a year after the appearance of *Political Justice*.

No doubt the poet's primary necessitarian influence was Godwin, as is indicated both by the circumstantial evidence of Godwin's preeminence at the time, and by their close friendship, which began in 1795 and continued until the death of the philosopher. But the existence of "Godwinian" ideas in the poet's works proves nothing; one of the reasons for the popularity of *Political Justice* was the very fact that it so well epitomized the liberal thought of the time. To note just a few examples, Godwin's belief in necessity was anticipated by Priestley, his economic theories by Mary Wollstonecraft, his concept of perfectibility by Condorcet and Price, and his emphasis on popular education by the Dissenters at large.[3]

---

[2] Coleridge, *Letters*, I, 102, 138; *The Life and Correspondence of the Late Robert Southey*, C. C. Southey, ed., 6 vols. (London: Longman, 1849-1850), I, 256-257; H. C. Robinson, *On Books and their Writers*, Edith J. Morley, ed., 3 vols. (London: Dent, 1938), I, 2-3; Hazlitt, *Works*, XI, 17. For a full account of the book's reception, see George Woodcock, *William Godwin: A Biographical Study* (London: Porcupine, 1946), pp. 98-110.

[3] There are many works which combine exactly the same ingredients that appear in *Political Justice*; Thelwall's *Rights of Nature, Against the Usurpations of Establishments. Part the Second*, 2nd ed. (London: Symonds, 1796), for example, is a complete duplication of Godwin's system, beginning with an espousal of "reason and moral justice" and proceeding to propound the sovereignty of the individual, to equate the "general good" with the personal, and to insist on the perfectibility of man.

Godwin himself acknowledged that his popularity was owing to the fact that his ideas "coincided in a great degree with the sentiments then prevailing in English Society". Autobiographical Note for 1794, appended to Godwin's Diary.

Likewise, Wordsworth strongly implies that more than one agent was responsible for his conversion to necessitarianism. Fairly early in *The Prelude* he tells Coleridge that he will later in the poem

> speak of an abasement in my mind
> Not altogether wrought without the help
> Of Books ill-chosen
>
> (V, 630-637; MS. M).

Noteworthy here is not just the plural "Books" but also the implication that the influence of his associates may have helped to effect his transformation. Similarly, as Havens has noted, when Wordsworth describes this period in Book X of *The Prelude*, no one book or author is named, or even implied, as the agent; the suggestion is that he merely succumbed to a current fad.[4] Consequently, if *Political Justice* is regarded as a résumé of the mechanical philosophy of the time, then it is a valid index of the nature of Wordsworth's thought in late 1794 and the spring of 1795; but it would be fallacious to insist upon its direct influence upon the poet in any one instance.

Godwin's system may be readily summarized.[5] A survey of the moral, political, and social evils of contemporary France and England illustrates his initial premise that government is responsible for most of the abuses in the world (I, 6-24). As he presents his "Principles of Government", he makes it clear that he looks primarily to Helvétius, Holbach, Rousseau, and Hume for inspiration, in opposition to the seventeenth-century English tradition; English Republicans are specifically criticized for regarding politics as one science and morality as another, and for relying on the social contract theory (I, 2-4, 183-193).

Godwin's Lockean corollary is that "the great stream of our voluntary actions essentially depends ... upon the decisions of the understanding". Likewise, involuntary actions are the consequences of "circumstances and events" (I, 26). In effect, then,

---

[4] *Mind of a Poet*, p. 543.
[5] The references are to *Enquiry Concerning Political Justice and Its Influence on Morals and Happiness*, F. E. L. Priestley, ed., 3 vols. (Toronto: University of Toronto Press, 1946).

environment and reason are the cornerstones of his system, while the concept of innate ideas is entirely negated. Since man possesses reason, perfectibility is the inevitable outcome: "Truth is omnipotent: The vices and moral weakness of man are not invincible: Man is perfectible, or in other words susceptible of perpetual improvement" (I, 85-86); above all, if the understanding of the people is improved, liberty will ensue as a matter of course (I, 96-104).

Closely tied to the concept of perfectibility is the theory of necessity, which evolved primarily from Hume, although Godwin's emphasis on environment made it an inevitable part of his philosophy. Simply stated, it negated all emotions and pictured man as a passive being, although "mental exertion" is necessary for the attainment of truth, justice, and happiness (I, 361-396). As a consequence, reason enables man to investigate every realm of the universe, particularly his own mind (I, 398-399).

In the process of formulating this system, Godwin enunciated many supplemental ideas. In terms of the "general good", a concept he adopted from Rousseau, men are of varying degrees of worth (I, 125-137). Similarly, no matter the type of government, it should be minimized for the good of its citizens (I, 239-246); but democracy is preferable because it has a "moral tendency", a result of its emphasis on reason (II, 114-123).[6] The constitution of a nation should also be held to a minimum, as a precaution against any idea of permanence.

On the surface, Godwin's insistence upon education and morality differs little from the Dissenting tradition of which he was himself originally a part. He shares the Dissenting idea that general, but not governmental, education is essential in developing the understanding, a necessary process before liberty and virtue can flourish (I, 194-214; II, 296-304). Moreover, men should be guided in their relations with other men by the principles of benevolence (I, 421-438). Yet Godwin's benevolence is based on reason and on the idea that the general good is equivalent to the

[6] It should be stressed that Godwin's concept of morality was atheistic in nature, repudiating both spiritual qualities and emotional benevolence – ideals central to Wordsworth's philosophy of 1793.

individual good. In his system, morality and education are likewise founded on reason alone, a reason that can encompass any area of human experience. In short, Godwin separates himself from the Dissenters by refusing to acknowledge any immaterial qualities and the consequent admission of a deity, the emotions, innate ideas, or the natural.

Nevertheless, *Political Justice* does express the thought of many of the more extreme radicals of its time. Thelwall has already been noted as one of these, as were Holcroft, Paine, and Mary Wollstonecraft.[7] And sometime in late 1794, impelled by a personal crisis and by the failure of the English and French governments to manifest any interest in the individual man, Wordsworth too became a convert to the philosophy which Godwin summarized.

That *The Prelude* refers to Godwinian necessitarianism is obvious. Even in describing his days with Beaupuy Wordsworth mentions that then he

> had a sounder judgment
> Than afterwards, carried about me yet
> With less alloy to its integrity
> The experience of past ages.
> (IX, 339-342).

That experience was seen in Chapters III and IV to be the example of the English Republicans, as continued by the Dissenters, whom Godwin repudiated and whom Wordsworth in effect renounced also by becoming an extremist. In Book X, when the poet describes this period in detail, he states that he was swayed by

> the Philosophy
> That promised to abstract the hopes of man
> Out of his feelings.
> (X, 806-809).

This can only refer to the anti-emotional, abstract systematizing of the philosophy of necessity. In the remainder of this section, he adds that implicit in this system is the exaltation of reason (X,

---

[7] For a discussion of the close similarity of Holcroft's thought to that of Godwin see Priestley's Introduction to *Political Justice*, III, 48.

815-830). As he describes it, he implies not only the effect it made upon his mind but also the criticisms that were later to disillusion him, the same objections which the Dissenters would have had:

> I was perplex'd and sought
> To accomplish the transition by such means
> As did not lie in nature, sacrificed
> The exactness of a comprehensive mind
> To scrupulous and microscopic views
> That furnish'd out materials for a work
> Of false imagination, placed beyond
> The limits of experience and of truth.
>
> (X, 842-849).

By "transition" Wordsworth simply means the amelioration of mankind, an ideal he had long hoped for; but he became impatient and fearful in 1794 about the possibility of its attainment through "natural" means. As a consequence, he became a fanatical systematizer, analyzing his emotions, his mental faculties, his motives; and going beyond himself, he

> took the knife in hand
> And stopping not at parts less sensitive,
> Endeavoured with my best skill to probe
> The living body of society
> Even to the heart; I push'd without remorse
> My speculations forward; yea, set foot
> On Nature's holiest places.
>
> (X, 873-879).

The description of the Solitary in *The Excursion* is so similar to this that Wordsworth's portrait, sharp and forceful as it is, must have come from his own personal experiences as well as from his distant observation of Joseph Fawcett. Here also "Abstraction" is seen as antagonistic to nature – and as an occasion for dissipation; likewise, it is suggested by the poet that political conditions accounted for the popularity of mechanical thought, as well as for his own conversion to that philosophy: all attempts to obtain political and social reforms had been

> quieted by iron bonds
> Of military sway. The shifting aims,

> The moral interests, the creative might,
> The varied functions and high attributes
> Of civil action, yielded to a power
> Formal, and odious, and contemptible.[8]

Such conditions, combined with Godwinism, helped to stifle the young writer, as *The Prelude* explains. Nature and mental comprehensiveness were the sources of his poetic inspiration; but the events of the time destroyed his ideals and his subsequent philosophy removed him from nature and focused his attention on "microscopic" analysis. It is small wonder, then, that from the middle of 1794 until he left London in August, 1795, Wordsworth wrote little or nothing; this is one reason why it is so pointless to look for necessitarianism in his poetry, for it was inimical to his inspiration. Wordsworth and Wrangham did plan a modern version of Juvenal's eighth satire while they were together in London, but little of it seems to have been written then. Even the later, extant fragments are vastly inferior to the poet's work of that time, and they are largely simple political invective. Possibly this is the "work/ Of false imagination" that Wordsworth referred to in *The Prelude* (X, 847-848).[9]

At any rate, judging from his accounts in *The Prelude* and in *The Excursion*, Wordsworth derived from the Godwinian system an exalted concept of reason – one which negated the emotions – a dependence on abstract systematizing of the universe, and a belief in necessity. It is important to note, however, that in each case he already had come to this position simply because it was part of the intellectual climate of his age; Godwin and other such philosophers merely helped him to carry them to extremes, to the point where his natural and Republican ideals were negated. Moreover, Wordsworth continued to believe in perfectibility, a doctrine implicit even in his "Letter to the Bishop of Llandaff", and in many of his political ideals, particularly his antagonism to monarchy and to war – beliefs which the Godwinian philosophers confirmed.

The poet arrived in London sometime in late January or

[8]   *Poetical Works*, V, 104.
[9]   See *Early Letters*, pp. 156-159, 172-178.

February, 1795.[10] Godwin noted in his diary on February 27 that he had tea that day at the home of William Frend, the company present being Holcroft, James Losh, John Tweddell, Jonathan Raine, Thomas Edwards, Wordsworth, Godfrey Higgins, William French, and Dyer.[11] This was apparently the first meeting between Wordsworth and the author of *Political Justice.* It could be dismissed as a mere chance had not the poet called on Godwin the very next morning and then joined him for breakfast – an honor Godwin usually reserved for well-established acquaintances – on March 10. It is evident that he was an intense admirer of the philosopher and that he lost little time in manifesting his admiration. Later visits of the poet took place on March 25, March 31, April 9, and April 22, after which Godwin left London for several weeks; but on July 14 he called on Wordsworth, who returned the visit on August 15 in company with Mathews, only to find the philosopher was not at home.

These visits strongly suggest that the poet's necessitarian period began sometime in 1794 and continued through the spring and summer of 1795. The chronology of *The Prelude,* which has been shown to be remarkably accurate, also implies that the turning point in his mental development was sometime late in 1794. These two sources together put the matter beyond all doubt.

Godwin's diary raises some important questions in other ways. In particular, who was responsible for Wordsworth's introduction to Godwin? And what was he doing at the home of William Frend, a young man who had been expelled from Cambridge two years before for his political and religious extremism and who had been closely connected with Dissenting circles for several years? Mrs. Moorman rightly emphasizes the fact that all of those in attendance at Frend's house on February 27 were liberals and that the majority of them were Cambridge men. But it should not be forgotten that Godwin's inevitable associate, Holcroft, was also there, or that at least two of those present – Dyer and Frend

10   *Early Letters,* p. 140.
11   Mrs. Moorman, pp. 263-264, briefly identifies all but two of the above. See also Schneider, p. 222, and Reed, p. 164.

– were Dissenters. Seen from this standpoint, Wordsworth's presence at Frend's gathering implies that he had at some time been introduced to the circle of Cambridge Dissenters who had taken up residence in London;[12] since the gathering was so soon after his return to London, it is likely that he had at least made the casual acquaintance of one or more of these Dissenters during his 1793 stay in the city.

Other Cambridge men also were important in his life during this spring. William Mathews was then working for an opposition paper, an occupation Wordsworth was considering before his arrival in London.[13] Possibly Mathews wrote for Daniel Stuart, one of the leading opposition publishers, who in 1795 purchased the *Morning Post* and who was active in the Society of the Friends of the People; the most likely alternative would be the *Morning Chronicle*, a more party-oriented paper run by James Gray and James Perry, two liberals with whom Wordsworth may have associated in 1793.[14] There is no evidence that Wordsworth wrote for these papers in 1795; but his connection with them through Mathews and his apparent sympathy with their cause are potentially significant, especially since the poet began contributing to the *Morning Post* in 1797 and since he later sent his pamphlet on the Convention of Cintra to that paper.

Apparently Mathews also fell prey to the fascination of Godwin about this time. On December 10, 1794, Godwin recorded in his diary that he had met a "Matthews" at the home of Thelwall, while on March 25 and 31, 1795, Wordsworth called on Godwin in company with "M", who would most likely have been Mathews.[15] At least it is certain that Mathews and Godwin later met many times.

Another Cambridge graduate with whom the poet associated

---

[12] Schneider offers the most complete discussion of the various personalities in this group who entered the poet's life.

[13] *Early Letters*, p. 135.

[14] *Ibid.*, p. 138.

[15] The reason for identifying "M" as Mathews is simply that later this spring Mathews alone accompanied Wordsworth on his visits to Godwin; Godwin used the initial of a person's name only when he had previously met him.

in 1795 was Francis Wrangham, a young man who had been a year ahead of Wordsworth at the University but who had lost an election to a fellowship in 1793 owing to his political principles.[16] Although he was an Anglican clergyman, he was severely critical of political and religious corruption, as is evidenced by the satire he and Wordsworth first began to write this spring.[17] Wrangham and Basil Montagu were close friends, the two jointly taking in pupils, so that it is probable that Wordsworth met Wrangham through Montagu.

Two other likely associates of Wordsworth on this visit were James Losh and John Tweddell, both of whom were present at Frend's tea with Dyer, Godwin, and Wordsworth. Both were Cambridge men, Tweddell a contemporary of the poet, and the three had many mutual friends. Both a liberal and a Unitarian, Losh was himself soon to become a close friend of Wordsworth. As early as January 1793 Tweddell was intimate with Dissenting circles; Rogers records dining with him at Dillys along with Parr and Priestley.[18] Both young men could thus have been among Wordsworth's means of entry into the Dissenting world.

Montagu appears to have been the poet's closest associate during this third visit to London. For part of the time, at least, the two stayed together in Montagu's quarters in Lincoln's Inn. Here was yet another disillusioned Cambridge graduate, a young man who also succumbed to the fascination of Godwinism and who in the spring of 1795 was undergoing much mental turmoil:

By an accident I became acquainted with Wm. Wordsworth. We spent some months together. He saw me, with great industry, perplexed and misled by passions wild and strong. . . . He unremittingly, and to me imperceptibly, endeavoured to eradicate my faults, and to encourage my good dispositions. I consider my having met Wm. Wordsworth the most fortunate event of my life.[19]

That Wordsworth should have attempted to rid Montagu of his

---

[16] Schneider, pp. 209-210.

[17] *Early Letters*, pp. 156-159, 167-168, 172-178.

[18] Clayden, *Rogers*, pp. 242-243. See also Mrs. Moorman, pp. 263-264, and Schneider, pp. 145-148.

[19] Montagu's unpublished autobiographical fragment; see *Early Letters*, p. 147n.

"passions" is added proof of the poet's dedication to reason at this time. Nevertheless, the emphasis on morality and on education which this account reveals suggests that Dissenting thought was still an important influence in his life. In fact, his association with these Cambridge dissentients, Losh, Mathews, Montagu, Tweddell and Wrangham, clearly connects Wordsworth with a form of political liberalism which was quite distinct from that of Godwin and Holcroft.

Godwin's separation from other liberals is best illustrated by a political pamphlet which he wrote in 1795: *Considerations on Lord Grenville's and Mr. Pitt's Bills*, "by a Lover of Order". Political agitation, especially that by John Thelwall, was the primary object of Godwin's censure, which included an attack upon the London Corresponding Society.[20] This was an immensely large organization in 1795, orderly in nature and dedicated to political reform and to a declaration of peace with France.[21] Godwin's pamphlet was greeted with scorn by many of these reformers,[22] for he was, after all, defending a further usurpation by the ministry of the liberties of the people. The continued opposition of Wordsworth to Pitt's repressive acts is suggested both by the political satire of his imitation of Juvenal and by his association with Mathews, Montagu, and Wrangham; the first of these, it must be remembered, was writing for an opposition paper, and he also met Godwin at the home of Thelwall, by far the most clamorous opponent of the ministry. Montagu and Wrangham likewise focused their attention on political and social abuses.

In yet another way are these young men distinguished from Godwin: there was a decided intellectual and social cleavage be-

---

[20]   Ford K. Brown, *The Life of William Godwin* (London: Dent, 1926), p. 100. See also John Binns, *Recollections of the Life of John Binns*, p. 43, for further evidence of the reaction of Godwin and Holcroft from reform societies; Binns implies that their about-face was the consequence of the threat of governmental prosecution. Another liberal, Joseph Ritson, had once admired Godwin but by 1794 had grown to dislike the man, especially for the disparity between his views and his actions. Ritson also ridiculed Holcroft. Bronson, *Ritson*, I, 161-165.

[21]   Maccoby, pp. 92-93.

[22]   Woodcock, pp. 113-114.

tween the Cambridge intellectuals and Godwin's circle.[23] Although
the two groups did fraternize, Godwin's diary reveals that the
Dissenting-Extremists dichotomy was still apparent in 1795. Two
of the older Cambridge dissentients, Dyer and Porson, may have
been responsible for the way in which the younger reformers
looked down at the philosophical extremists. Coleridge, for example, preceded Wordsworth to London in the fall of 1794, when
he met Porson through his familiarity with several of the Cambridge liberals. In December he wrote of his first introduction to
London radical circles: "My God! to hear Porson *crush* Godwin,
Holcroft &c – They absolutely tremble before him!"[24] Undoubtedly, their debate centered on "self love and God", subjects which
were currently on Godwin's mind (see his Diary, December 21,
23, 1794) and about which the two disagreed completely.

Likewise, Dyer would not have agreed with Godwin's atheism,
with his negation of the emotions, or with his opposition to the
reform cause; the two, in fact, associated little. Yet Dyer was one
of the Cambridge Dissenters present at Frend's when Wordsworth met Godwin, and it is possible that the poet's introduction
to Dyer – if this was their first meeting – was as important to
him as his introduction to Godwin. This scholarly Dissenter, it
was noted in Chapter IV, shared Wordsworth's ideals in many
ways, not the least of which was his connecting everyday language
with political and spiritual freedom. The idea was first expressed
in Dyer's biography of Robinson, which was published in 1796;
in all probability he was writing the book at the time he met the
young poet. As will be seen, Coleridge and Wordsworth both
later manifested much admiration for this man and his books,
which would imply that the unobtrusive Dyer played an important role in the lives of both men by combatting the atheistic
and necessitarian climate which surrounded them.

A slight shred of evidence connects Dyer directly with Wordsworth at this time, for on a letter which Coleridge wrote to Dyer
on March 10, 1795, someone (presumably Dyer) has written:

[23] The author is indebted to Professor Lewis Patton for first calling this
to his attention.
[24] Coleridge, *Letters*, I, 138.

"Wm Wordsworth No. 15 Chalton Street Sommers Town".[25] This was likely the poet's residence during the early part of his 1795 London stay; it is probably also not a coincidence that this address was only a few doors from Godwin's house. On the other hand, his relationship with various Dissenters and reformers points to the conclusion that he was torn between two groups of associates and thus between two political philosophies. Godwin's diary shows that the poet visited the philosopher frequently during the first weeks after their meeting, but that in the last months of his stay in London his calls became more infrequent, which might indicate either that Dissenting criticism had disenchanted him about Godwin's system or that he was unable to resolve the two points of view.

This interpretation is confirmed by *The Prelude*, for, describing his conversion to necessitarianism, Wordsworth relates the consequent confusion and then despair that came over him:

> Thus I fared,
> Dragging all passions, notions, shapes of faith,
> Like culprits to the bar, . . .
>   now believing,
> Now disbelieving, endlessly perplex'd
> With impulse, motive, right and wrong, the ground
> Of moral obligation, what the rule
> And what the sanction, till, demanding *proof*,
> And seeking it in everything, I lost
> All feeling of conviction, and, in fine,
> Sick, wearied out with contrarieties,
> Yielded up moral questions in despair,
> And for my future studies, as the sole
> Employment of the enquiring faculty,
> Turn'd towards mathematics, and their clear
> And solid evidence.
>   (X, 889-905).

The duration of this mood may be defined with reasonable accuracy, since it began while he was in the city — indeed, as a result of his visit there — and it ceased when Dorothy, nature, and Coleridge combined to restore his original ideals. Moreover, this passage from *The Prelude* focuses on the very issues over which the Dissenters and the atheistic necessitarians must have disputed: benevolence as opposed to self-love, emotions as opposed to reason, family obligations as opposed to the "general good", God as opposed to necessity. Perhaps Wordsworth's gradual conversion to necessity was imperceptible to him, so that when he returned to London in 1795 he was dismayed to find that he no longer possessed an intellectual kinship with his earlier Dissenting acquaintances.

Coleridge's letters reveal admiration for the high humanitarian idealism of such men as Dyer and Porson,[26] and Wordsworth clearly shared that opinion. It is apparent that liberal intellectual circles in London during 1794 and 1795 were the setting for a bitter engagement between the proponents of reason and those who insisted that the rational must be reconciled with the emotions and the transcendent. Wordsworth's inner torment at this very time may thus be seen as parallel to, and doubtless a consequence of, the intellectual milieu around him. If this interpretation is correct, Wordsworth's great crisis must have begun in the late spring of 1795 and lasted until the end of that year or the beginning of 1796, although its repercussions were to remain with him long after that.

The usual view of this crisis is probably best summarized by Rader, who relates Wordsworth's development to the three stages described in "Tintern Abbey". To Rader, the poet's "sensationalist" period began after his return from France, progressing "until at the time of the moral crisis of 1795, the personality was reft in a 'two-fold frame of body and mind'".[27] This conventional reason-sense dichotomy is acceptable in the abstract, but it muddies Wordsworth's relationships with the intellectual climate of his time. His healthy earlier (and later) phase involved a Dissenting combination of the rational and the emotional. To be precise, then, the crisis should be called a conflict for Wordsworth, as for his intellectual world, between pure reason holding

---

[26]   *Ibid.*, I, 97-98, 100-101, 138-139.
[27]   Rader, *Presiding Ideas*, pp. 139-140.

absolute dominion over the mind and a synthesis of all the facets of perception and thought.

Painful as his last days in London must have been, they performed the valuable service of making Wordsworth aware of some of the flaws in Godwin's system. Possibly he was influenced by the somewhat socially motivated disdain that the Cambridge liberals manifested toward Godwin and his friends. More likely he was shocked to discover the extent to which Godwin and Holcroft carried their necessitarian philosophy; although *Political Justice* does not reveal it, Godwin was virtually an atheist, as Coleridge discovered to his disgust.[28] Much of Wordsworth's perplexity must have come from the fact that the necessitarian system nowhere explains how the "omnipotence of truth" will be manifested; Godwin and his colleagues amplified Rousseau's concept of the general will, but like Rousseau they failed to indicate how a nation's administrators could determine what that might be.

In the last analysis, however, an extreme mechanical system was simply alien to Wordsworth's innermost nature. This was so not only because of its atheistic overtones but also through its repudiation of the spirituality of nature, of the emotions, and of the individual will; this last was potentially most important, for, although Godwin attempted to leave room in his system for a free will, he still subordinated individual motives and rights to the forces of necessity and to the general good. And, as Wordsworth himself discovered, Godwinian determinism led to intellectual fragmentation, as opposed to the organic comprehensiveness towards which he normally inclined.

It is possible to argue that, after Wordsworth "rebelled from Godwin", he still retained much of his system. His continued friendship with the philosopher, for instance, suggests that his revulsion from him was not as great as some scholars would have it; Coleridge many years later declared that he visited Godwin "notwithstanding he could not approve even of Wordsworth's feelings and language respecting Godwin".[29] Yet few scholars

---

[28] Coleridge, *Letters*, I, 102.
[29] H. C. Robinson, *On Books and Their Writers*, I, 29, March 30, 1811.

agree as to what precisely Wordsworth did retain of his extreme systematizing: to some, it was the idea of perfectibility; to others, the outlines of necessity; and finally, there are those who say that his revulsion was complete, leaving no Godwinian mark on his subsequent poetry.[30]

What all this disagreement seems to indicate is that the poet actually took little from Godwin; although their ideas were similar in many instances, once again it must be recalled that the concepts of necessity and perfectibility, among others, were implicit in the thought of many writers in the 1790's. Hence, Wordsworth's enduring affection for Godwin must be ascribed simply to friendship and to a very limited intellectual affinity.

When the second edition of *Political Justice* appeared, the poet wrote to Mathews about it:

I expect to find the work much improved. I cannot say that I have been encouraged in this hope by the perusal of the second preface, ... Such a piece of barbarous writing I have not often seen. ... I have attempted to read Holcroft's *Man of Ten Thousand*, but such stuff![31]

Why would he have "expected" the second edition to be improved? The obvious answer is that he had talked to Godwin about flaws in the first edition, or had heard others mention them, and knew that the latter was contemplating changes along the lines of the criticism which had been presented to him. The reference to Holcroft is an added suggestion that Wordsworth now viewed Godwin's circle with intellectual disdain, while regarding Godwin himself as a worthwhile associate.

Presumably, then, the changes that were made in the second edition were those which Wordsworth anticipated. Generally speaking, the new version makes more of an allowance for the

---

[30] Brown, *Godwin*, pp. 74-75; Beatty, *William Wordsworth: His Doctrine and Art in Their Historical Relations*, pp. 23-31; Fairchild, *Religious Trends*, III, 154-160; Legouis, pp. 270-278, 309n; J. R. MacGillivray, "The Date of Composition of *The Borderers*", *MLN*, XLIX (1934), 110; Meyer, pp. 176-191.
[31] *Early Letters*, pp. 170-171.

emotions and for intuition.[32] And in the Preface to *St. Leon* (1799) Godwin revealed how consciously his adjustments had been made:

Some readers of my graver productions will perhaps, in perusing these little volumes, accuse me of inconsistency; the affections and charities of private life being every where in this publication a topic of the warmest eulogium, . . . for more than four years, I have been anxious for opportunity and leisure to modify some of the earlier chapters of [*Political Justice*] in conformity to the sentiments inculcated in this. . . . I apprehend domestic and private affections inseparable from the nature of man, and from what may be styled the culture of the heart. [33]

This is far removed from the mechanistic exaltation of reason that characterized the first edition of *Political Justice*, and Godwin's entire circle, for that matter. "More than four years", moreover, implies that the philosopher had first realized the flaws in his system as early as 1794-1795. Although Godwin's editor has suggested that Coleridge was responsible for this change of heart, through his criticism in the *Watchman* and in *Conciones ad populum*,[34] a more plausible agent for the transformation would be the Dissenting world, particularly Dyer and Porson. Godwin had after all only just met the young Coleridge, whereas his association with Dissent had been longstanding; certainly in the mid-1790's Dyer and Porson would have carried greater weight with him than Coleridge would have.

Mentally perplexed and sick at heart, the young Wordsworth sought refuge from London in August, 1795, by returning to the world of nature and to Dorothy. The very opening of *The Prelude* describes his sense of liberation from the city, appropriately so, because the poet concludes the chronological description of his mental development with his attainment of a natural philosophy. The poem as a whole was designed to show the stages through which the author went in arriving at his philosophy, and so he

---

[32]   F. E. L. Priestley's Introduction to *Political Justice* contains an analysis of Godwin's continuing alterations in his philosophy. III, 88-107.

[33]   Godwin, *St. Leon*, 4 vols. (London: Robinson, 1799), I, viii-ix.

[34]   *Political Justice*, III, 106-107.

began it with his departure from London in 1795, an act that was
symbolic of his repudiation of artificial, mechanical systems: [35]

> Oh there is blessing in this gentle breeze
> That blows from the green fields and from the clouds
> And from the sky: . . .
>   O welcome Friend!
> A captive greets thee, coming from a house
> Of bondage, from yon City's walls set free,
> A prison where he hath been long immured.
> Now I am free, enfranchis'd and at large,
> May fix my habitation where I will. . . .
> The earth is all before me: with a heart
> Joyous, nor scar'd at its own liberty,
> I look about, and should the guide I chuse
> Be nothing better than a wandering cloud,
> I cannot miss my way.
>   (I, 1-19).

This passage may be regarded as a perfectly accurate indication of the poet's feelings at that time. He clearly expresses intense
relief at leaving the city; he seems to have faith in the ability of
nature to direct him. This, then, is a man who is reacting from
mechanical necessitarianism and from the intellectual controversy
of the city: he exults in his personal liberty and in the knowledge
that blind forces do not direct his life. Further, the religious overtones ("blessing" and "guide" particularly) reveal both his need
for spiritual solace and his belief in the transcendental nature of
the universe; he realizes that the "heart" is as important as reason.

Wordsworth thus left London with hope and determination,
as well as perplexity, since he sensed what his proper environment and his life's work should be. And he was taking with him
the younger Basil Montagu,[36] to educate the boy by means of
nature, rather than by means of the abstract systematizing which
Godwin recommended. He was aware that the ideals he derived
from the seventeenth century and from Dissenting liberals could
be correlated with nature.

---

[35] Mrs. Moorman, pp. 272-275, presents other evidence in behalf of the
contention that these lines refer to the poet's third departure from London.
[36] *Early Letters*, p. 147n.

Yet it must be stressed that this was the poet's mood only at the time he left London, for he was still to undergo periods of doubt during which he was unable to write and when his faith in man and in nature weakened.[37] It was many months before he could fully recover from the confusion in his mind that had originated in the intellectual climate in London, nor did the continually oppressive political atmosphere help him. Only after months of wavering did he completely regain his former ideals.

Indications of the poet's mental unrest are, therefore, primarily evident during the first year of the Racedown period. Some poetry belongs to this portion of his career, proving that he periodically gained an insight into the philosophy he sensed but could not yet define; but few complete works emerged. One of the exceptions, *The Borderers*, suggests its author's frame of mind by its mood – gloomy and gothic, hesitantly postulating an optimistic philosophy in the face of events that appear to represent only complete nihilism.

Deeper insight into Wordsworth's feelings is provided by the several short poems and fragments that preceded the writing of *The Borderers*: "The hour-bell sounds", "Fragment of a Gothic Tale", "The Convict", "Address to the Ocean", and the two fragments numbered XVI, a, b.[38] Aside from their fragmentary and inferior quality, these pieces are characterized by a close similarity of tone; in them the natural world is hostile and desolate, the speakers are downcast and isolated, and an atmosphere of unexplainable fear surrounds them. "The Convict" is particularly interesting as an attempt to reassert the beliefs of 1793 in

---

[37]   Legouis, p. 285, is one of many who take this to extremes and claim that the Racedown period was full of gloomy pessimism for Wordsworth, when he was able to do little work. The account in *The Prelude* confutes the former, while the many manuscript versions of poems which date from this period, especially its later months, disprove the latter.

[38]   *Poetical Works*, I, 287-295, 312-314; J. R. MacGillivray, "An Early Poem and Letter by Wordsworth", *RES*, N.S. V (1954), 62-65; R. S. Woof, "Wordsworth's Poetry and Stuart's Newspapers: 1797-1803", *Studies in Bibliography*, XV (1962), 160-164, 171. Woof feels that the manuscript version of "The Convict" reveals an "anti-religious feeling", but it is probably more accurate here to stress Wordsworth's continued hostility to established religion for its part in the war and domestic distress.

the face of the dejection of 1796. At the conclusion, the poet directly addresses the convict:

> Poor victim! no idle intruder has stood
>   With o'er weening complacence our state to compare;
> But one whose first wish is the wish to be good,
>   Is come as a brother thy sorrows to share.
>
> At thy name, though compassion her nature resign,
>   Tho' in virtue's proud mouth thy report be a stain
> My care, if the arm of the mighty were mine,
>   Would plant thee where yet thou might'st blossom again.
>
> Vain wish! yet misdeem not that vainly I grieve –
>   When thy soul shall repose from that heartgnawing flame
> My pity thy children and wife shall reprieve
>   From the dangers that wait round the dwellings of shame.

The ideals of humanitarian service and virtue are paralleled by the metrical form, which was a favorite with Dissenting poets. Yet here, as in the rest of the poem, this affirmation is but a feeble hope in comparison with Wordsworth's ambitious plans of 1793-4.

Further proof of his feelings at this time is supplied by *The Excursion*, where the Wanderer reminds the Solitary of the powers of nature and the evils of materialism and narrowness of vision. Presumably the Wanderer represents the course of action Wordsworth did take, the Solitary that which he might have taken had he remained a disciple of the extremists; but the issue was by no means decided in 1796. The Wanderer's language often resembles that of a converted Godwinian, now applying necessity in a spiritual context:

> One adequate support
> For the calamities of mortal life
> Exists — one only; an assured belief
> That the procession of our fate, howe'er
> Sad or disturbed, is ordered by a Being
> Of infinite benevolence and power;
> Whose everlasting purposes embrace
> All accidents, converting them to good. [39]

[39] *Poetical Works*, V, 110.

The positive side of Wordsworth's life at Racedown was that which involved nature, Dorothy, and their small charge, Basil Montagu; before very long, Coleridge also entered the picture. *The Prelude* proves that the beneficial influence of nature and his associates began while he was still disconsolate and lacking in conviction; he makes no distinction in chronology between the advent of Dorothy and that of Coleridge, merely noting that it was "about this time" that he met the latter (X, 905-941).

Biographers need not be disturbed by the fact that the poet and his sister first moved to Racedown in September, 1795, while Coleridge did not begin to play an important role in his life until the spring of 1796;[40] in *The Prelude*, Wordsworth was speaking of the time when the combined spiritual solace of his surroundings first affected him noticeably. In other words, not until the spring of 1796 did the poet begin to overcome his depression. The letters of the winter of 1795 substantiate this, since he refers repeatedly in them to his inability to write, to his loneliness, and to his melancholy.[41]

Dorothy, it would appear, was at first most instrumental in the poet's recovery:

> though impair'd and chang'd
> Much, as it seem'd, I was no further chang'd
> Than as a clouded, not a waning moon:
> She, in the midst of all, preserv'd me still
> A Poet, made me seek beneath that name
> My office upon earth, and nowhere else,
> And lastly, Nature's Self, by human love
> Assisted, . . .
> Revived the feelings of my earlier life,
> Gave me that strength and knowledge full of peace, . . .
> Which through the steps of our degeneracy,
> All degradation of this age, hath still
> Upheld me.
>
>   *(The Prelude*, X, 916-930).

Dorothy was not the source of any of his ideas. She merely urged him to maintain his faith in the human universe despite the ad-

---

40   Mrs. Moorman, pp. 276, 291-292.
41   *Early Letters*, pp. 153-154, 156-159, 169.

verse political and social situation. Then nature revived his former idealism, giving him at the same time conviction and an enlarged vision; he dedicated himself to voicing the lofty humanitarianism which he first acquired in France and in London during 1792 and the spring of 1793. As he came to realize, his ideals were needed all the more because of the "degradation of this age".

The works of the Racedown period reveal a noticeable progression in the poet's thought, for the earliest are obsessed with political and economic conditions or their consequences, containing little more than bitter invective or frustrated lamentation; but gradually a more positive attitude emerges as Wordsworth slowly worked his way to a meaningful philosophy. During his first winter at Racedown, before he began to feel the beneficial influence of his environment, he centered his attention on his adaptation of Juvenal, fragments of which remain from letters to the co-author, Wrangham.[42] The poet himself accurately described the tone of the poem and its occasion in a letter to Mathews in the early spring of 1796:

Not however entirely to forget the world, I season my recollection of some of its objects with a little ill-nature, I attempt to write satires! and in all satires whatever the authors may say there will be found a spice of malignity. [43]

No other poetry Wordsworth ever wrote is as bitter as this satire. But the vituperation consists in more than just name-calling, though there is a good deal of that; the poet's repeated criticism is that the actions of the ministry and of the courts are tyrannical, immoral, and irrational. The war with France is still the object of most of the poet's scorn; after excusing the Duke of York's ineptitude in battle because of his youth, he goes on to say that

> twas other cause than lack of years
> That moistened Dunkirk's sands with blood and tears,
> Else had Morality beheld her line
> With Guards and Uhlans run along the Rhine,

[42] *Ibid.*, pp. 156-159, 172-178.
[43] *Ibid.*, p. 169.

> Religion hailed her creeds by war restored,
> And Truth had blest the logic of his sword. [44]

A Uhlan was a Tartarian lancer, used especially in the Prussian armies, so that Wordsworth is criticizing by implication England's compact with the nations responsible for the rape of Poland. Those who would say that he was still a Godwinian at this time, however, should take a closer look at this passage. "Morality" could conceivably be the "political justice" that Godwin advocated, but the reference to religion makes that dubious; the only alternative is that Wordsworth is here again adopting the Dissenting correlation of rationalism with religious morality. Further, it must be remembered that Godwin had denounced political agitation, in contrast to the London Dissenters, especially the younger group with which Wordsworth associated.

Throughout the poem, moreover, he consciously borrows lines from Milton, and he even recalls the earlier period in English history when the sins of the government provoked the wrath of genuine patriots:

> What arts had better claim with wrath to warm
> A Pym's brave heart, or stir a Ham[p]den's arm? [45]

These references at once reaffirm his affinity with the Dissenters and imply that he continued to admire the English Republicans, whose ideals were far removed from the mechanical philosophy to which he had recently fallen prey.

On November 27, 1795, he wrote to Wrangham about another poem, which is clearly an expanded version of "Guilt and Sorrow", judging from his description:

I have a poem which I should wish to dispose of provided I could get any thing for it. I recollect reading the first draught of it to you in London. But since I came to Racedown I have made alterations and additions so material as that it may be looked on almost as another work. Its object is partly to expose the vices of the penal law and the calamities of war as they affect individuals. [46]

[44] *Poetical Works*, I, 303.
[45] *Ibid.*, I, 305.
[46] *Early Letters*, p. 159.

De Selincourt has thoroughly analyzed the nature of the poet's changes:

MS. 1 shows him an ardent humanitarian, keenly alive to horrors of war and to the wrongs of a social system in which the lot of the poor and oppressed compares unfavourably with that of the primitive savage, but with his optimistic faith still undimmed in the ultimate triumph of reason: in MS. 2 (Oct. 1795) this faith has vanished, he is at the 'lowest ebb' of his moral crisis; and whilst his humanitarianism is as passionate as ever, his picture of the injustice of social conditions is drawn in still darker colours. [47]

The story of the sailor is now added, the poet sparing no opportunity to lash out at social injustice. The Female Vagrant likewise elaborates her tale in terms far more bitter than the 1793 version. This more savage tone is especially illustrated in the concluding stanza of the 1795 manuscript, where a postscript to the hanging of the sailor is appended:

> They left him hung on high in iron case,
> And dissolute men unthinking and untaught,
> Planted their festive [   ] beneath his face;
> And to that spot, which idle numbers sought,
> Women and children were by Fathers brought. [48]

It is almost unnecessary by now to note that in the midst of his sarcastic conclusion Wordsworth has still ascribed immorality to ignorance and to the failure to use reason. But the predominant mood of the alterations is that of melancholy bitterness, a mood supported by the gothic setting.

The fact remains, however, that "Guilt and Sorrow" suffered the same fate as the imitation of Juvenal. The story of the Female Vagrant was included in *Lyrical Ballads*, but the poem as a whole was not completed until 1842 – in a form far removed from the spirit of the 1795 manuscript.

Wordsworth's important project in 1796 was *The Borderers*, a play that reflects at once the continuing gloom of his outlook and his gradually reappearing idealism. Once the object of much debate as to its implications, the play is now generally thought to

[47] *Poetical Works*, I, 333.
[48]   *Ibid.*, I, 127.

be a renunciation of Godwin on the part of the author.[49] This cannot be disputed, provided that one important qualification is added: as in *The Prelude*, the poet here is attacking no one work or man, but a world-view. Oswald, the Iago-like villain of the play, is the personification of all the defects of rationalism that Wordsworth began to record the next year when he undertook to describe his mental development for Coleridge.

Other scholars have disagreed about the central theme of the play and about its indications of Wordsworth's frame of mind at the time of its composition. For instance, Fairchild resolves the play into a question: "How could intellectual power and benevolistic feeling be harmonized in a single personality?"[50] To Hartman, "the central issue of the play [is]: can the intellect yield true moral judgments?"[51] Explicitly autobiographical are the interpretations of James and Smith. The former asserts that Oswald "voices most of Wordsworth's thought and feeling of the time", the two of them existing in a "condition of intellectual hate"; the play thus represents Wordsworth's discovery of evil.[52] Smith, conversely, claims that the play "represents the healed and restored poet's reasoned judgment" about the errors of his past.[53]

Fairchild and Hartman are in basic agreement. But their approach to the play may be further clarified by reference to Wordsworth's intellectual development. What is fundamentally at conflict in the play is the disinterested humanitarianism of the Dissenting tradition and the awe-inspiring but self-centered intellectualism of the rationalists. This rationalism may be associated

---

[49]   Bateson, pp. 122-123; Legouis, p. 270; Mrs. Moorman, pp. 303-307; Schneider, pp. 231-234; Welsford, pp. 45-50. See in opposition Garrod, p. 92; Meyer, p. 175; Todd, pp. 86-89, all of whom in effect claim that the play does not reject Godwin because no character in it is truly guided by reason. The problem with this interpretation is that Wordsworth was not interested in presenting a good Godwinian, or a bad one; rather he is portraying the inevitable consequences of any form of Godwinism.

[50]   Fairchild, *Religious Trends*, III, 159.

[51]   Hartman, *Wordsworth's Poetry*, p. 129.

[52]   D. G. James, *Scepticism and Poetry; An Essay on the Poetic Imagination* (London: George Allen and Unwin, 1937), pp. 151-155.

[53]   J. H. Smith, "Genesis of *The Borderers*", *PMLA*, XLIX (1934), 922-930. These various interpretations constitute a representative sampling of the traditional approaches to the play.

not only with the Godwinians but also with the all-powerful repressive ministry of Pitt and its apologists. Marmaduke's helplessness in the face of Oswald's machinations would thus parallel the plight of the Dissenters in the 1790's: the humbly good minority abused by power and corruption.

That there is hatred in the play, as James asserts, cannot be denied. But that the work represents a "discovery" of evil is doubtful. This discovery, occurring in stages, had come earlier. The evil of misused power had become apparent to Wordsworth as early as 1791 through the example of Lord Lonsdale. Similarly, when visiting London in 1791 he had come to see the potential evil in human nature. Certain Godwinians (who would have been in sharp contrast to the Dissenters he knew) would have taught him something about intellectual evil. The evil in *The Borderers* is primarily this last, supplemented by the other two. Torn between two views of life in London in 1795, Wordsworth only gradually came to see that rationalism, apparently an intellectual panacea, was in fact not only inadequate as a way of life but pernicious as well. (Hence we may reject Smith's claim that the play represents Wordsworth's "reasoned judgment" about the subject.) The gothicism in the play, then, is not a pose to agreeably terrify the reader into a sense of the sublime, but a sincere evocation of his mood; and more than that: it is an intellectual indictment of an entire way of life.

Briefly, Oswald's errors are his overemphasis of reason, his obsession with minute analysis, and his repudiation of emotion. Every action of the villain reflects his distorted commitment to reason, in contrast to the innocent Marmaduke and his band, who represent the natural affections;[54] Marmaduke, in fact, symbolizes his creator, in that he too was seduced away from his ideals by the attraction of reason. Oswald's portrayal of him aptly describes the poet's turmoil in 1795:

> This Stripling's mind
> Is shaken till the dregs float on the surface;
> And, in the storm and anguish of the heart,
> He talks of a transition in his Soul,

[54] See especially *Poetical Works*, I, 171-172, 187.

> And dreams that he is happy. We dissect
> The senseless body, and why not the mind? [55]

Reason, to Oswald and to a good necessitarian, repudiated the emotions:

> Wisdom, if Justice speak the word, beats down
> The giant's strength; and, at the voice of Justice,
> Spares not the worm. . . .
>   The wiles of woman,
> And craft of age, seducing reason, first
> Made weakness a protection, and obscured
> The moral shapes of things. His tender cries
> And helpless innocence – do they protect
> The infant lamb?

At this point, one of Marmaduke's uncontaminated colleagues blurts out: "By heaven, his words are reason!" [56] Wordsworth is surely being satirical here, for these lines effectively criticize the extremist's ability to rationalize cruelty and unnaturalness in the name of reason and justice; one has only to think of Godwin's famous example to realize what the poet was referring to: were Fénelon and one's wife in the same house when it caught fire, the philosopher is to be rescued first for he is of the greater service to mankind.

In short, Wordsworth's ultimate objection here is exactly what he also asserted in *The Prelude* and in *The Excursion* with regard to Fawcett: that rationalism carried to extremes occasions immorality. Equally condemned for its adverse moral influence is tyranny, both social and political. [57] But governmental institutions as such are not subjected to his scrutiny in the play, an indication that he is beginning to go beyond particular grievances to more basic problems. Consequently, the idea of misused power, which had been one of his favorite criticisms ever since he adopted it from the English Republicans, is now extended beyond the realm of politics:

---

[55] *Ibid.*, I, 174.
[56] *Ibid.*, I, 171-172; Marmaduke, once warped by Oswald, makes the same point with regard to children. I, 177. See also I, 348.
[57] *Ibid.*, I, 187.

> there needs no other motive
> Than that most strange incontinence in crime
> Which haunts this Oswald. Power is life to him
> And breath and being; where he cannot govern,
> He will destroy. [58]

This summation of Oswald is an important insight into Wordsworth's thought, since it shows him undertaking to apply political criteria to life at large.

In contrast with the sinister philosophy of the villains, several characters in *The Borderers* are mouthpieces for virtue and sensitivity. Admittedly, they are overshadowed by Oswald, and their voices are often weak, indicating that Wordsworth had not yet fully regained his earlier confidence; nevertheless they do express a higher idealism which is reminiscent of the poet's philosophy of 1792 and 1793. Herbert, the innocent victim of Marmaduke's blindness, and his daughter, Idonea, both manifest moral sensibility, in direct contrast with Oswald; Marmaduke's failure is that he listened to the latter, rather than to the precepts of Herbert:

> Learn, young Man,
> To fear the virtuous, and reverence misery,
> Whether too much for patience, or, like mine,
> Softened till it becomes a gift of mercy. [59]

And when he later discovers that he has murdered an innocent man, he laments being "In such a wilderness – to see no thing,/ No, not the pitying moon!" [60]

Sometime in 1797 Wordsworth wrote a prefatory essay explaining his intentions in the play. He makes it obvious that Oswald was the object of most of his attention, and he describes him in terms similar to his portrait of the Solitary in *The Excursion*. The villain began as

a young man of great intellectual powers yet without any solid princi-

---

[58] *Ibid.*, I, 184. See also Wordsworth's prefatory note of 1842, in which he associates Oswald's "hardening of the heart" with the effects of the French Revolution. I, 342; on power, see I, 345.
[59] *Ibid.*, I, 180-181.
[60] *Ibid.*, I, 213.

ples of genuine benevolence. His master passions are pride and the love of distinction. He has deeply imbibed a spirit of enterprise in a tumultuous age. He goes into the world and is betrayed into a great crime.

As a consequence, the young man became a sceptic, shaking off "the obligations of religion and morality in a dark and tempestuous age".[61] Except for the "great crime", this is surely a self-portrait, for the poet had likewise lost his grip on his principles when he returned to London in 1795, and he too was over-burdened by the times in which he lived. Consequently, the play as a whole may be regarded as an accurate index of Wordsworth's state of mind in late 1796, when he was still dejected by the political situation and by the memory of his necessitarian period, but when he was nevertheless beginning to reaffirm the Dissenting concept of benevolence and to relate it to an active and beneficial nature.

Todd's approach may profitably be used as a touchstone to illustrate Wordsworth's continued political concerns and Dissenting influences in the play. Todd claims that "the play is carefully set in a region and a time which leave the actors free from all social influences and restraints". He goes on:

The fact that Wordsworth was drawing on his experience of the French Revolution in this portrayal of the power of evil gives the play its political point. ... In the vaunted reason this power of evil could possess a lethal weapon, but the significant discovery embodied in the play is the poet's realization that the real source of evil was in the individual, not in the society; the consequence of this discovery was a growing concern rather with the regeneration of the individual than with that of the society.

And, Todd notes, "It is not extravagant to point out that this conviction of an active power of evil at work in the world, ... was the beginning of Wordsworth's return to orthodox Christianity."[62]

Contrary to Todd's view, Wordsworth's choice of place and time for the play would seem to have been dictated, at least in

[61] *Ibid.*, I, 345-347.
[62] Todd, pp. 87, 88-89, 88n.

part, by the gothic cult of his age. As such, the Border region
during the medieval period would have been for him synonymous
with tyranny and anarchy, the one helping to bring about the
other and the medievalism further suggesting a time when truth
had been subverted by "superstition". There are thus clear political implications in the facts that Marmaduke's band must
pillage to survive, must hide in Robin Hood fashion to escape
tyranny, and must in effect resort to anarchy to remain free. The
parallels with England in the 1790's are apparent, especially in
MS. A of the play when, for example, Rivers exclaims "now let
friendship cease, since Liberty/ Is banished from this world".[63]

Consequently, while the play does emphasize individual guilt,
it also indicates the role of society in occasioning that guilt. At
one point Oswald claims:

> We subsist
> In slavery; all is slavery; we receive
> Laws, but we ask not whence those laws have come. [64]

Oswald here shows the intellectual slavery of absolute reason; but
he is also obviously referring to the slavery of a repressive society.
Anarchist that he is, any society would be repressive to Oswald,
but the rest of the band is escaping specifically from tyranny.
Oswald repudiates freedom of any sort:

> a great mind
> Contemns its age, and is pursued with obloquy
> Because its movements are not understood
> I felt that truly to be the world's friend
> We must become the object of its hate. [65]

Oswald describes the course of political extremists who depart
from the Dissenting ideals of an all-encompassing intellectual
freedom and of a moderate non-subversive correction of a nation's
ills. Wordsworth may be recalling here that a number of the
extremists of the 1790's either had retreated into a desperate and
hardened hostility to the world or had recanted, in effect sub-

[63] *Poetical Works*, I, 350.
[64] *Ibid.*, I, 202.
[65] *Ibid.*, I, 200 and n.

mitting to the tyranny of the ministry. There are elements of both extremes in Oswald.

To return to Todd, the implicit religious values in the play can be called Christian, but they are hardly those of the bland Establishment to which Wordsworth later turned. The religion implied here is one of simple purity and humility, of steadfastness to universal truth, of respect for life, and of relevance and involvement – all of which correspond far more closely to the Dissent than to the Anglicanism of the 1790's. Oswald reveals the negation of all these religious values in that he is complex and proud, steadfast only to his own limited view of truth, disrespectful of life, and – both in words and in deeds – indifferent and alienated.

The converse of Oswald is represented not only by the opposing characters but also, and more importantly, by the resolution of the play. Those who argue for a tragic conclusion to the work fail to recognize the Christian elements there, apparent most especially in the themes of forgiveness, endurance, and ultimate heavenly mercy.[66] That Marmaduke can go on, and not seek the immediate death that Oswald so readily embraces, is testimony to the religious forces at work upon him. Above all, these three themes are directly parallel with the religious emphases of the Dissenters, particularly in the 1790's.

As might be expected, the fragmentary remains of MS. A contain more direct political comment and more parallels with Dissent than the later manuscripts of the play. The scene with the "holy Pilgrim", deleted from later versions, manifests the conventional Dissenting values of simplicity, humility, naturalness, and love:

> this old man knows there is a power,
> Even in the common offices of love
> And friendly ministration, to revive
> Nature within thee, bid thee smile again
> With those that smile, and weep with those
> that weep. [67]

In terms of its religious and political themes, then, MS. A of the

---

[66]   *Ibid.*, I, 223-225.
[67]   *Ibid.*, I, 355.

play shows that by the end of 1796 Wordsworth was beginning to regain certain positive convictions. These beliefs, to be sure, were held not with an easy optimism, but with a kind of grim assurance – of their rectitude if not of their durability.

Wordsworth's continued interest in politics during his Race-down period is indicated not only by his writings and his persistent association with known radicals but also by his reading. On November 26, 1795, Azariah Pinney wrote to him: "I shall send you ... Luesdon [sic.] Hill, & Louvet, but will keep Madame Roland till I have the pleasure of seeing you ... Beddoe's [sic.] 2nd Pamphlet I will also forward to you; Miss Williams's Letters I will bring when I go to Race-down, as I propose giving them a second reading."[68] Later, in March, 1797, James Losh sent the poet a bundle of magazines and pamphlets, including Burke's *Letters on a Regicide Peace* and *Letter to the Duke of Portland,* Coleridge's *Conciones ad Populum* and *Ode to the Departing Year,* Thomas Erskine's *View of the Causes and Consequences of the Present War,* and "some sermons against atheism" by J. P. Estlin.[69]

These titles again reveal Wordsworth's Dissenting and liberal orientation at Racedown. Besides the French political writers, three of the names mentioned above were prominently connected with Dissenting circles: Beddoes, Estlin, and Helen Maria Williams. The first two were among Joseph Johnson's authors. Beddoes was a scientist, the friend of Watt, Davy, and Coleridge; his "second pamphlet" probably refers to "A Word in Defense of the Bill of Rights", published by Johnson in 1795. Estlin was a well-known Unitarian minister at Bristol and a friend of Coleridge also. Two of his sermons that Wordsworth likely received from Losh were: *Evidences of Revealed Religion, ... stated with reference to a Pamphlet called the Age of Reason* (Johnson, 1796) and *The Nature and the Causes of Atheism* (Johnson,

---

[68] Quoted in Carol Landon, "Wordsworth's Racedown Period: Some Uncertainties Resolved", *Bulletin of the New York Public Library*, 68 (1964), 100-109.

[69] Quoted in Mrs. Moorman, p. 309. Erskine, a Foxite, had become famous in 1794 for defending the accused in the notorious treason trials of that year.

1797). Carol Landon asserts that Pinney was "probably" referring to Helen Maria Williams's *Letters Containing a Sketch of the Politics of France,* a work from which Wordsworth borrowed the phrase "The hour-bell sounds".[70]

Between the summer of 1796 and spring 1797, several poems occupied Wordsworth's attention, all of them reflecting his progression away from pessimism and towards a renewed faith in man. Furthermore, all of them are far more assured in tone than the works of the two previous years, although the reaction from mechanical systems is still apparent in them. The fact that at least two of them are set in the poet's boyhood environment may well indicate that he had regained his confidence, and explain how he regained it.

"Lines left upon a Seat in a Yew-tree" especially illustrates his frame of mind. It is the story of a gifted man who was afflicted with too much pride and who withdrew from the world, feeling it had neglected him; but he could not forget

> those beings, to whose minds,
> Warm from the labours of benevolence,
> The world, and man himself, appeared a scene
> Of kindred loveliness: then he would sigh
> With mournful joy, to think that others felt
> What he must never feel: and so, lost man!
> On visionary views would fancy feed,
> Till his eye streamed with tears. [71]

Here is another Joseph Fawcett, as colored by the poet's own experience; he too has deserted the ideals of the liberal Dissenters – humanity, morality, and science – and turned to gloomy solitude.

At the end of the poem, Wordsworth adds an admonition to others:

> If thou be one whose heart the holy forms
> Of young imagination have kept pure,
> Stranger! henceforth be warned; and know, that pride,
> Howe'er disguised in its own majesty,

---

[70]   Miss Landon, pp. 100-109.
[71]   *Poetical Works,* I, 92-94, 1798 version.

> Is littleness; that he, who feels contempt
> For any living thing, hath faculties
> Which he has never used.

False pride, excessive introspection, and the inability to appre-
ciate humble forms of life were all failings that he would have
attributed to Godwinism. In place of that outlook, Wordsworth
now confidently offers an idealism centered on the imagination –
not so much emphasizing the benefits of the imaginative life as
its prerequisites. His focus is illustrated, again negatively, in a
portrait from the contemporary fragment "The Baker's Cart":

> The words were simple, but her look and voice
> Made up their meaning, and bespoke a mind
> Which being long neglected, and denied
> The common food of hope, was now become
> Sick and extravagant, – by strong access
> Of momentary pangs driven to that state
> In which all past experience melts away,
> And the rebellious heart to its own will
> Fashions the laws of nature. [72]

Clearly necessary for imaginative growth is a healthy environment, which we can understand to involve both an unimpeded
view of the past and freedom from economic and political distress.

Likewise, imaginative health requires a profound sense of
otherness. Such poems of this period as "The Ruined Cottage",
"Description of a Beggar", and "Old Man Travelling" reveal
Wordsworth's renewed insistence on the inherent worth of all
forms of human life. Through Margaret in "The Ruined Cottage"
he is attempting to arouse pity and compassion in the reader, the
sort of benevolent enlargement that Dyer was seen to insist upon.
Margaret's distress was directly owing to war and to the resultant
economic depression, while the beggar and the old man (eliciting
interest on their own terms) are in part replies to "political
economists" and their schemes for "houses of industry".[73] But
criticism occupies only a small portion of these poems; these
portraits are now illustrative of positive values which are far

[72] *Ibid.*, I, 316.
[73] *Ibid.*, V, 379-404; IV, 235-247. See also IV, 445-446, for Wordsworth's
later remarks on the poor laws.

more important to the poet than accusations against an unfeeling ministry. These people, natural and whole and healthy, have attained a "peace so perfect, that the young behold/ With envy", as he says of the "Old Man Travelling". And artistically, by virtue of their objectivity, distance, and detail, these poems show that Wordsworth himself was increasingly in possession of a healthy sense of otherness.

Another way to put it is that Wordsworth was returning to nature at Racedown. It should be stressed that this "return" was in fact just that: a renewed faith in the natural universe, not only harking back to his childhood experiences with nature, but also recalling his days as a moderate liberal in France and then in London. The conventional view that the return to nature constituted for Wordsworth a repudiation of his earlier political commitment is false, both because his political involvement did continue at Racedown and above all because it was English Dissent as early as 1793 that helped to lead him to an exalted view of nature.

Benziger has noted that the return to nature was Wordsworth's attempt to reawaken "the old sense of a Divinity within and above things".[74] This sense of the divine, apparent especially in the later works of the Racedown period, does not represent a return to Anglican theology. It is instead a reassertion of such Dissenting ideals as the respect for all forms of existence, the love of the simple and the insignificant, and the insistence on a whole view of life. It was almost a commonplace among the Dissenting philosophers and scientists (notably Priestley) to regard the natural universe as alive. With their concept of a loving and benevolent God, it was an easy step to find God's grace immanent in life at large. Dissenting thought thus tended to synthesize scientific enquiry, traditional Christianity, liberal politics, and a respect for the natural universe.[75] These same four elements are

[74]   James Benziger, *Images of Eternity; Studies in the Poetry of Religious Vision from Wordsworth to T. S. Eliot* (Carbondale: Southern Illinois University Press, 1965), p. 5.
[75]   Piper has noted the connection between science, political liberalism, and the concept of a vital nature on the part of many Dissenters in the 1790's. *Active Universe*, pp. 3-7, 115. See also Beach, who relates Wordsworth's

to be found repeatedly in the poems of Wordsworth's last year at Racedown.

With no forewarning, Coleridge appeared at Racedown on June 6, 1797, in effect heralding the final stage in Wordsworth's early development. Scholars have spent much time trying to decide who gave what to whom in this relationship. It should be obvious that any friendship as close as theirs requires a complete intellectual affinity – mutual interests and agreement on controversial topics. The ideals of Coleridge and Wordsworth were by 1797 incredibly similar. In terms of their interests and principles, the two, in reality, did no more than duplicate one another.

A brief summary of Coleridge's opinions and intellectual sources will illustrate the extent of their resemblance to those of Wordsworth. Like his friend, Coleridge looked primarily to the English liberal tradition; although he too had once admired the French Revolution, his primary political ideals derived from the seventeenth-century Republicans and their successors, the Dissenters, not from Rousseau or Montesquieu.[76]

In 1795, only two years after his graduation from Cambridge, Coleridge delivered a series of political lectures at Bristol, his object being to present "a comparative view of the English Rebellion under Charles the First, and the French Revolution".[77] The prospectus of the series reveals a detailed knowledge of the Republican theorists, showing that Coleridge had early become interested in his nation's political heritage. Other remarks by him

---

concept of an active principle in nature to, among other sources, the "materialism" of Joseph Priestley. *The Concept of Nature in Nineteenth-Century English Poetry* (New York: Macmillan, 1936), pp. 12-13.

[76] Unlike Wordsworth, Coleridge has not suffered from inattention to his political thought, although there is no study focusing particularly on his debt to the Dissenters. Among those who analyze his social and political background, the foremost are Harold Beeley, "The Political Thought of Coleridge", *Coleridge: Studies by Several Hands*, Edmund Blunden and E. L. Griggs, eds. (London: Constable, 1934), 149-175; E. K. Chambers, *Samuel Taylor Coleridge* (Oxford: Clarendon Press, 1938); John Colmer, *Coleridge, Critic of Society* (Oxford: Clarendon Press, 1959); John H. Muirhead, *Coleridge as Philosopher*; Carl R. Woodring, *Politics in the Poetry of Coleridge* (Madison: University of Wisconsin Press, 1961).

[77] Joseph Cottle, *Reminiscences of Samuel Taylor Coleridge and Robert Southey*, 2nd ed. (London: Houlston, 1848), pp. 17-18.

indicate that his sympathy was wholly with the Republicans, and that he regarded contemporary leaders as being oblivious of their tradition:

Sages and patriots that being dead do yet speak to us, spirits of Milton, Locke, Sidney, Harrington! that still wander through your native country, giving wisdom and inspiring zeal! the cauldron of persecution is bubbling against you, – the spells of despotism are being muttered. [78]

From the Republicans, Coleridge derived essentially the same ideas as Wordsworth: "they teach ... that to govern well is to train up a nation to true wisdom & virtue." [79] Moreover, his abiding concern was also with Milton, whose works are referred to extensively in the notebooks; [80] when the "Convention of Cintra" pamphlet appeared, he appropriately recalled Wordsworth's acknowledged political example, terming the work "assuredly the grandest politico-moral work since Milton's Defensio Pop. Anglic." [81] All his life he retained his admiration for the Republicans, reading their works and quoting them in his own writings,[82] just as did his fellow poet.

Of the contemporary liberal factions, Coleridge likewise numbered himself with the Dissenters. It is well known that in the late 1790's he was a Unitarian; but he also applied his religious convictions to politics, thus arriving at essentially Republican ideals. Godwin's diary is partial evidence of Coleridge's connection with the liberal Dissenters, as is the series of letters he wrote to Dyer in 1790's. Dyer's mentor, Robinson, and Dr. Beddoes were both admired by Coleridge,[83] while his last publication be-

[78] *The Plot Discovered* (Bristol: 1795), pp. 10-11; see also Woodring, pp. 83-85, on Coleridge's political heroes.
[79] *Notebooks*, ed. by Kathleen Coburn, Vol. I: 1794-1804 (London: Routledge and Kegan Paul, 1957), entry 110; see also Colmer, p. 44.
[80] *Ibid., Notes*, xx.
[81] Coleridge, *Letters*, III, 273.
[82] *Biographia Literaria*, J. Shawcross, ed., 2 vols. (London: Oxford University Press, 1949), I, 38; *Notes, Theological, Political, and Miscellaneous*, The Rev. Derwent Coleridge, ed. (London: Moxon, 1853), pp. 189-193, 196-197, 201-202, 213-214. See also Roberta Florence Brinkley, *Coleridge on the Seventeenth Century* (Durham: Duke University Press, 1955).
[83] *Notes*, pp. 112-126; *The Watchman* (Bristol: Published by the Author, 1796), pp. 74-76.

fore *Lyrical Ballads – Fears in Solitude –* was issued by Wordsworth's first publisher, Johnson. Moreover, as Woodring has shown, he respected Gilbert Wakefield, a member of Johnson's circle, and his thought in the *Conciones* of 1795 is especially close to that of Wakefield.[84]

Priestley, however, was the Dissenter most influential on Coleridge, both in religion and in politics. This is particularly seen in his notebooks, where he records several references to Priestley, including one of 1796 which well reveals that he and Wordsworth were moving in the same direction:

Doctrine of necessity rendered not dangerous by the Imagination which contemplates immediate, not remote effects – hence vice always hateful & altho equally monotonous as Virtue. [85]

Specifically political admiration is expressed in a sonnet on Priestley which Coleridge published in the *Morning Chronicle* on December 11, 1794, and it is implied in the famous story of his toasting "Dr. Priestley" before a group of provincial conservatives.[86]

While Coleridge's admiration for the English Republicans and for the Dissenters, and his belief in the moral and educational responsibilities of government, all remained constant, he did undergo many changes in his political outlook. One of his first political utterances, for example, *The Fall of Robespierre*, reveals an intense hatred for the extremists in the revolution, with a corresponding sympathy for the cause as a whole. By the spring of 1795, Coleridge had become embittered by the turn of events in France and in England, the result being his extremely caustic *Conciones ad Populum*.[87] Yet by 1796 he had recovered from

---

[84] Woodring, pp. 114-115.

[85] *Notebooks*, I, entry 156; see also entry 150.

[86] *The Poems of Samuel Taylor Coleridge*, Ernest Hartley Coleridge, ed. (London: Oxford University Press, 1935), pp. 81-82; *Letters*, I, 89-91. Lamb's letters are further proof of Coleridge's interest in Priestley: "Coleridge, in reading your Rs. Musings I felt a transient superiority over you: I *have* seen Priestly. I love to see his name repeated in your writings. I love and honor him almost profanely." *The Letters of Charles Lamb*, E. V. Lucas, ed., 3 vols. (New Haven: Yale University Press, 1935), I, 11, see also I, 78, 86.

[87] *The Fall of Robespierre* (Cambridge: Flower, 1794), was dated Sep-

this mood, now turning to moderate reform and to non-political means of improving morality. His change was announced in poetry:

> Sweet is the tear that from some Howard's eye
> Drops on the cheek of one he lifts from earth: . . .
> I therefore go, and join head, heart, and hand,
> Active and firm, to fight the bloodless fight
> Of Science, Freedom, and the Truth in Christ. [88]

This is a good summary of the ideals of the humanitarian Dissenter, as illustrated by the careers of Howard and Dyer; the emphasis on the emotions is as indicative as the Dissenting juxtaposition of science, politics, and religion. In a sense, *The Watchman*, which Coleridge published this same spring of 1796, is an expansion of these principles, while illustrating another necessary ideal, the dissemination of morality and knowledge.

As to his philosophy of man, Coleridge's early involvement in the Pantisocracy scheme proves that he too at one time possessed a faith in human nature that time eventually refuted. But, again like Wordsworth, he did retain a faith in the ultimate perfectibility of man through nature, as indicated by *The Watchman*, where he proves his point by quoting Condorcet, the probable origin of Wordsworth's concept of human improvement.[89]

Finally, and most conclusively, Coleridge shared his new friend's literary ideals. Each was enthusiastic about the poetry of Cowper, while disdaining most of the poetry of the eighteenth century. Coleridge also turned to narrative poetry, and he too attempted to use it as a medium for his ethical principles. And at a very early age he admired the sonnets of Bowles for possessing "natural diction".[90]

---

tember 22, 1794; *Conciones ad Populum* (Bristol: 1795), appeared in February, 1795. See also Cottle, pp. 19-20, for an account of Coleridge's high regard for the defendants in the treason trials of 1794.

[88] *Poems*, pp. 106-108.

[89] *The Watchman*, pp. 329-330. Coleridge's political thought in 1799 and in 1800 is revealed in a series of articles in the *Morning Post*, entitled *Essays on His Own Times*, Sara Coleridge, ed., 3 vols. (London: Pickering, 1850).

[90] *Biographia Literaria*, p. 16 and n; see also Lamb's *Letters*, I, 9.

All this, then, was the basis for the friendship between Wordsworth and Coleridge. If the latter introduced the former to any significant new influence, it was in the realm of philosophy; but that occurred at Alfoxden after their friendship had been well established, not at Racedown. Until Wordsworth's departure from Racedown in the summer of 1797, he obtained from Coleridge only confidence in his ideals and dedication to his career.

Racedown may be summed up as the locale in which Wordsworth regained his faith in man and discovered the restorative powers of nature. If there is any logic to his organization of Books XI and XII of the first version of *The Prelude*, both of which are entitled "Imagination, How Impaired and Restored", it may well be that Book XI deals with his natural philosophy which he evolved at Racedown, while Book XII centers on the expansion of it that Coleridge helped to inspire at Alfoxden.

This is plausible, since Book XI does not investigate the transcendental theory of the imagination that is manifested in the poetry of the later Alfoxden period. Instead, it focuses on the predominant themes of his Racedown works – nature in contrast to reason, the essential worth of all men, and the value of a comprehensive mental vision. All these have been seen to be both reactions from political extremism and reversions to his earlier idealism. Thus in summarizing his state of mind at Racedown, Wordsworth appropriately makes use of political language:

> Gladly here, . . .
> Would I endeavour to unfold the means
> Which Nature studiously employs to thwart
> This tyranny, summons all the senses each
> To counteract the other and themselves,
> And makes them all, and the objects with which all
> Are conversant, subservient in their turn
> To the great ends of Liberty and Power.
> (XI, 176-184).

Similarly, the book ends, not with a positive statement of his philosophy, but with yet another allusion to his earlier mental states:

> Behold me then
> Once more in Nature's presence, thus restored
> Or otherwise, and strengthened once again
> (With memory left of what had been escaped)
> To habits of devoutest sympathy.
>
> (XI, 393-397).

"What had been escaped" was certainly mechanical systematizing. By the same token, the "once again" must refer to his regaining the idealism of 1792 and 1793. It seems to be evident, then, that at Racedown Wordsworth consciously returned to the outlines of the philosophy he formulated through the inspiration of Beaupuy, the English Republicans, and the Dissenters. During this time his most important intellectual development was the extension of these political principles to the natural universe at large; he ceased being a political reformer and became a philosophic poet – not to the negation of reform but for its enlargement.

VII.

ALFOXDEN AND *LYRICAL BALLADS*

In early July, 1797, Wordsworth and his sister accompanied Coleridge to his home at Nether Stowey. Through the assistance of a local radical, Thomas Poole, the poet and Dorothy settled at Alfoxden House, only a short distance from Stowey, their "principal inducement" being "Coleridge's society". Dorothy's three letters of this summer are sufficient proof of their enchantment with the locality and with their associates, a mood that was not to disappear during their year at Alfoxden.[1]

During the first months of their association, however, Wordsworth and Coleridge wrote little. Not that their surroundings were alien; rather, their first concern was the interchange of ideas – an exchange that undoubtedly helped each poet to clarify in his mind the details of his belief. The poetry that soon ensued testifies to the beneficial influence of their association and their environment. But it also shows that they were still primarily concerned with the political and social situation – and still essentially liberals – as is suggested also by their acquaintances in the Stowey area. This fact must be kept in mind, for it indicates that the thought which the two young poets evolved was occasioned by the state of England at the time; in particular details their thought may have clear literary antecedents, but the direction of their thinking resulted from contemporary circumstances.

Foremost among their Stowey associates was the genial Thomas Poole, farmer, liberal intellectual, and patron of promising young writers. In the midst of the general local hostility to the two poets, Poole's friendship was readily welcomed. He had gone through

[1] *Early Letters*, pp. 189-191.

many of the same crises that had faced them, especially as a consequence of the war with France and the repression of reform. But despite the political and social climate, Poole retained his faith in man's perfectibility and in his essential goodness; in addition, he admired the English Republicans while offering a telling criticism of Godwin: "I have never read Godwin's work; but I fear in pampering the mind, he has destroyed the heart." [2] In contrast with some of his earlier associates, Wordsworth must have found Poole an enlightening combination of intense liberalism and a simple yet intellectual morality. Indeed, the man was possibly an important influence on the poet's glorification of rural simplicity in *Lyrical Ballads*.

Shortly after the Wordsworths' arrival, there appeared another liberal, John Thelwall, a man who had earned notoriety for his vehement support of reform and who was seeking a more sympathetic environment than London offered him. Thelwall was something of an embarrassment to Wordsworth and Coleridge, not because they found him objectionable but because his presence attached an even greater stigma to themselves in the eyes of the local citizens. Therefore, when Thelwall later desired to settle permanently at Stowey, Coleridge was forced to discourage him, while still siding with his cause; he called Thelwall

Perhaps the only *acting* Democrat, that *is* honest for the *Patriots* are ragged cattle – a most execrable herd — arrogant because they are ignorant, and boastful of the strength of reason, because they have never tried it enough to know its *weakness*. – O my poor Country! The Clouds cover thee – there is not one spot of clear blue in the whole heaven. [3]

This outburst is a repudiation not of reform but of extreme reformers, for Coleridge clearly states in his letters that he sides with those reformers who combine morality and the emotions with their rational schemes.

Coleridge's statements do not necessarily mean that Words-

---

[2] Mrs. Henry Sandford, *Thomas Poole and His Friends*, 2 vols. (London: Macmillan, 1888), I, 93-94, 167-168; II, 4.
[3] Coleridge, *Letters*, I, 339-342; Coleridge's use of the word "patriot" was common in the 1790's, the term connoting both sympathy with the French Revolution and atheistic libertarianism. See Woodring, pp. 87-91.

worth shared these views, but other evidence does point to the conclusion that the poet still retained his liberal ideals. Aside from his poetry of the period, which will be discussed later, the primary proof of this is his continued acquaintance with liberals during the Alfoxden period. Besides the Wedgwoods, who were mainly interested in Coleridge, there was James Tobin, whom Wordsworth probably met in London during his 1796 visit to the city.[4] Tobin belonged to the group of Bristol liberals to which Coleridge had been introduced earlier, and the three continued their friendship during the winter of 1797-1798; the consequence was Tobin's being immortalized in the original opening line of "We are seven": "A simple child, dear brother Jim".[5]

Further, on April 26, 1798, Dorothy noted in her journal that "William went to have his picture taken".[6] The painter was William Shuter, another local associate of the poets and evidently also a liberal, judging from his appearance in Godwin's diary on December 18, 1794, when he visited with Godwin, Holcroft, and Thelwall.

What particularly reveals Wordsworth's opinions at this time, however, is his reception in the Stowey area, indicating that he was a liberal in the eyes of his provincial neighbors, at least. The consequence was the famous incident which Coleridge described in his *Biographia Literaria*, when the government sent a spy to investigate the young poets at the hysterical entreaty of some local alarmists.[7] Neither of them was a threat to the national security, but it is important to realize that in their political and social ideals – as well as in their literary methods – they were part of a very small minority.

Once the two young men had arrived at what they regarded as a meaningful philosophy, they turned to poetry in order to com-

[4] Godwin's Diary, entries for June 18 and June 25, 1796; Wordsworth also corresponded with Tobin in the spring of 1798.
[5] *Lyrical Ballads*, R. L. Brett and A. R. Jones, eds. (London: Methuen, 1963), pp. 66, 279-281.
[6] *Journals of Dorothy Wordsworth*, Ernest de Selincourt, ed., 2 vols. (New York: Macmillan, 1941), I, 16.
[7] The incident is fully explored by A. J. Eagleston, "Wordsworth, Coleridge, and the Spy", *Coleridge, Studies by Several Hands*, pp. 71-87.

municate it. Consequently, the spring and summer of 1798 constituted one of the most productive periods either poet ever experienced, their inspiration no doubt arising in large part from the sense of confidence and fulfillment which the two felt on finally attaining a satisfactory set of ideals. The letters of Wordsworth and of his sister at this time repeatedly refer to the poet's continuing creativity and his high spirits; early in the spring Dorothy mentioned specifically that her brother's

> faculties seem to expand every day, he composes with much more facility than he did, as to the *mechanism* of poetry, and his ideas flow faster than he can express them. [8]

The results of this new-found assurance included both the majority of the poems in *Lyrical Ballads* and 1300 lines of the poet's projected masterpiece, *The Recluse*. As he wrote to Tobin, it was meant

> to convey most of the knowledge of which I am possessed. My object is to give pictures of Nature, Man, and Society. Indeed I know not any thing which will not come within the scope of my plan. [9]

The poetry of the Alfoxden period proves that Wordsworth had fully matured as a poet – in his thought as well as in his style; and the fact that he should have undertaken as ambitious a work as *The Recluse* indicates that he was fully aware of his fulfillment. But it must also be stressed that these works – again both in thought and style – are direct consequences of their author's social and political thought as it evolved from his youthful republicanism.

Likewise, Coleridge was writing some of his finest poetry at this time. "The Ancient Mariner", *Fears in Solitude*, and "France: An Ode" are particularly worth noting since all three contain political overtones, if in varying amounts. Woodring has fully analyzed Coleridge's political implications in these poems, especially showing that they reflect their author's "renunciation of government as a source of freedom" – a result not only of the French invasion of Switzerland but also of "current events in

---

[8] *Early Letters*, p. 200.
[9] *Ibid.*, p. 212.

London".[10] Woodring fails, however, to admit the possib
Wordsworth might have had something to do with Cc
development; the former had himself recently renounced
institutions and reform in favor of nature and universal enlightenment, so it is highly possible that he induced Coleridge to
take the same step.

In the summer of 1798 Wordsworth and his sister toured the
Wye valley, which the poet had visited five years before and
which now occasioned the greatest of his poems in *Lyrical Ballads*, "Lines written a few miles above Tintern Abbey". Five
years before Wordsworth had just left London and the company
of liberal Dissent, his mind full of plans to effect his new-found
Republican and Dissenting ideals. "Tintern Abbey" provides
clear evidence that the summer of 1793 had been a joyful one
for the poet,[11] and it would indicate that his liberalism of that
time had been associated in his mind with the beauty of the Wye
valley, the two together – his ideals and nature – supporting him
through the political and personal crises of the next three years.
That the poem is obviously an inspired work of art may be
attributed not just to Wordsworth's return to the actual scene
but more importantly to his recovery of his state of mind and of
his humanitarianism of 1793.

When the Wordsworths rejoined Coleridge, final arrangements
were made for the publication of *Lyrical Ballads* by Cottle of
Bristol, after which the three went to London in preparation for
a trip to Germany. The next month Coleridge wrote to his wife:

In London I visited Mrs Barbauld; but before that I had introduced
myself to Johnson, the Bookseller, who received me civilly the first
time, cordially the second, affectionately the third – & finally took
leave of me with tears in his eyes. – He is a worthy Man. [12]

[10] Woodring, pp. 180-187.
[11] See especially lines 1-23 of the poem. *Lyrical Ballads*, pp. 111-112.
[12] Coleridge, *Letters*, I, 420. Johnson was sufficiently impressed by Coleridge to help finance the German tour and to offer to send him several of
his publications, including volumes by Malthus and Horne Tooke. *Ibid.*, I,
417. See also Mrs. Sandford, pp. 285-286. The Mrs. Barbauld referred to
was the sister of John Aikin and was one of Johnson's most prolific authors;
moreover, she was intimate with the Martineau family, the famous Unitarians of Norwich, whom Dorothy Wordsworth also knew. *Early Letters*,

Although he introduced himself, Coleridge surely was accompanied by Wordsworth on some of these visits to the publisher. This is suggested by two letters of the following spring from Wordsworth to Cottle. In the first, the poet wrote to inquire about the London publication of *Lyrical Ballads*:

The day before I left England I wrote to you to request that you would transfer your right to the *Lyrical Ballads* to Mr. Johnson, on account of its being likely to be very advantageous to me. [13]

Clearly, the poet and his first publisher had agreed that the latter would undertake the venture; unfortunately, Cottle had made arrangements with Arch in London before receiving notice to that effect. When Wordsworth learned of Cottle's transaction, he was annoyed:

I still, however, regret it upon the same grounds as before, namely, that I have lost a good opportunity of connecting myself with Johnson; that I think the poems are not so likely to have a quick sale as if they were in his hands; and also that they must necessarily be separated from any thing which I may hereafter publish. You ought not to have mentioned in your letter to Johnson, that the poems were *sold* to you, as I had told you that I had not acquainted him with that circumstance. [14]

Such a peevish outburst towards his good friend can only have been the result of intense disappointment. Admittedly, much of the poet's eagerness must have stemmed from the fact that Johnson was one of London's most reputable publishers; but his motives could not have been purely financial, for several London houses could have assured the volume as large a sale as could Johnson. Wordsworth simply wanted *Lyrical Ballads* to appear under the imprint of the publisher with whom he felt the greatest intellectual kinship. Moreover, the second letter to Cottle implies that he intended to have his ensuing work brought out by Johnson. It may be concluded, then, that Wordsworth still regarded the leading Dissenting bookseller as "my publisher", and that he

---

p. 42; Harriet Martineau, *Autobiography*, 2 vols. (Boston: Osgood, 1877), I, 228-229.

[13] *Early Letters*, p. 259.

[14] *Ibid.*, pp. 262-263, see also p. 260.

was fully aware that the *Lyrical Ballads* were perfectly in keeping with Dissenting ideals.

Although it is but a sketchy outline of the principles Wordsworth enunciated in the Preface of 1800, the "Advertisement" to the first edition of *Lyrical Ballads* indicates that the poet had these principles in mind when he conceived the volume:

It is the honourable characteristic of Poetry that its materials are to be found in every subject which can interest the human mind. The evidence of this fact is to be sought, not in the writings of Critics, but in those of Poets themselves.

The majority of the following poems are to be considered as experiments. They were written chiefly with a view to ascertain how far the language of conversation in the middle and lower classes of society is adapted to the purposes of poetic pleasure. Readers accustomed to the gaudiness and inane phraseology of many modern writers, . . . will perhaps frequently have to struggle with feelings of strangeness and aukwardness [sic]: . . . such readers . . . should ask themselves if it contains a natural delineation of human passions, human characters, and human incidents; . . .

[The poems] are either absolute inventions of the author, or facts which took place within his personal observation or that of his friends. [15]

What is most noticeable about the "Advertisement" is Wordsworth's empirical, essentially scientific approach to poetry: we are to consider his poems as "experiments". The logical corollary to this is his insistence on the authenticity of the style and the incidents of the poems. This concern with fact, suggestive of the empirical tradition of Locke, Newton, and Hartley, should actually be placed more immediately in the context of the Dissenting-scientific milieu of the 1790's, when the empirical method was applied to all realms of human activity. Also, like the Dissenting scientists, Wordsworth here reveals an ideal he first acquired in 1793 and reverted to after 1795, namely the glorification of the intellect for its scope and synthesizing ability. Contemporary

---

[15] *Lyrical Ballads*, pp. 7-8. See also G. L. Little, "An Important Unpublished Wordsworth Letter: December 18th, 1800", *Notes and Queries*, CCIV (1959), 313-316; in this letter Wordsworth reaffirms the revolutionary nature of the volume.

criticism, traditional though it may be, severely limits the scope of the poet; contemporary poetry, with its "gaudiness and inane phraseology", is neither natural nor intellectually stimulating. Finally, it should be noted that the particular center of Wordsworth's attention is on man, not the natural universe, thus placing the volume squarely in the tradition of late eighteenth-century humanitarianism, not in the picturesque movement or the "Return to Nature" school.

The favorable reception accorded the volume by the Dissenting *Analytical Review* has been noted previously; Johnson's reviewer did not miss the implications of Wordsworth's announced style. In a very real sense, the acceptance of the political *status quo* was equivalent to the complacent reception accorded "the gaudiness and inane phraseology of many modern writers". In one of his most perceptive articles, Hazlitt, who was in a position to know what Wordsworth personally intended, also discerned the political overtones of the poet's style and subject matter:

It is one of the innovations of the time. It partakes of, and is carried along with, the revolutionary movement of our age: the political changes of the day were the model on which he formed and conducted his poetical experiments. His Muse... is a levelling one. It proceeds on a principle of equality, and strives to reduce all things to the same standard. ... Kings, queens, priests, nobles, the altar and the throne, the distinctions of rank, birth, wealth, power, ... are not to be found here. [16]

Havens, likewise, feels that the poet's "reaction from the abstract theorizing into which Paine, Godwin, and the French radical philosophers had led him resulted in an absorption in the concrete, the immediate, and the contemporary".[17] This is acceptable in its outlines, provided two important qualifications are added: Wordsworth's "reaction" was from one view of reform to another, namely from that of Godwin and his fellow radicals to

[16] Hazlitt, *Works*, XI, 87. *The Monthly Review* was not oblivious of the democratic implications of Wordsworth's first collection either, for it repeatedly denounced his "ballads" for their dangerous tendencies. XXIX (June, 1799), 202-210.

[17] Havens, *Mind of a Poet*, I, 17; see also Fink, Review of Todd, *Modern Philology*, LVI (1958), 137-139; Todd, pp. 99-100; Watson, pp. 534-536.

that of the "levelling" Dissenters – especially Dyer; and he is occasionally, in his seeming obsession with the concrete, mocking eighteenth-century materialism as it evolved from Locke and Newton. In other words, Wordsworth's literary approach may be regarded as a reply to both extremes – the extravagant systematizing of the Godwinians *and* the smug assurance of the conservatives, social as well as political.

The style of *Lyrical Ballads* may be said to reflect the Dissenting emphasis on simplicity and purity; in this sense, Wordsworth was still attacking his old foes, formalism and what he called "superstition". In 1801, Coleridge, who was far more communicative than Wordsworth about the implications of their literary practices, wrote a letter to Wilberforce for his colleague, explaining their methods:

When the material forms or intellectual ideas which should be employed to represent the internal state of feeling, are made to claim attention for their own sake, then commences . . . a passion for gaudy ornament & violent stimulants in morals; & in our literature bombast and vicious refinements, an aversion to the common conversational language of our Countrymen. [18]

Their style, then, was meant to be unobtrusive, to avoid detracting from the reader's apprehension of the essential thought and emotion of the poem. Such an idea is traceable to the "Roman ideals" of the simple and frugal life which Wordsworth shared with the English Republicans and the French Girondins; but it was the Dissenting writers who systematically carried these ideals into the realm of style.[19] Thus Coleridge's comparison of literary excesses to moral "stimulants" reveals that the two poets were consciously replying to contemporary social tastes and religious practices, as well as to the political situation. And, it must be

[18]   Coleridge, *Letters*, II, 666.
[19]   Hanspeter Schelp has suggested that in writing his "Daffodils" Wordsworth probably made use of a hymn by Charles Wesley, "When quiet in my house I sit". "Wordsworth's 'Daffodils' Influenced by a Wesleyan Hymn?" *English Studies*, XLII (1961), 307-309. Certainly the poet knew of the large body of Evangelical and Dissenting hymns, many of which he would have heard when he attended the Old Jewry meetinghouse. It is entirely possible that these hymns reinforced the influence of Dyer and other Dissenting writers in shaping Wordsworth's style.

added, their style was designed to approximate the natural and the permanent in language – as Wordsworth implied in his "Advertisement" – in order to parallel their emphasis on the natural and the permanent in the universe at large.[20]

These stylistic implications are thoroughly borne out when the thought of *Lyrical Ballads* is examined. At this juncture, however, it should be made clear that more of the poems than most readers have hitherto realized were written with a touch of humor, if not even in the spirit of satire; since the volume as a whole is conspicuously rebellious in many ways, the comic spirit was almost inevitable, even if it was alien to Wordsworth's talent.[21]

Ever since his days with Beaupuy, the poet had dedicated himself to the cause of mankind; this became the entire rationale of his existence, especially after he had adopted the Dissenting emphasis on moral edification. It will be remembered that he was financially aided by Raisley Calvert because the latter thought he would prove to be of service to humanity. Similarly, all his poetry after 1793 attempts in some way to impart moral principles. And this is especially true of *Lyrical Ballads*, since by 1798 he was assured of his humanitarian ideals.

[20] W. J. B. Owen examines at length Wordsworth's linguistic and natural concepts of permanence. *Wordsworth's Preface to Lyrical Ballads, Anglistica*, IX (Copenhagen: Rosenkilde and Bagger, 1957), pp. 11-14.

On the other hand, Robert Mayo has presented elaborate evidence to prove that Wordsworth was heavily dependent on magazine verse of the time and that his volume is not so revolutionary as scholars think. "The Contemporaneity of the *Lyrical Ballads*", *PMLA*, LXIX (1954), 486-522. Admittedly the volume is "contemporary" in spirit, but it is also consciously rebellious, in thought and in style; Wordsworth himself looked upon it as such in his various prefatory essays. Moreover, in the country he probably had little access to the various London periodicals; when he was able to see them, he dismissed their poetical selections as "the trash which infests the magazines". *Early Letters*, p. 126. Also, as Owen has pointed out, one essential difference between Wordsworth and other writers of the 1790's is that, in writing of the victims of society, he "is not concerned to pity so much as to understand", *Lyrical Ballads. 1798* (London: Oxford University Press, 1967), pp. xxix-xxx.

[21] John E. Jordan presents a convincing case for the presence of humor in much of Wordsworth's poetry, although he only alludes in passing to the poet's use of satire and he does not concern himself with the philosophical or political implications of his humor. "Wordsworth's Humor", *PMLA*, LXXIII (1958), 81-93.

The central premise established by *Lyrical Ballads* is the importance of the natural in every area of human life. As such, Wordsworth is not advocating a "return to nature". The external landscape is not even a requisite for a natural way of life (see "Poems on the Naming of Places": II. "To Joanna", 1-8),[22] although it is conducive to the natural by representing, much of the time, an analogue to the ideal human existence. Wordsworth's indulgence in the pathetic fallacy has often been ridiculed, but in all fairness it should be admitted that the ascription of human traits to nature, far from being a sentimental attempt to "humanize" the world of nature, is actually his way of "naturalizing" the human world. Invariably, the central thrust even of his poems of pure scenic description is human nature. In "Lines written in early spring", "every flower / Enjoys the air it breathes".[23] In contrast to much of human society, the flowers (and the birds as well, and so presumably the whole of nature) are seen to live in joyful harmony with their environment. The contrast between harmony and discordance is seen in "The Waterfall and the Eglantine" and "The Oak and the Broom". In the former, the Eglantine asks, "Why should we dwell in strife?" It attempts to live in accord with its surroundings, both giving and receiving in its own humble way. In the latter poem, the Broom is seen to cling tenaciously but meaningfully to existence.[24] The human context is apparent if implicit in both poems.

In order for nature to be made a proper analogue in human life, it must be first approached empirically. Brett and Jones have noted that the poems in the volume are in large part based upon the sensationalist empiricism of Hartley.[25] A large number of the poems were the result of direct observation, as the "Advertisement" to the first edition, the Preface to the 1800 edition, and the Fenwick notes all reveal.

Wordsworth was well aware, however, that the empirical ap-

---

[22]   *Lyrical Ballads* (1800), p. 213.
[23]   *Ibid.*, pp. 68-69.
[24]   *Ibid.* (1800), pp. 152-157. See also "Ruth", ll. 121-150 (pp. 180-181) for another instance where nature represents an analogue to man.
[25]   Brett and Jones, *Lyrical Ballads*, pp. xxxiii-xxxv.

proach could be perverted, becoming an end in itself and so seriously limiting the mental vision of the observer. The repeated attacks on science and philosophy in the volume, while not criticisms of these disciplines when correctly approached, are Wordsworth's attempts to show the destructiveness of empiricism when improperly used. "Expostulation and Reply" and "The Tables Turned" are the most obvious examples of his reaction from mechanistic philosophies that abused empiricism. Both poems were probably occasioned by a conversation with the young William Hazlitt, a visitor at Nether Stowey in the spring of 1798, who was then writing his *Essay on the Principles of Human Action*, a survey from Hobbes to Hartley, and who was "somewhat unreasonably attached to modern books of moral philosophy".[26] Wordsworth's lines are well known:

> Our meddling intellect
> Misshapes the beauteous forms of things;
> — We murder to dissect.[27]

A similar statement appears in "A Poet's Epitaph":

> Physician art thou? One, all eyes,
> Philosopher! a fingering slave,
> One that would peep and botanize
> Upon his mother's grave?

> Wrapp'd closely in thy sensual fleece
> O turn aside, and take, I pray,
> That he below may rest in peace,
> Thy pin-point of a soul away![28]

It should be stressed here that such close analysis is not merely destructive of nature's beauty (insofar as it deprives man of that beauty) but of natural beauty, that of the human "form" and "soul". To Wordsworth, thinkers like Godwin ignored aesthetic and spiritual elements alike by being too concerned with the minutiae of the physical universe.[29]

---

[26]   *Ibid.*, p. 288. Hazlitt's *Essay* was published by Johnson in 1805.

[27]   "The Tables Turned", *Ibid.*, p. 105.

[28]   *Ibid.* (1800), p. 207.

[29]   Brett and Jones admit that Wordsworth is attacking Godwin in poems such as "Expostulation and Reply" (p. 288), but they repeatedly find Godwin's influence elsewhere in the volume (pp. 276-277, 278, 285). Rather

When carried out properly, however, an empirical examination of nature would lead to a sense of permanence and of peace, an awareness of place, and above all to a morality that is based on mutual giving and receiving. All of these ideals have evident socio-political connotations. Peace and permanence were inevitable liberal ideals in the 1790's, stemming both from the anti-war position of most liberals and from their dismay with the aimlessness of those in authority, who seemed to be impeding the process of perfecting human life. (Certainly the very idea of an ideal existence in nature owes something to the schemes of perfectibility of the political reformers.) The concept of permanence in *Lyrical Ballads* has been pointed out by Owen.[30] Peace as a consequence of experiencing nature is found in a number of places:

> Oh glide, fair stream! for ever so;
> Thy quiet soul on all bestowing,
> 'Till all our minds for ever flow,
> As thy deep waters now are flowing.

>   He is by nature led
> To peace so perfect, that the young behold
> With envy, what the old man hardly feels. [31]

Likewise, an awareness of place is understandable among those who found themselves aliens in their native land, at least in human society. They logically turned to the natural scene, not out of any patriotic love for the current ministry, but to identify with at least some element of their environment. Even in such apolitical poems as "Tintern Abbey" and the series entitled "Poems on the Naming of Places", nature is presented as a refuge from the woes of human society; we should remember that Wordsworth has in mind not just any society, but that specifically of England in the

---

than ascribe all empirical and necessitarian ideas in *Lyrical Ballads* to Godwin and Hartley, it would seem more plausible to relate them to a source that combines hostility to Godwin on the above grounds and agreement with him in other areas. English Dissent perfectly fits this description.

[30]   Owen, pp. 11-21.

[31]   "Lines written near Richmond", *Lyrical Ballads*, p. 102; "Old Man Travelling", *Ibid.*, p. 106.

1790's. That he regarded this as an instinctive and natural re-
course for those wearied or abused by human life is shown by
the frequency with which even the insane in Wordsworth's poetry
turn to nature.

Above all, nature can educate man in terms of morality. The
stress in the volume on the moral should also be seen initially as
an extension of Wordsworth's liberal hostility to the various areas
of Establishment life, all of which he had long charged with
immorality. To avoid this, nature must be an essential component
of any child's education – a point Coleridge also makes in "The
Foster-Mother's Tale" and in "The Nightingale". From this
standpoint, "Anecdote for Fathers" illustrates the harmful, if not
also immoral, potentialities of over-abstraction; the speaker's
question was in effect a Godwinian one which forced the little
boy to lie because it could not be answered in natural terms.
Likewise, in "We are seven" the poet again assumes the mask of
the materialist as he confronts the small girl who whiles away her
time at the grave of her brother and her sister; the narrator cannot
see what she sees intuitively – that in spiritual, natural terms they
are alive. In both instances, humor stems not from the narrator's
superior air, but from the ironic fact that his assurance prevents
him from comprehending a simple truth.[32]

Nature's most elementary moral lesson is the worth of all life
– a point that has obvious socio-economic relevance to the late
eighteenth century. For years Wordsworth had seen examples of
indifference on the part of authorities – in the government, in the
church, and in society; he had seen the pleas for reform go un-
heeded, and he had confronted apathy himself in the Lonsdale
lawsuit. It is no wonder that most of the poems in the volume
insist that nature can teach man to regard every person as an
individual of value. In such poems as "The Oak and the Broom"
and "The Waterfall and the Eglantine" Wordsworth shows that
the most trivial parts of the natural scene are both beautiful and
necessary. The same idea is applied specifically to the animal
kingdom in "Hart-Leap Well", and to man in the numerous poems

---

[32] *Ibid.*, pp. 63-68.

that emphasize the worth even of beggars and the aged. A personal statement of the same theme appears in the description of the poet at the end of "A Poet's Epitaph".[33]

Respect for all life can come only through an awakening of the spiritual resources in man – something Godwinians and political leaders alike were unable to do in Wordsworth's eyes. With this spiritual enlightenment would come an awareness of the holiness of all things. The Christian elements in Wordsworth's poetry of the late 1790's have been generally ignored, many scholars evidently acquiescing to the eighteenth-century Establishment's premise that all men were either Anglicans or infidels. Yet the idea of an active power of virtue, emanating from above throughout the natural world, is apparent in several places in *Lyrical Ballads*.[34] To notice but two examples, in "Tintern Abbey" we see that nature can produce in man a "blessed mood", and "Lines written near Richmond" concludes:

> – The evening darkness gathers round
> By virtue's holiest powers attended. [35]

With this spiritual awakening, man can feel at one with all existence, loving in his heart every form of life. This theme was of course stated most memorably by Coleridge:

> He prayeth best who loveth best,
>   All things both great and small:
> For the dear God, who loveth us,
>   He made and loveth all. [36]

The words "love" and "heart" echo throughout Wordsworth's poems in the volume also, not for the sake of a sentimental pose, but to suggest a sincere and profound response to his sense of identity with the universe at large.[37] The following lines from

---

[33] *Ibid.* (1800), pp. 206-208.

[34] David Rogers finds Christian elements in "Expostulation and Reply", and he feels that at this time Wordsworth "does not deny God as a transcendent being, but simply says he apprehended God through nature". "Wordsworth's Rediscovery of Religion", *Universitas*, I (1963), 79-93.

[35] *Lyrical Ballads*, pp. 112, 102.

[36] *Ibid.*, p. 34.

[37] Among the many examples of Wordsworth's use of these two words, the following may be singled out: "Tintern Abbey", ll. 23-36; "Hart-Leap

"The Tables Turned" especially show how Wordsworth reconciled the several elements we have noted:

> Come forth, and bring with you a heart
> That watches and receives.

Here Wordsworth synthesizes humanitarian concern ("heart"), the empirical mode of examining nature ("watches"), and the passive receptivity due to the active power of the world ("receives").

Besides respect for life, Wordsworth's "natural" morality includes a rigorous but non-puritanical sense of virtue, simplicity, and work. These qualities he found embodied in the peasants of the Lake Country, but they all also have broader socio-political implications. Humble virtue and simplicity are repeatedly stressed in such poems as "Michael", and the other sketches of the life of the North country farmers. Work and responsibility, frequently said to have first appeared as themes in Wordsworth only with the "Ode to Duty", are likewise emphasized in many places. "Michael", "Simon Lee", and "The Idle Shepherd-Boys" enunciate the themes in human terms, while such poems as "The Oak and the Broom" and "The Waterfall and the Eglantine" apply them in the context of nature per se.

These last two poems illustrate a parallel point as well. Just as external nature can be an analogue to man in terms of the good, so can it parallel the evil in man. In these two poems, as also in "The Two Thieves" and especially in "Ruth", nature is seen to have a potentiality for evil that can in fact have an adverse effect on man. Wordsworth's nature is not a Rousseauistic glorification of the natural state, but rather a quasi-Christian concept influenced by the idea of original sin and by the rugged life of the North country. We may note, for example, the hardy acceptance of death manifested time and again by the central characters of *Lyrical Ballads*, as in "The Brothers" and "Old Man Travelling".

Although Wordsworth's view of life in *Lyrical Ballads* led him

---

Well", ll. 163-168; "The Brothers", ll. 207-241; "The Two Thieves", ll. 45-48; "A Poet's Epitaph", ll. 37-52; and "Michael", ll. 457-459.

to stress the effects of nature, the central focus of the volume, as has been noted, is man. Every poem either directly comments on human life or can be indirectly related to mankind. Wordsworth's favorite human types are of course children and the aged. Singled out in part because they are the poet's way of emphasizing the elemental in human nature, these two types are also chosen because they were most susceptible to current economic, educational, political, and social practices.[38]

The natural reaction to human life that Wordsworth advocates would involve a sense of identity with and an awareness of the worth of these people. As such, the essential point about human life that the poet is making in *Lyrical Ballads* is that man must be able to feel. The volume may thus be regarded as a conscious reply to an age whose intellectual leaders, in Wordsworth's estimation, had lost all sense of feeling by exaggerating reason and whose political leaders were callously indifferent to humanity. Such a man was Harry Gill. A man of property who felt no sympathy for his fellowman, he lived by the letter of the law – a law that was often pernicious in the poet's eyes. He is unnatural in his lack of feeling for Goody Blake. That he is "a lusty drover", "stout of limb", underlines his callous, physical nature, in contrast to Goody Blake, who is "old and poor, / Ill fed . . . and thinly clad".[39]

Another source of Wordsworth's reaction here is the cult of the sentimental, which can be described as the glorification of a false, unnatural feeling. Sentimentalism is unnatural because it is impermanent, unpeaceful, disordered, and above all oriented towards self only. Proper feeling can take many forms, but invariably it would lead to a sense of peace and permanence, it

---

[38] "As with Blake, there are political overtones to Wordsworth's vision of innocence". Brett and Jones, *Lyrical Ballads*, p. xxix. On man in *Lyrical Ballads*, see also Benziger, pp. 38-42; Hartman, pp. 141-162; Leavis, *Revaluation; Tradition and Development in English Poetry* (New York: Norton, 1963), pp. 154-185; Owen, pp. 93, 102; and Charles Ryskamp, "Wordsworth's *Lyrical Ballads* in their Time", *From Sensibility to Romanticism*, F. W. Hilles and Harold Bloom, eds. (New York: Oxford University Press, 1965), pp. 357-372.

[39] *Lyrical Ballads*, pp. 54-58. A parallel example of callousness appears in "Andrew Jones", *Ibid.* (1800), pp. 169-170.

would be characterized by an essential simplicity of thought and expression, it would have clear moral connotations, and it would be humanitarian in orientation. In *Lyrical Ballads*, natural feeling generally takes one of three forms: pity, gratitude, and love (the first two having direct, and the third indirect, socio-political implications).

Pity appears in such poems as "Goody Blake, and Harry Gill", "Simon Lee", "Andrew Jones", "The Old Cumberland Beggar" and "Poems on the Naming of Places": IV. "A narrow girdle of rough stones".[40] In most of them Wordsworth specifically espouses pity as a necessary response to human life; in all of them he carefully avoids sentimentality both by generalizing his description and by adopting a frequently ironic or at least jaunty manner. In "Simon Lee" the generalized description leads to a kind of understatement that evokes pity while avoiding sentimentalism:

> A scrap of land they have, but they
> Are poorest of the poor.
> This scrap of land he from the heath
> Enclosed when he was stronger;
> But what avails the land to them,
> Which they can till no longer? [41]

A physical age, ignorant of spiritual qualities, allows only those who are strong and healthy, or wealthy, to survive; others are left to fare as best they can. Similarly, in "Goody Blake, and Harry Gill", we have seen an obsession with the material leading to an unnatural disregard for the unfortunate. The description here again is generalized, and delivered in a tone that obviates a sentimental reaction:

---

[40]   Brett and Jones say that Wordsworth's attitude in "Goody Blake, and Harry Gill" is "characteristically Godwinian", and then go on to say that "The idea of warmth and cold is clearly ... metaphorically linked with Wordsworth's appeal to humanitarian principles". *Lyrical Ballads*, pp. 276-277. This last point is certainly correct, but it would be difficult to reconcile with the assertion that the poem is Godwinian, since Godwin repudiates the emotions.

[41]   *Ibid.*, p. 62.

> All day she spun in her poor dwelling,
> And then her three hours' work at night!
> Alas! 'twas hardly worth the telling,
> It would not pay for candle-light. [42]

In Wordsworth's scheme, gratitude is as essential as pity; it is a spiritual quality also, an acknowledgment that things are given man other than that which he earns, and therefore it is basically Christian in spirit. It appears incidentally in a number of poems ("Tintern Abbey" for instance), but its most direct expression appears in "Simon Lee":

> — I've heard of hearts unkind, kind deeds
> With coldness still returning.
> Alas! the gratitude of men
> Has oftner left me mourning. [43]

Wordsworth is of course not depreciating Simon's reaction. The old man's excessive gratefulness points up his total dependence on others and shows that he is unaccustomed to such assistance; it thus dramatizes and fuses extreme need and complete indifference to that need. Legouis has rightly asserted that the poem in part attacks Godwin's notion that gratitude can have "no part of justice or virtue", which would appear to contradict his statement elsewhere that Wordsworth and Godwin "are at one in deploring the unreasonableness of gratitude".[44] It is only to the extent that society and the economic system have mistreated Simon that his gratitude is unreasonable. The reflection is on society, not on Simon.

The most elemental form of natural affection is love. "The Idiot Boy" illustrates both the extensiveness and the efficacy of pure love. In writing to John Wilson in June, 1802, Wordsworth claimed that he was largely prompted by noticing the "loathing" many people felt at the sight of an idiot, a reaction he had never seen in a member of the lower class (but which he had no doubt seen frequently on the part of the Establishment towards all

---

[42]   *Ibid.*, p. 55.
[43]   *Ibid.*, p. 63.
[44]   *Lyrical Ballads*, pp. 277-278; Legouis, "Some Remarks on the Composition of the *Lyrical Ballads* of 1798", *Wordsworth and Coleridge*, pp. 10-11.

beneath it).[45] The idiot's mother, in her unfailing love for the boy, is the poet's testimony to the strength which can be derived from purity and naturalness.[46] The converse to this poem is "The Mad Mother", in which it is the mother who is deprived of her sanity. She can still, however, love her child passionately, her intuition telling her that her innocent child is worthy of her love. Most important, this love gives meaning to her life.[47] The poem was published immediately prior to "The Idiot Boy" in 1798, and in 1800 the two were on either side of "Love", suggesting that Wordsworth consciously related all three poems as variations on the same theme.

Another poem expressive of this idea is "Lines written at a small distance from my House". Here Wordsworth makes the most expansive statement of the volume about love, showing that it is a profoundly meaningful experience and that his emphasis on it is directly motivated by the intellectual climate of his time:

> Love, now an universal birth,
> From heart to heart is stealing,
> From earth to man, from man to earth,
> – It is the hour of feeling.
>
> One moment now may give us more
> Than fifty years of reason;
> Our minds shall drink at every pore
> The spirit of the season.
>
> Some silent laws our hearts may make,
> Which they shall long obey;
> We for the year to come may take
> Our temper from to-day.
>
> And from the blessed power that rolls
> About, below, above;
> We'll frame the measure of our souls,
> They shall be tuned to love. [48]

[45] *Early Letters*, pp. 352-358.
[46] *Lyrical Ballads*, pp. 85-101.
[47] *Ibid.*, pp. 82-85.
[48] *Ibid.*, pp. 59-60. Other poems which explicitly express the necessity of love and its powers are "Michael", "The Brothers", and of course "Tintern Abbey", in the speaker's relationship to his sister. See also footnote 37.

This poem illustrates how love operates in man. It tacitly indicates a belief in free will, behind which lies natural "necessity". If men only choose to open their hearts to the workings of the natural universe, then they would learn to love all forms of life. To the poet, man had lost this feeling of unity with all earthly beings because he had, in every realm of existence, substituted mechanical, physical forces for spiritual ones. Thus attempts at spirituality in literature, for example, merely resulted in awkward and artificial sentimentality; attempts at humanitarianism on the part of the political leaders similarly led to unnatural workhouses. The deeper, more worthwhile spiritual forces can be grasped only by negating the physical. Time and again, therefore, the poet in this volume contrasts, as he does here, motion and stillness – the latter being his metaphor for spirituality; both are seen as necessary in human life.

The most obvious indication of the absence of spirituality in contemporary life were the socio-economic conditions, of the peasants particularly. Although the Wordsworth of the late 1790's has usually been described as more concerned with the general than with the particular, a surprisingly large number of specific references to social and economic conditions appears in *Lyrical Ballads*. Their number, in fact, indicates that such conditions loomed large in his mind while he was writing the poems of the volume. In the 1798 edition we may note specific socio-economic comments in "Goody Blake, and Harry Gill", "Simon Lee", "The Last of the Flock", "Old Man Travelling", and in the earlier poem, "The Female Vagrant". Criticism is also strongly implied at the end of "Lines written in early Spring". The edition of 1800 added "The Brothers", "The Old Cumberland Beggar", "A Poet's Epitaph", and "Michael". In addition many poems present situations that are analogues to contemporary socio-economic conditions. Such may be said of "The Complaint of a forsaken Indian Woman", "The Oak and the Broom", and "The Waterfall and the Eglantine". In this last, for example, the proud and disdainful waterfall may be regarded as a metaphor for indifferent men of power and wealth, while the meek and seemingly insignificant eglantine is ignored, and at the end, swept away by the waterfall.

Three themes are especially stressed by Wordsworth in these allusions. One is that the poor frequently spend long hours at very arduous work, but to no economic benefit; such is the lot of Goody Blake, Simon Lee, Michael, and Walter Ewbank and his forefathers in "The Brothers". A second is that the inherent worth of the poor is often unappreciated by others. The most obvious example of this theme would be "The Old Cumberland Beggar"; but it appears in other poems as well, explicitly as in "The Two Thieves", "A Poet's Epitaph", and "Poems on the Naming of Places": IV, and implicitly in such poems as "Goody Blake, and Harry Gill", "The Idiot Boy", and "Old Man Travelling". In fact, in one way or another, this second theme appears in virtually every poem in the volume. Though it may at times be deprived of its socio-economic context, there can be no doubt what was in Wordsworth's mind in each case.

The third and most explicit theme is that current socio-economic practices are depriving the peasants of their ability to make a living. Simon Lee is victimized by enclosure, Walter Ewbank and his forefathers by anti-agrarian economic policies that make generations of toil completely fruitless. The list of such instances could be much expanded. One of the most poignant and devastating appears in "The Last of the Flock". Here an English farmer has been forced to sell his sheep one by one, the only possession he could claim, because he was refused parish assistance. Once again, the criticism is pointed at rational systems that have no logic in human terms; the poem represents the conflict between the individual and the blind, unfeeling "they" who are responsible for the farmer's dilemma.[49]

Although much attention has been given to Wordsworth's emphasis on natural feeling in *Lyrical Ballads*, it should be stressed that his philosophy of man encompasses the intellect as well. The volume in effect postulates a natural state of mind as well as a natural state of the heart. In its outlines, his concept of the natural state of mind involves a sense of the unity of all life, derived from an all-encompassing intellectual awareness. What is apparently insignificant in physical terms is actually a vital part

[49] *Ibid.*, pp. 78-81.

of the living whole, in spiritual terms. The insignificant is made important not because of its place on a chain of being or because of its function in a machine, but because it is part of an organic, living unity. To realize this, a non-empirical spiritual perception is required; Wordsworth's description of the death of a stag in "Hart-Leap Well" is indicative:

> This beast not unobserv'd by Nature fell,
> His death was mourn'd by sympathy divine.
>
> The Being, that is in the clouds and air,
> That is in the green leaves among the groves,
> Maintains a deep and reverential care
> For them the quiet creatures whom he loves.
>   * * *
> One lesson, Shepherd, let us two divide,
> Taught both by what she shews, and what conceals,
> Never to blend our pleasure or our pride
> With sorrow of the meanest thing that feels. [50]

Just as nature can be an analogue to teach man natural feeling, so the spiritual processes of life can be instructive to man. But such edification requires not only empirical study to discover "what she shews", but also intuition to perceive what nature "conceals".

Paradoxically, then, the mind should be aware of the significance of the trivial yet also be capable of grasping a larger view of things. To Wordsworth, the gravest intellectual error is the failure to acquire a broad mental vision, the failure of the Physician and of the Moralist in "A Poet's Epitaph". The Physician is caught up in the senses and the minute; the Moralist is simply caught up in himself:

> He has neither eyes nor ears;
> Himself his world, and his own God;
>
> One to whose smooth-rubb'd soul can cling
> Nor form nor feeling great nor small,
> A reasoning, self-sufficing thing,
> An intellectual All in All! [51]

---

[50]   *Ibid.* (1800), p. 131.
[51]   *Ibid.* (1800), p. 207.

In his preoccupation with reasoning, the Moralist neglects not only the empirical evidence of his senses but more important the spiritual powers of his mind. The traditional idea that Wordsworth borrowed heavily from Hartley in the late 1790's is obviously correct; but it should be stressed that Hartleyan sensationalism, even in *Lyrical Ballads*, was but an initial intellectual step, to be ultimately supplanted by an awareness of spiritual forces, whose characteristics are a non-Hartleyan emotional sympathy and mental scope.

Ultimately, the mind, besides possessing empirical faculties, has also an active, creative power of its own, making it receptive to the active, spiritual power of the universe. This idea has often been noted in "Tintern Abbey", as something of an exception in the volume as a whole. But signs of a transcending vitalism are apparent almost everywhere in the book. We may cite some of the more explicit instances:

> Oh glide, fair stream! for ever so;
> Thy quiet soul on all bestowing,
> 'Till all our minds for ever flow,
> As thy deep waters now are flowing.[52]

> Nor less I deem that there are powers,
> Which of themselves our minds impress,
> That we can feed this mind of ours,
> In a wise passiveness. [53]

> In sleep I heard the northern gleams;
> The stars they were among my dreams;
> In sleep did I behold the skies,
> I saw the crackling flashes drive;
> And yet they are upon my eyes,
> And yet I am alive. [54]

This last excerpt, from "The Complaint of a forsaken Indian Woman", suggests that even in a person who is physically of little worth, the mind can be receptive. The active universe can

---

[52] "Lines written near Richmond", *Ibid.*, p. 102.
[53] "Expostulation and Reply", *Ibid.*, p. 103.
[54] *Ibid.*, p. 107.

work directly on her mind without the intermediary agency of the senses.

The idea of unity is the key to Wordsworth's concept of the spiritual power of the mind. The natural universe has inherent qualities which man, if he so desires, can comprehend by "communion" with it. This communion involves, as we have noted, both empirical study and a state of "wise passiveness," by which "we are laid asleep / In body, and become a living soul" ("Tintern Abbey", ll. 46-47). By doing this, man not only overcomes the lower evils of a social and political order, but conquers as well spiritual blindness; he attains

> a sense sublime
> Of something far more deeply interfused,
> Whose dwelling is the light of setting suns,
> And the round ocean, and the living air,
> And the blue sky, and in the mind of man,
> A motion and a spirit, that impels
> All thinking things, all objects of all thought,
> And rolls through all things. [55]

Through this imaginative power of the mind, nature reveals the essential spiritual unity of the universe. This unity encompasses not only all "things" but also all moral truth; natural truth is universally true.

Although "Tintern Abbey" is Wordsworth's most explicit statement of his transcendental philosophy in *Lyrical Ballads*, that philosophy is implicit in the volume as a whole; it is the inherent world-view that permits him to arrive at the conclusions and reactions he describes in the other poems. Similarly, there can be no doubt that these transcendental overtones were the central portion of his repudiation of the primary philosophic point of view of the eighteenth century, a point of view that

---

[55] *Ibid.*, p. 114. In his recent book, Jonathan Wordsworth has some excellent remarks along these same lines. In particular he stresses the idea of the "One Life", although I feel he somewhat exaggerates its place in Wordsworth's thought in 1798; is it, finally, any more of a keystone than, say, the "Inner Light", the active universe, or the natural? *The Music of Humanity* (London: Nelson, 1969), *passim* and especially pp. 256-258.

culminated, to the poet, in political stagnation, social heartlessness, and literary insensitivity.

These last two points may be illustrated by noting that the mind's attainment of a sense of unity requires certain definite qualities that are delineated in several poems and that represent clear reactions to eighteenth-century attitudes. In "Ruth", we see that one of the reasons for the corruption of Ruth's lover is his own lack of "self-controul".[56]

> His genius and his moral frame
> Were thus impair'd, and he became
> The slave of low desires;
> A man who without self-controul
> Would seek what the degraded soul
> Unworthily admires.

Whether on the part of the devotees of reason or the powerful who were indifferent to humanity, self-interest involved a lack of self-discipline and prevented them from attaining a sense of the oneness of life. Hence their cruel neglect of the poor and the weak. Luke's fall from a natural state in "Michael" is likewise occasioned, not by the city per se, but by his own lack of will power: he "began / To slacken in his duty" and eventually "*gave himself* / To evil courses" [italics mine].[57] The converse of this is suggested in "The Old Cumberland Beggar", where Wordsworth emphasizes the role that "habit" must play in forming proper attitudes of mind.[58] With willpower, discipline, and responsible mental habits, then, the mind will be ready to respond to the active powers of the universe and thus acquire that intellectual enlargement which is the ultimate step in Wordsworth's concept of mental fulfillment.

The thought of *Lyrical Ballads* may be approached from another relevant angle – namely the audience for which the volume was intended. Wordsworth frankly noted in his Preface that he thought many of his poems would be objectionable to many readers. Perkins has commented on this subject as follows:

[56] *Ibid.* (1800), pp. 180-181.
[57] *Ibid.* (1800), p. 233.
[58] *Ibid.* (1800), p. 202.

The style and subjects of the *Lyrical Ballads* are ... deliberately calculated to offend and correct the feelings of the sort of person who usually reads poetry – that is, members of the middle and upper classes. In other words, both his attitude to the public, and, at least in his opinion, the attitude of the public to his work, should be explained in connection with his still liberal politics. To show and urge how all men are alike may be consistent with any political faith. Wordsworth prided himself on it even when he was sunk in Toryism. On the other hand, the approach can easily involve an implicit questioning of the social order, and this subversive tendency seemed to emerge in the *Lyrical Ballads*. It bristled even in the primitivism, the use of lower-class or rustic persons to exemplify human nature. At least to his own satisfaction, Wordsworth proves that the "maternal passion" is the same in Betty Foy with her idiot child as it is in a fine lady. [59]

Although I would quibble with a number of Perkins' incidental points here, the essential idea cannot be disputed: that *Lyrical Ballads* is a didactic attempt to influence the minds of its readers, to direct them towards a more liberal and one might add a more intellectual response to life. Certainly Wordsworth is also striving to reach a larger audience than that of most contemporary poetry. It is noteworthy that, as much of the foregoing evidence indicates, the second edition of the volume is, if anything, more openly liberal and didactic than the first.

It should be evident by now that the parallels between much of the previous discussion and the thought of liberal Dissent are striking, both in their number and in their similitude. In no instance does Wordsworth's thought in *Lyrical Ballads* conflict with his idealism of 1793. This is not to say that the volume is merely a restatement of his Republican-Dissenting thought; rather it represents the evolution of that thought and its expansion and application to new areas. [60] Most immediately apparent are the reforming motives of the volume at large (Wordsworth in this

[59] *Wordsworth and the Poetry of Sincerity*, pp. 151-152.
[60] There are several *prima facie* connections between *Lyrical Ballads* and Dissent. As Wordsworth said later, "The Ancient Mariner" was originally meant to be included in a new magazine which Dr. Aikin, the Dissenter, intended to edit. *Poetical Works*, I, 360-361. Likewise, the probable source

regard not being hostile to England as such but merely trying to correct certain apparent abuses) and his scientific approach to his subject and his style. Equally typical of Dissent is his habit of synthesizing the various modes of existence, particularly human society and nature.

In his concern for man, Wordsworth continues the humanitarian idealism that was the legacy of his days as a Dissenting-Republican. The particular ingredients of his concept of man perfectly parallel Dissenting thought. Men are to be concerned for each other; no matter how worthless a man may seem, there is some good and utility in him. The ideal human way of life combines simplicity, virtue, hard work, and economic well-being. Like Wordsworth, the Dissenters revealed a respect for property, even the peculiarly Wordsworthian sense of the home – something to be highly valued as giving one roots and permanence, yet in itself so very precarious, as many Dissenters came to realize and as Wordsworth often presents it in his poetry. The paradox in Wordsworth's view of man has been noted, Hartman calling it a "blend of benevolence and necessitarianism",[61] Mac-Lean in turn seeing it as a fusion of the sentimental and the economic.[62] This distinctive combination of opposing elements is as typical of Dissent as it is of Wordsworth.

Wordsworth's morality is likewise similar to that of English Dissent. Such Dissenting moral-philosophers as Priestley and Price were able to reconcile a moralistic repudiation of the English Establishment with Christian virtue, a reconciliation not found in the thought of the more extreme reformers or that of the orthodox Anglicans. Wordsworth and the liberal Dissenters alike emphasize a simple, humble virtue, repeatedly stressing that it must be natural and not affected. The ultimate goal of the moral life, for both, is love. Likewise, for both, truth is universal, something to be apprehended both by the mind and the heart.

---

of "Goody Blake, and Harry Gill" (Erasmus Darwin's *Zoönomia*) was published by Joseph Johnson.

[61] *Wordsworth's Poetry*, p. 376.

[62] *Agrarian Age: A Background for Wordsworth*, "Yale Studies in English", CXV (New Haven: Yale University Press, 1950), p. 98.

And finally both acknowledge the active presence of evil in the world: socio-political wrong occasioned by ignorance and poverty (as with virtually all liberal reformers) and natural evil in man and nature (which many radicals repudiated).

To both Wordsworth and the Dissenters, again, moral truth and the ultimate unity of things are to be perceived through a fusion of two modes of thought: empirical observation and the more profound workings of the heart. The latter is a necessary complement to their concept of the active power of the universe. Both then combine traditional eighteenth-century sensationalism and the new cult of the transcendental. For both an appeal to tradition (particularly native tradition) is a crucial aspect of experience; hence, their mutual emphasis on education. And for both the ultimate goal of the mind is total intellectual enlargement.

While the foregoing discussion argues that *Lyrical Ballads* represents Wordsworth's return to his ideals of 1793, it must be emphasized that his later point of view had evolved away from Dissenting thought in certain respects. Dissenting Platonism is more fully developed, Wordsworth now arriving at his concept of the imagination, which would seem to have no direct parallel in Dissenting thought. Nature's role in the life of man is now made more explicit and more extensive. Similarly, the glorification of place, and particularly the peasant life of the Lake Country, has no parallel among the Dissenters. Nevertheless, these departures in no way represent repudiations of Dissent but rather logical extensions of its thought.

In conclusion, it is necessary to turn to the last two books of *The Prelude* and to equate Wordsworth's mature philosophy with the intellectual and political forces that conditioned him. Again, the social and political situation must be acknowledged as the primary impelling force behind his work of the 1790's; he loved man, but his poetry would not have been written if the human amelioration of his dreams had been an actuality. Years later, Aubrey de Vere came to know the aged Wordsworth closely, and his record of the poet's conversation is revealing:

The more impassioned part of his nature connected itself especially with his political feelings. He regarded his own intellect as one which united some of the faculties which belong to the statesman with those which belong to the poet; and public affairs interested him not less deeply than poetry . . . Yet his political sympathies were not with his own country only, but with the progress of humanity. [63]

If this was true of the Wordsworth of the 1840's, how much more true it must have been of the young poet.

Few of his poems are devoid of political or social implications of some kind, even when they are primarily concerned with nature. The natural universe, in fact, seems to have made him more optimistic about the state of man; more especially, nature was not alien to society – unless man made it so. In *The Prelude* the poet tells of sitting with Coleridge beside streams

> To ruminate with interchange of talk
> On rational liberty, and hope in Man,
> Justice and peace.
>
> (IX, 396-402).

Coleridge, writing to his brother in the spring of 1798, explicitly indicates that the two poets had the political situation in mind and that they did not envision any absolute dichotomy between the human and the natural universes:

one good consequence which I expect from revolutions, is that Individuals will see the necessity of individual effort; that they will act as kind neighbours & good Christians, rather than as citizens & electors; and so by degrees will purge off that error, . . . of attributing to Governments a talismanic influence over our virtues & our happiness – as if Governments were not rather effects than causes. . . . yet they are in the wisdom & goodness of Nature; & not only are they physically necessary as effects, but also as causes they are *morally* necessary in order to prevent the utter dissolution of the patient. [64]

The two of them had arrived at one important qualification to general liberal ideals – that government reform will not by itself perfect man; the individual must by himself be perfected from within. The heady confidence of Wordsworth and Coleridge as

---

[63]   *Essays Chiefly on Poetry*, 2 vols. (London: Macmillan, 1887), "Recollections of Wordsworth", II, 281-282.
[64]   Coleridge, *Letters*, I, 395-396.

they plotted their careers in 1798 derived from their assurance that they had found the means for that inward perfection.

At the same time, to say that every man is potentially capable of such improvement is to imply a deep faith in human nature. With the Dissenters, the two believed that man was good and valuable because he possessed spiritual qualities; he was a creature of divine origins: "the inner frame is good,/ And graciously composed" (*The Prelude*, XII, 278-286). Such a concern with man in the abstract was likewise a consequence of their interest in political reform. But whereas the average radical simply concerned himself with the physical rights of man, the two poets – again like the Dissenters – centered on his spiritual rights, which he had only to discover in order to claim them as his own.

With his full faith in man restored, Wordsworth states that he was then

> prepared to find
> Ambition, folly, madness in the men
> Who thrust themselves upon this passive world
> As Rulers of the world, to see in these,
> Even when the public welfare is their aim,
> Plans without thought, or bottom'd on false thought
> And false philosophy: . . .
>   and thereby perceiv'd
> The utter hollowness of what we name
> The wealth of Nations.
>   (*The Prelude*, XII, 69-92).

Hence he repudiates the eighteenth-century obsession with the material and economic components of nations: the true wealth of a country lies in its individual citizens, provided the inherent worth in them is cultivated. Unfortunately, however, contemporary manners permitted people to be aware only of

> the outside marks by which
> Society has parted man from man,
> Neglectful of the universal heart.
>   (XII, 205-219).

Nevertheless, under the right circumstances man can perceive his "universal heart", and it was this potentiality that made

Wordsworth an ardent believer in man's perfectibility. Always, when he refers to man in *The Prelude*, his attention centers on the human mind,[65] surely a concern that was indebted to the heavy emphasis placed on the mind by the political philosophers. But while the rationalists subscribed to the tradition of Locke and Hartley in its repudiation of innate ideas and in its insistence on the mechanical nature of the mind, Wordsworth came to feel that the mind could perceive spiritual qualities. This was a necessary conclusion, since it supplied him with a philosophical defense of his acceptance of the emotionally oriented Dissenting theory of benevolence. Like these humanitarians, he was attempting to refute not only the material, necessitarian atheists but also the unfeeling conservatives in their acceptance of the political *status quo* and of the corrupt and even immoral social conditions.

Wordsworth's theories about the natural universe which was essential to man may also be related meaningfully to his political background. In the first place, he realized that he owed to nature the rediscovery of his earlier ideals, for he found that it lifted "The Being into magnanimity" and made him scorn again whatever "we blazon with the pompous names/ Of power and action". Thus he came to believe once more in the objects of life that were simply and quietly pure (*The Prelude*, XII, 1-55). So his reaction in yet another instance was political in origin and derived from his thought of 1793, when he was already denouncing the misused power and the inconsequential activity that prevailed in the governments of the world.

Further, he came to believe that nature could shape "the character of nations", that it was more influential on man and his society than thinkers had hitherto believed. In his earlier political reading, the poet would have discovered Montesquieu's emphasis on climate as the origin of national character, and perhaps Hume's insistence that government was the formative influence. The poet did accept the political concept of national characteristics; but here also he consciously reacted against tradition by ascribing a nation's traits to natural conditions, especially its topography.

[65]   As instances, see *The Prelude*, II, 321-341; XIII, 1-122.

Moreover, he felt that in countries like England the national character was obscured by legalism and materialism.[66]

But the most important function of external nature to Wordsworth was its ability to make man aware of the essential unity of all life. The quest of the Romantic thinkers for a transcendental oneness was as much dependent on the political and social conditions of their time as it was a consequence of literary or philosophical influences. The early chapters of this work have attested to Wordsworth's involvement in the political events of his youth, and such was the case with all the other Romantics; indeed, public affairs were difficult to ignore in the 1790's. The inevitable consequence, especially to the hopeful and idealistic minds of young men, was confusion and disillusionment, for England had become hardened in its conservatism. No matter how worthy a cause was, it was defeated in Parliament; agitation and unrest prevailed at home, while war and revolution continued on the foreign scene.

Their minds perplexed by a tumultuous age and their hopes shattered by an antagonistic nation, the young intellectuals of the time looked elsewhere for a means to mankind's amelioration. This they found in external nature, a realm that supplied them not only with a faith in man but also with a sense of the permanent, of the unified.[67] But their liberal hopes for humanity were retained; working outside of the political world, they still sought essentially the same goals as the political reformers – that man should be happy, peaceful, and good.

Wordsworth usually shows his concern with unity in the two large works that permitted him to expand the subject. In *The Excursion*, for example, the Wanderer appropriately ends his discourse with "a legitimate union of the imagination, affections, understanding, and reason":

[66]   *Early Letters*, pp. 353-354; see also pp. 255-256.
[67]   Coleridge indicates several times in his letters that the complex state of national affairs depressed him and made him turn to nature for a unifying principle. *Letters*, I, 349, 354-355, 397. See also H. C. Robinson, *On Books and Their Writers*, I, 60, on Hazlitt.

> Thus deeply drinking-in the soul of things,
> We shall be wise perforce; and, while inspired
> By choice, and conscious that the Will is free,
> Shall move unswerving, . . .
>   along the path
> Of order and of good. [68]

The emphasis on free will here is an obvious denial of mechanical necessity; but his hopes for man's attainment of wisdom, peace, and goodness are plainly prompted by the failings he had found in society.

Similarly, the concluding book of *The Prelude* centers entirely on the vision of harmony and unity that the mind acquires through communion with nature:

> Oh! who is he that hath his whole life long
> Preserved, enlarged this freedom in himself?
> For this alone is genuine Liberty.
>   (XIII, 120-122). [69]

Freedom of the soul, then, was essential before mere political liberty could be attained. It is thus significant that *The Prelude* should end with a political statement, revealing that the poet regarded himself mainly as a reformer, not of institutions, but of man; years from now, when the author and his friend are old men,

> Then, though, too weak to tread the ways of truth,
> This Age fall back to old idolatry,
> Though men return to servitude as fast
> As the tide ebbs, to ignominy and shame
> By Nations sink together, we shall still
> Find solace in the knowledge which we have,
> Bless'd with true happiness if we may be
> United helpers forward of a day
> Of firmer trust, joint-labourers in a work . . .
> Of their redemption, surely yet to come.
> Prophets of Nature, we to them will speak
> A lasting inspiration, sanctified
> By reason and by truth; what we have loved,
> Others will love; and we may teach them how;

[68] *Poetical Works*, V, 149-150.
[69] See also *The Prelude*, XIII, 70-73, variant of 1804.

> Instruct them how the mind of man becomes
> A thousand times more beautiful than the earth
> On which he dwells, above this Frame of things
> (Which, 'mid all revolutions in the hopes
> And fears of men, doth still remain unchanged)
> In beauty exalted, as it is itself
> Of substance and of fabric more divine.
>
> (*The Prelude*, XIII, 428-452).

Thus he concludes his great philosophical poem by asserting the spiritual nobility of mankind, even though it is obscured by physical circumstances. Moreover, his faith is dependent on the outlines of his political idealism of 1793 – not the outer details of reform but the more essential dedication to the natural, the true, and the good.

In the light of the earlier discussion of *Lyrical Ballads*, the last two books of *The Prelude* (Books XII and XIII in the 1805 version) may thus be seen as an accurate description of Wordsworth's state of mind at Alfoxden and in the months thereafter. Although his chronological narration ceases at this point, the poet now telescopes the various influences upon him and his varied reactions much as he telescoped his description of London. This departure from the chronological is both factually accurate (for the various influences of this period were literally fused in time) and appropriate to his mood of the time (in that it produces a feeling of culmination, just as Wordsworth's own intellectual career reached a culmination at this point). Above all, it must be insisted that *The Prelude* does have a logic to its ordering, in intellectual and psychological terms.[70] To be sure, there is not a consistent philosophy in the poem, simply because Wordsworth's description is totally immersed in his thought of the particular phase each book covers. But when Books XII and XIII are seen as descriptions of his state of mind at Alfoxden, and when we come to realize that that state of mind was the fulfillment of his earlier years of intellectual searching, then we can discover that the poem follows a consistent intellectual and psychological

---

[70] By contrast, see Herbert Lindenberger, *On Wordsworth's "Prelude"* (Princeton: Princeton University Press, 1963), pp. 188-197.

pattern. It is, after all, descriptive of a "growth", and not an account of a static frame of mind.

We have seen that Wordsworth's thought began as a more or less continuous sweep of the pendulum from childhood conservatism through a moderate liberalism of 1793 to the extreme radicalism of 1795. This was followed by a return of the pendulum to a moderate liberalism akin to that of 1793 – followed by a long and gradual final movement back to conservatism. To conclude with the publication of *Lyrical Ballads* and the years described in the final portions of *The Prelude* is thus appropriate, for the thought of the poet to this point has a unity of its own. His days at Alfoxden represent the culmination of his years of intellectual enquiry, resulting in the fusion of his earlier Dissenting-Republican idealism and his own poetic idiom.

BIBLIOGRAPHY OF PRIMARY WORKS CITED

Aikin, John, *Poems* (London: Johnson, 1791).
——, *The Spirit of the Constitution and that of the Church of England, compared* (London: Johnson, 1790).
Aikin, Lucy, *Memoir of John Aikin, M.D., with a Selection of his Miscellaneous Pieces, Biographical, Moral and Critical* (Philadelphia: Abraham Small, 1824).
The Analytical Review. First Series, I-XXVIII (1788-1798); Second Series, I (1799).
The Anti-Jacobin. Fourth edition (London: Wright, 1799).
Binns, John, *Recollections of the Life of John Binns* (Philadelphia: by the author, 1854).
Bogue, David, and James Bennett, *History of the Dissenters, From the Revolution in 1688 to the Year 1808.* 4 vols. (London: for the authors, 1808-1812).
Cartwright, John, *An Appeal, Civil and Military, on the Subject of the English Constitution.* Second edition (London: for the author, 1799).
Christie, Thomas, *Letters on the Revolution of France, and on the new Constitution established by the National Assembly* (London: Johnson, 1791).
Coleridge, Samuel Taylor, *Biographia Literaria.* Edited by J. Shawcross, 2 vols. (London: Oxford, 1949).
——, *Collected Letters of Samuel Taylor Coleridge.* Edited by Earl Leslie Griggs, 4 vols. (Oxford: Clarendon Press, 1956-1959).
——, *Conciones ad Populum, or Addresses to the People* (Bristol, 1795).
——, *Essays on His Own Times.* Edited by Sara Coleridge, 3 vols. (London: Pickering, 1850).
——, *The Fall of Robespierre, An Historic Drama* (Cambridge: Lunn and Merrill, 1794).
——, *The Notebooks of Samuel Taylor Coleridge.* Edited by Kathleen Coburn, Vol. I (1794-1804) (London: Routledge and Kegan Paul, 1957).
——, *Notes, Theological, Political, and Miscellaneous.* Edited by The Rev. Derwent Coleridge (London: Moxon, 1853).
——, *The Plot Discovered; or An Address to the People, against Ministerial Treason* (Bristol, 1795).

——, *The Poems of Samuel Taylor Coleridge*. Edited by Ernest Hartley Coleridge (London: Oxford, 1935).

——, *The Watchman* (Bristol: by the author, 1796).

Condorcet, Antoine-Nicolas de, *Sketch for a Historical Picture of the Progress of the Human Mind*. Translated by June Barraclough (London: Weidenfeld and Nicolson, 1955).

Cooper, Thomas, *A Reply to Mr. Burke's Invective against Mr. Cooper, and Mr. Watt*. Second edition (London: Johnson, 1792).

Cooper, Thomas, and James Watt, *Discours de MM. Cooper et Watt, Députés de la société constitutionnelle de Manchester, prononcé à la société des amis de la constitution, séante à Paris* (Paris: Société des Amis de la Constitution, 1792).

Cottle, Joseph, *Reminiscences of Samuel Taylor Coleridge and Robert Southey*. Second edition (London: Houlston and Stoneman, 1848).

The Critical Review. First Series, LXIII-LXX (1787-1790); Second Series, I-XVIII (1791-1796).

De Quincey, Thomas, *The Collected Writings of Thomas De Quincey*. Edited by David Masson, 14 vols. (London: Black, 1896-1897).

Dyer, George, *The Complaints of the Poor People of England*. Second edition (London: Ridgway and Symonds, 1793).

——, *Memoirs of the Life and Writings of Robert Robinson* (London: Robinsons, 1796).

Fawcett, Joseph, *The Art of War* (London: Johnson, 1795).

——, *Poems* (London: Johnson, 1798).

——, *Sermons delivered at the Sunday-Evening Lecture, for the Winter Season, at the Old Jewry*. 2 vols. (London: Johnson, 1795).

Frend, William, *Peace and Union*. Second edition (Cambridge: Robinsons, 1793).

The Gentleman's Magazine. LIX-LXVIII (1789-1798).

Godwin, William, Diary. Unpublished typescript copy in the possession of Professor Lewis Patton, Duke University.

——, *Enquiry concerning Political Justice and its Influence on Morals and Happiness*. Third edition. Edited by F. E. L. Priestley, 3 vols. (Toronto: University of Toronto, 1946).

——, *St. Leon: A Tale of the Sixteenth Century*. 4 vols. (London: Robinsons, 1799).

Gunning, Henry. *Reminiscences of Cambridge*. Edited by D. A. Winstanley (Cambridge: University Press, 1932).

Harrington, James, *The Political Writings of James Harrington: Representative Selections*. Edited by Charles Blitzer (New York: Liberal Arts Press, 1955).

Haydon, Benjamin Robert, *The Diary of Benjamin Robert Haydon*. Edited by Willard Bissell Pope, 2 vols. (Cambridge: Harvard, 1960).

Hazlitt, William, *The Complete Works of William Hazlitt*. Edited by P. P. Howe, 21 vols. (London: Dent, 1932).

Helvétius, Claude-Adrien, *De L'Esprit; De L'Homme; Notes, Maximes et Pensées; Le Bonheur Lettres*. Edited by Albert Keim. Quatrième édition (Paris: Mercure de France, 1909).

Holcroft, Thomas, *The Life of Thomas Holcroft*. Edited by Elbridge Colby, 2 vols. (London: Constable, 1925).

Kippis, Andrew, *An Address, delivered at the Interment of the late Rev. Dr. Richard Price* (London: Cadell and Johnson, 1791).

Knowles, John, *The Life and Writings of Henry Fuseli*. 3 vols. (London: Colburn and Bentley, 1831).

Lamb, Charles, *The Letters of Charles Lamb*. Edited by E. V. Lucas. 3 vols. (New Haven: Yale, 1935).

Lofft, Capel, *Remarks on the Letter of the Rt. Hon. Edmund Burke, concerning the Revolution in France* (London: Johnson, 1790).

Ludlow, Edmund, *Memoirs of Edmund Ludlow. With a Collection of Original Papers, and the Case of King Charles the First* (London: T. Becket, 1771).

Martineau, Harriet, *Autobiography*. Edited by Maria Weston Chapman. 2 vols. (Boston: Osgood, 1877).

Milton, John, *The Works of John Milton*. Edited by Frank Allen Patterson, et al. *18 vols*. (New York: Columbia, 1931-1938).

The Modern Catalogue of Books, ... containing the Books which have been published in London since the Year 1792 (London: Bent, 1803).

Montesquieu, M. De Secondat, Baron de, *The Spirit of Laws*. Translated by Mr. Nugent. Third edition, 2 vols. (London: Nourse and Vaillant, 1758).

The Monthly Review. I-XXIX (1790-1799).

The Morning Chronicle. 1790-1798.

The Morning Post. 1793-1795.

Muirhead, James Patrick, *The Life of James Watt, with Selections from his Correspondence* (New York: Appleton, 1859).

Nichols, John, *Literary Anecdotes of the Eighteenth Century*. 10 vols. (London: for the author, 1812-1815).

The Parliamentary History of England. XXVIII-XXIX (1789-1792) (London: Hansard, 1816-1817).

Pistorius, Herman Andrew, *Notes and Additions to Dr. Hartley's Observations on Man*. Translated (London: Johnson, 1791).

Priestley, Joseph, *An Answer to Mr. Paine's Age of Reason* (London: Johnson, 1795).

——, *An Essay on the First Principles of Government; and on the Nature of Political, Civil, and Religious Liberty* (London: Dodsley, ... Cadell, ... and Johnson, 1768).

——, *Letters to the Philosophers and Politicians of France, on the Subject of Religion* (London: Johnson, 1793).

Robinson, Henry Crabb, *The Correspondence of Henry Crabb Robinson with the Wordsworth Circle*. Edited by Edith J. Morley, 2 vols. (Oxford: Clarendon Press, 1927).

——, *Henry Crabb Robinson on Books and their Writers*. Edited by Edith J. Morley, 3 vols. (London: Dent, 1938).

Rousseau, Jean Jacques, *The Confessions of Jean Jacques Rousseau*. Translated by W. Conyngham Mallory (New York: Boni, n.d.).

——, *The Social Contract*. Translated by G. D. H. Cole (London: Dent, 1938).

Ruggles, Thomas, *The History of the Poor; Their Rights, Duties and the Laws respecting Them.* 2 vols. (London: Deighton, 1793-1794).

Sidney, Algernon, *Discourses concerning Government.* 2 vols. (Philadelphia: Wayne, 1805).

Southey, Robert, *The Life and Correspondence of the Late Robert Southey.* Edited by Charles Cuthbert Southey, 6 vols. (London: Longman, 1849-1850).

Thelwall, John, *Rights of Nature, against the Usurpations of Establishments. A Series of Letters to the People, in Reply to the False Principles of Burke.* Second edition (London: Symonds and March, 1796).

The Times. London, 1791-1798.

Wakefield, Gilbert, *An Examination of the Age of Reason* (London: Kearsley, 1794).

——, *A Reply to the Second Part of the Age of Reason* (London: Symonds, 1795).

——, *The Spirit of Christianity, compared with the Spirit of the Times in Great Britain.* Third edition (London: Kearsley, 1794).

Whig Club, instituted in May 1784 (London: Barr, 1792).

Wordsworth, Christopher (1774-1846). *The Early Wordsworthian Milieu, A Notebook of Christopher Wordsworth with a Few Entries by William Wordsworth.* Edited by Z. S. Fink (Oxford: Clarendon Press, 1958).

Wordsworth, Christopher (1807-1885). *Memoirs of William Wordsworth.* 2 vols. (London: Moxon, 1851).

Wordsworth, Christopher (1848-1938). *Social Life at the English Universities in the Eighteenth Century* (Cambridge: Deighton, Bell, 1874).

Wordsworth, Dorothy, *Journals of Dorothy Wordsworth.* Edited by Ernest de Selincourt, 2 vols. (New York: Macmillan, 1941).

Wordsworth, John, *The Letters of John Wordsworth.* Edited by Carl H. Ketcham (Ithaca: Cornell, 1969).

Wordsworth, William, *The Letters of William and Dorothy Wordsworth. The Early Years, 1787-1805.* Second edition. Edited by Chester L. Shaver (Oxford: Clarendon Press, 1967).

——, *The Letters of William and Dorothy Wordsworth. The Middle Years, 1806-1820.* Edited by Ernest de Selincourt, 2 vols. (Oxford: Clarendon Press, 1937).

——, *The Poetical Works of William Wordsworth.* Edited by Ernest de Selincourt and Helen Darbishire. 5 vols. (Oxford: Clarendon Press, 1940-1949).

——, *The Prelude, or, Growth of a Poet's Mind.* Edited by Ernest de Selincourt. Second edition, revised by Helen Darbishire (Oxford: Clarendon Press, 1959).

——, *The Prose Works of William Wordsworth.* Edited by the Rev. Alexander Grosart, 3 vols. (London: Moxon, 1876).

——, *Wordsworth: Representative Poems.* Edited by Arthur Beatty (New York: Odyssey, 1937).

——, and Samuel Taylor Coleridge, *Lyrical Ballads.* Edited by R. L. Brett and A. R. Jones (London: Methuen, 1963).

——, *Lyrical Ballads. 1798.* Edited by W. J. B. Owen (London: Oxford, 1967).

Wyvill, the Rev. Christopher, *A Defence of Dr. Price, and the Reformers of England* (London: Johnson, 1792).

Young, Robert, *An Examination of . . . the First Book of Sir Isaac Newton's Principia* (London: Johnson, 1788).

INDEX

F3